Hough on the Hill
Hykeham North
Ingoldsby
Irnham
Kirkby la Thorpe
Kirkby Underwood
Kyme North
Kyme South

Langtoft
Leadenham
Leasingham
Lenton, Keisby and Osgodby
Little Bytham
Londonthorpe and Harrowby
Market Deeping
Marston
Martin
Metheringham
Morton nr Bourne
Navenby
Newton and Haceby
Nocton
Normanton
Norton Disney
Old Somerby
Osbournby
Pickworth
Pointon and Sempringham
Ponton Great
Ponton Little and Stroxton
Potter Hanworth
Quarrington
Rauceby North
Rauceby South
Rippingale
Ropsley and Humby
Rowston
Roxholm
Ruskington
Scarle North
Scopwick
Scredington
Sedgebrook
Silk Willoughby
Skellingthorpe
Skillington
Sleaford New
Sleaford Old
Stamford
Stapleford
Stoke Rochford
Stubton
Swaton
Swayfield
Swinstead
Swinderby
Syston
Tallington
Temple Bruer with Temple High Grange
Thorpe on the Hill
Threckingham
Thurlby
Thurlby nr Bourne
Timberland
Toft with Lound and Manthorpe
Uffington
Waddington
Walcot
Walcot nr Folkingham
Washingborough
Welbourne
Welby
Wellingore
Westborough and Dry Doddington
Wilsford
Witham on the Hill
Witham North
Witham South
Woolsthorpe
Wyville with Hungerton

Boston and South Holland

AN HISTORICAL ATLAS OF
LINCOLNSHIRE

AN HISTORICAL ATLAS OF
LINCOLNSHIRE

edited by

Stewart Bennett and Nicholas Bennett

with contributions by

Rodney W. Ambler, John Aram, Ian Beckwith,
Alan Bilham-Boult, Mike Fenton, Bill Goodhand,
Terry Hancock, Hilary Healey, Michael J. Jones,
Stephen J. Kemp, Tom Lane, Jeffrey May, Dennis Mills,
Ann Mitson, Peter Muskett, Susan Noble, Richard Olney,
Julie O'Neill, Simon Pawley, Peter Raspin, Charles Rawding,
David Roberts, David Robinson, David Roffe, Rex C. Russell,
Brian Sandham, Brian Simmons, David Start, Alan Vince,
Ben Witwell, Neil Wright, Jane Young

Maps drawn by

Keith Scurr, Helen Palmer-Brown, Rex C. Russell,
and Stephanie Sykes

Phillimore

2001

First edition published by the University of Hull Press, 1993
Reprinted 1994

Published by
PHILLIMORE & CO. LTD.
Shopwyke Manor Barn, Chichester, West Sussex

ISBN 1 86077 166 1

Printed and bound in Great Britain by
BUTLER AND TANNER LTD.
London and Frome

CONTENTS

CONTRIBUTORS

Rodney W. Ambler, BA, PhD, FRHistS., FSA.	Senior Lecturer in History, University of Hull
John Aram, BEd, FRGS.	Geological Consultant
Ian Beckwith, BA.	Anglican Priest, Open University Tutor and author
Nicholas Bennett, MA, DPhil.	Vice Chancellor and Lincoln Cathedral Librarian
Stewart Bennett, BEd, MA, PhD.	PGCE History Tutor, Hull University and freelance teacher
Alan Bilham-Boult, BA.	Head of Freiston Hall Field Centre
Mike Fenton, BA.	Head of History, Carres Grammar School
Bill Goodhand, BA, MA.	Part-time Tutor, Adult Education Dept., Nottingham University. Formerly Head of Geography Department, Bishop Grosseteste College
Terry Hancock, ALA.	Author and Principal Librarian, Lincolnshire Library Service
Hilary Healey, NDD, MPhil, FSA.	Artist, archaeologist and local historian
Michael J. Jones, MA, FSA, MIFA.	Director, City of Lincoln Archaeology Unit
Stephen J. Kemp, BA, Dip. TP., MRTPI.	Former Principal Planning Assistant, Lincoln City Council
Tom Lane, MIFA.	Field Officer, Heritage Trust of Lincolnshire
Jeffrey May, MA, FSA.	Senior Lecturer in Archaeology, University of Nottingham
Dennis Mills, MA, PhD, PGCE.	Editor of *Twentieth Century Lincolnshire* Vol XII in the History of Lincolnshire Series
Ann Mitson, MA, PhD.	Researcher and part-time lecturer
Peter Muskett, MA, MEd.	Former Schools Administrative Officer, Lincoln Diocese Education Office
Susan Noble, MA, DAA.	Public Services Manager, Lincolnshire Archives Office
Richard Olney, MA, DPhil, FRHistSoc.	Assistant Keeper, Royal Commission on Historical Manuscripts
Julie O'Neill, BA, MA, PhD.	Part-time lecturer and researcher
Simon Pawley, MA, PhD.	Teacher and local historian
Peter Raspin, MA, MA, MRTPI.	Principal Planning Officer, Lincolnshire County Council
Charles Rawding, BA, MA, DPhil.	Geography Teacher at Waltham Toll Bar School, Grimsby
David Roberts, PhD.	Architectural historian
David Robinson, MSc.	Formerly Senior Lecturer, Nottingham University
David Roffe, MA, PhD, FSA, FRHist Soc.	Leverhulme Research Fellow, University of Sheffield
Rex C. Russell, BA.	Formerly Senior Tutor in Local Studies, University of Hull
Brian Sandham, BEd, MA.	Lecturer in History, Grantham College
Brian Simmons, MA, FSA, MIFA.	Formerly Director of the Trust for Lincolnshire Archaeology
David Start, BSc, MIFA.	Director, The Heritage Trust of Lincolnshire
Alan Vince, BA, PhD, FSA, MIFA.	Assistant Director, City of Lincoln Archaeology Unit
Ben Whitwell, PhD, FSA.	Archaeology Manager, Humberside Archaeology Unit
Neil Wright, DMA.	Industrial archaeologist and local historian
Jane Young	Medieval Pottery Researcher, City of Lincoln Archaeology Unit

Acknowledgements

We wish to thank all those who have helped in the production of the Atlas: David Dymond and Edward Martin, for their initial help and advice; Gershom Knight and Rod Ambler, for their assistance in the early stages; Phil Holmes and Miss Jean Smith, for their forbearance and for the work they have done behind the scenes, and Keith Scurr. The editors gratefully acknowledge the availability of the Scorer Collection including technical services. Illustrations on pp. 66, 67 are kindly provided by David Roberts. Most importantly, we thank the contributors, who have been prepared to put up with our hounding over more than three years. Many have given advice and support beyond writing their own contributions.

The *Historical Atlas of Lincolnshire* is the first publication to treat such a breadth of topics about the historic County. There are 74 pages of maps with short explanatory text by over thirty contributors. Most of the maps are the product of recent research, or bring up to date work previously published. They reflect the wide variety of research currently being undertaken into Lincolnshire's past. While most maps give a perspective of the whole county, some attention has been given to specific areas, such as the fens, the coastline, and Lincoln as the county town.

The main objective of the Atlas is to inform the general reader about the historical geography of the county. Many people want to find out more about the area in which they live. To this end, most of the maps are detailed to show the boundaries of both ecclesiastical and civil parishes, making it possible to see how individual parishes fit into the county perspective. The names of the parishes are given on two larger scale pull-out maps at the back of the volume. Each contribution is followed by suggestions for further reading. We hope that the Atlas, with its wide range of topics, will be of value to the general reader and the specialist alike, providing a stimulus for further research.

The variety of the landscape of one of the largest counties in the country has had a fundamental effect on human activity. The topography ranges from chalk upland of more than 130 metres above sea-level to extensive areas which are less than one metre above sea-level and the inter-relationship of landscape and human activity is the central theme of this volume. Using a chronological framework, the Atlas includes contributions about the development of the landscape and its geology. These are followed by studies of the county during prehistoric, Roman and Anglo-Saxon times, based on archaeological research carried out over the last two or three decades. From the middle ages,

when the sources become more varied and plentiful, there are contributions relating to political, social, religious, industrial and commercial aspects of Lincolnshire's past. Attention has also been paid to changes in the county during the last fifty years of the 20th century, including the connections with the RAF. As well as illustrating the wide range of historical research being undertaken at the present time, we hope that the Atlas also demonstrates something of the methodology associated with this work.

Although the modern county of Lincolnshire is included in the East Midlands region, its economic and social basis is very different from that of Nottinghamshire or Leicestershire which is why we feel that it is right to treat the county as a separate entity. Despite its size, Lincolnshire has in a sense always been isolated from the rest of the country. The main reasons for this were the natural barriers of the Humber in the north and the fens in the south, Although the city of Lincoln became one of the most important regional centres both under the Romans and later under the Normans, by the later middle ages both city and county had declined in importance. At a time of tremendous economic change from the middle of the 19th century, Lincolnshire remained a largely rural county and even today elements of this isolation can be seen by glancing at a map of the modern motorway network.

Inevitably, any single volume which covers such a long period of history will he piecemeal: although a number of the contributions do show change over substantial periods of time, most provide a snap-shot of a particular issue. As historical research is a continuous process, many contributions should only be seen as interim, reflecting the state of research at the present time. With so many contributors, it is not surprising that interpretations may differ and even conflict. We make no apology for this.

THE MAPS

THE MAKING OF THE LANDSCAPE

John Aram, Alan Bilham-Boult and Bill Goodhand

Introduction: Lincolnshire landscapes are principally the result of the interaction of a variety of processes over a long period of time upon Triassic, Jurassic and Cretaceous ages *(see* Solid Geology Map p.5). During the last half million years the climate has fluctuated several times between full glacial and tundra, to conditions warmer than the present day *(see* chronology in note 1).

The Anglian Effects: In the cold glacial climate of the Middle Pleistocene (c.300,000-250,000 BP–the Anglian glaciation), the entire county was overwhelmed by a vast continental ice-sheet hundreds of metres in depth. The ice-sheet suppressed the pre-existing drainage system and eroded huge quantities of rock, deepening the clay vales by as much as thirty metres. At the end of the Anglian glaciation, the melting of these huge ice-sheets left behind large tracts of till (often referred to as the Older Drift). The character of these tills varies throughout the county, their colour and texture being related to the source rocks eroded by the ice. Near Gainsborough they are reddish due to the high proportion of Mercian Mudstone (Keuper Marl), while in central Lincolnshire the Wragby till is blue-grey due to the inclusion of much Oxford and Kimmeridge clays. Till containing a high proportion of chalk and flint are frequently described as 'chalky boulder clay'. Many tills now only survive patchily on the interfluves between valleys, where they seldom reach more than five metres in thickness; however exceptional thicknesses of up to seventy-five metres have been recorded in the Kesteven Uplands, where they fill buried channels of pre-Anglian rivers.

Late Anglian to Late Devensian Glaciations: As the Anglian ice-sheet retreated, peri-glacial conditions gave way to a temperate climate during the Hoxnian stage. The few known deposits of this age in Lincolnshire include shell-bearing beach gravels and peat deposits at Kirmington, and gravels containing derived vertebrate fossils and hand axes at Welton le Wold. Widespread 'cambering' of scarp edges, bulging of valley floors and solifluction lobes on steep slopes occurred during the late Anglian stage. In the past some 'chalky tills' have been assigned to a 'Wolstonian' glaciation, but there is no indisputable evidence for this event, although a brief cold stage has been recorded *(see* chronology table in note 1).

At Tattershall, pollen and molluscs from a basal peat bed indicate warm temperate conditions with woodlands during the Ipswichian stage. Sea-level rose from-100 metres OD to about +8 metres OD, drowning a wide coastal plain and cutting a sloping platform into the eastern side of the Wolds. To the west, high terraces of the Rivers Trent and Witham have been dated to the Ipswichian on the evidence of hippopotamus remains. Beds overlying Ipswichian deposits contain cold fauna vertebrates including mammoths and reindeer, whilst the sediments contain frequent ice-wedge casts and cryoturbation features indicative of a return to tundra conditions. Fluvial sands and gravels deposited after the Anglian but before the Devensian on the Fen margins are similarly affected.

Devensian ice-sheets reached Lincolnshire only briefly before retreating after 13000 BP; 'North Sea Ice' from Scotland and north-east England was deflected by 'Scandinavian Ice' into the Humber estuary, one lobe reaching the Ancholme valley. Ice originating in the Lake District and advancing across the Pennines and down the Vale of York filled the northern part of the lower Trent valley. In the east a possible maximum ice advance position may be marked by the Stickney moraine extending southwards from the Wolds. Low ridges of recessional moraines (as at Hogsthorpe) mark stages in the retreat of this last ice-sheet.

One major consequence of these ice advances was a temporary blocking of river outfalls into the Humber and the Wash; lakes of varying sizes would have resulted, extensive in the Trent valley and Fenlands, very localised in the Wolds valley. As the ice front retreated the tundra conditions returned to all areas; widespread solifluction and slumping of saturated clays and sands spread down the slopes to infill valley bottoms. On frequently frozen land surfaces devoid of vegetation many pockets of fine wind-blown sands accumulated in sheltered locations.

The Post Glacial Period. With the melting and retreat of the ice sheets from the maximum of the Devensian glacial event sea-level rose rapidly, perhaps as much as ten metres in 1,000 years in the period around 8,000 BP. Known as the Flandrian transgression, this rise extinguished the land bridge with Europe and established Britain as a continental offshore island. The early coniferous forests established as the climate ameliorated were overcome by the advancing sea, their remains now being found as stumps and roots revealed at low tide on beaches such as Huttoft Bank. Sea-level continued to rise and, despite the rise in the land surfaces due to isostatic recovery, the sea rose more rapidly, flooding over the low-lying areas of the present Fenlands and Humber estuary to perhaps a maximum of +5 metres OD (*c*.2000 BP).

The sea therefore spread across the Fenland beyond Spalding and Bourne, close to the present site of Billingborough and the gravel islands at Market Deeping. Associated with the rise in sea-level, the major rivers entering the Humber and Fenland must have been subject to heavy deposition, rapidly filling the broad deep valleys cut when the sea-level was lower. They were thus transformed in their upper and middle courses to wide, flat-floored, ill-drained areas, typified by the River Trent. After 2000 BP sea-level regressed; in the Fens this phase being represented by the deposition of coastal silts (the Romano-British silts), creating a ridge known in the Fenlands as the 'townlands'. Landward of this ridge lowland basins fed by freshwater streams accumulated deep and extensive peat deposits over the next 1500 years or so.

Notes and further details on page 136.

Pre-Anglian—Anglian period

Devensian period

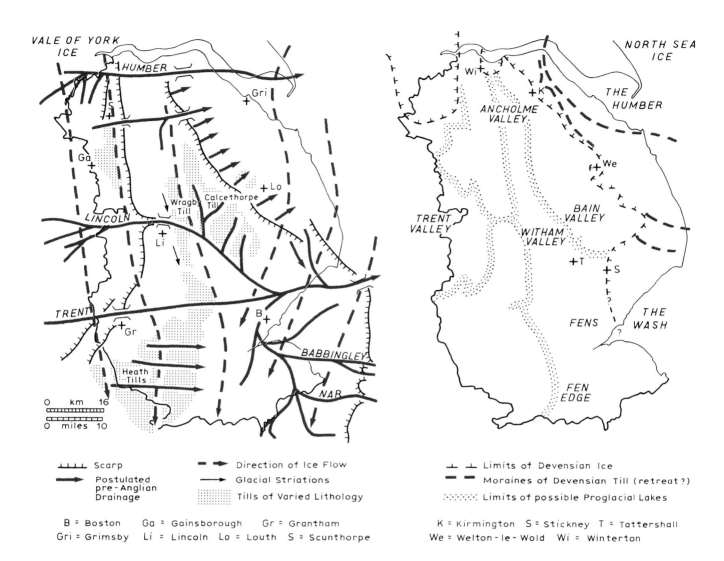

VALE OF YORK ICE
HUMBER
Gri
Ga
Calcethorpe Till
Wragby Till
+ Lo
LINCOLN
Li
TRENT
B
+Gr
Heath Tills
BABBINGLEY
NAR

NORTH SEA ICE
Wi
K
THE HUMBER
ANCHOLME VALLEY
We
TRENT VALLEY
BAIN VALLEY
WITHAM VALLEY
T
S
FENS
THE WASH
FEN EDGE

O km 16
O miles 10

⊥⊥⊥⊥ Scarp
→ Postulated pre-Anglian Drainage
⇢ Direction of Ice Flow
→ Glacial Striations
⋯ Tills of Varied Lithology

B = Boston   Ga = Gainsborough   Gr = Grantham
Gri = Grimsby   Li = Lincoln   Lo = Louth   S = Scunthorpe

⊥ ⊥ Limits of Devensian Ice
⇢ Moraines of Devensian Till (retreat?)
⋯⋯ Limits of possible Proglacial Lakes

K = Kirmington   S = Stickney   T = Tattershall
We = Welton-le-Wold   Wi = Winterton

Post-glacial period

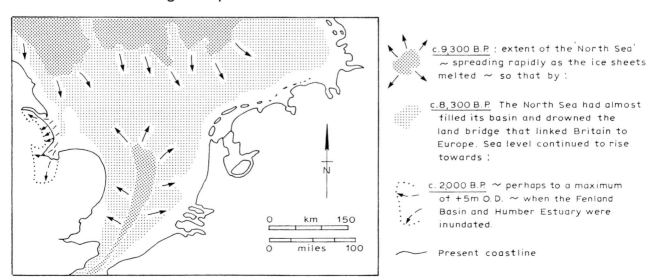

O km 150
O miles 100

↗ c.9,300 B.P : extent of the 'North Sea' ~ spreading rapidly as the ice sheets melted ~ so that by :

c.8,300 B.P The North Sea had almost filled its basin and drowned the land bridge that linked Britain to Europe. Sea level continued to rise towards :

c.2,000 B.P ~ perhaps to a maximum of +5m O.D. ~ when the Fenland Basin and Humber Estuary were inundated.

— Present coastline

3

The 'solid' geology of Lincolnshire consists of sedimentary rocks of Mesozoic ages, the oldest being the Triassic beds, approximately 220 million years, that underlie the extreme north-west of the county. Overlying strata form a series of north-south strips, with Jurassic strata dipping eastwards beneath progressively younger Cretaceous beds. This pattern is modified in the Jurassic by a thinning of individual beds and a slight increase in dip angle towards the north, causing a narrowing of outcrop widths. The increasing width of outcrops southwards combines with a change to a more south-easterly dip direction to the south of Grantham causing the Lower Jurassic beds to swing westwards into adjacent counties. Earth movements and a break in sedimentation towards the end of the Jurassic period resulted in the Lower Cretaceous beds being deposited unconformably with a north-easterly dip direction across the different beds of the Upper Jurassic.[1] Recent deep exploration programmes have proved the character of pre-Triassic rocks beneath parts of the county; with coal seams beneath Gainsborough at more than 750 metres below mean sea-level, and near Lincoln at depths greater than 1,000 metres.[2] Beneath the Carboniferous rocks lie mainly pre-Cambrian volcanic and metamorphic rocks, with localised granites of presumed Caledonian age.

Triassic The oldest rocks to outcrop in the area are of Upper Triassic age–the Mercia Mudstone Group (formerly 'Keuper Marls') and the Penarth Group (formerly 'The Rhaetic'). Near Gainsborough they consist of a lower series of variable red calcareous silts and clays ('marls'), with thin lenses of gypsum, an upper series of greenish to grey siltstones and clays 'Tea Green Marls'). Dark grey-black shales of the Westbury Formation (Penarth Group) follow, then the Cotham member of the Lilstock Formation with a nodular limestone bed beneath pale grey to greenish clays that become reddened towards the north. The Penarth Group increases in thickness from a few metres near Grantham to a maximum of twenty metres near Gainsborough, before thinning again northwards.

Jurassic A resistant group of limestone beds at the base of the Lower Lias (Lower Jurassic) caps a low north-south 'Rhaetic Scarp'. Otherwise, shales with thin limestones and sandstones predominate in the south, giving way northwards to the Frodingham ironstone. The Middle Lias consists of sands and clays, overlain by a calcareous ironstone ('Marlstone Rock') that forms a thin nodule bed in the north but thickens to form a continuous bed of iron ore south of Navenby. In contrast the Upper Lias consists almost entirely of blue-grey mudstones and shales, with only thin nodular limestones towards the top. The thickness of the Lias is approximately 200 metres over most of the county, but decreases sharply north of Scunthorpe.

The Middle Jurassic begins with the Northampton Sand Ironstone, a greenish-blue rock that weathers to an orange-brown sandy material. The overlying Grantham Formation, absent locally in the Lincoln area, reaches up to eight metres of coloured sands, silts and clays to the south and north. The overlying Lincolnshire limestone thins away from a maximum thickness of over thirty metres near Grantham; the lower beds being particularly variable towards the northern and southern margins.[3] More uniform oolitic limestones in the Upper Lincolnshire limestone provide high-grade building stones, such as 'Ancaster Stone'. Estuarine beds of multi-coloured clays, silts, sands and carbonaceous material often lie upon a reddened surface of the weathered oolitic limestone. The Great Oolitic Limestone is rarely oolitic in this area, consisting of a few metres of rubbly limestone with marly partings, dying away north of Brigg where it is overlapped by green and blue clays and shales of the Blisworth Clays. The Combrash, rarely more than two metres thick, forms a strip of rubbly, sandy limestones.[4] Clays dominate the Upper Jurassic. Up to eighty metres of blue-grey shales, clays and mudstones form the Oxford Clay, and up to 130 metres of dark blue clays and mudstones with oil shales comprise the Kimmeridge Clay beds, as proved during the Wash Barrage investigations.[5]

Cretaceous The Spilsby Sandstone, with a maximum thickness of twenty-five metres in the southern Wolds, thins both northwards and eastwards. The lower beds tend to be coarser and greenish with the mineral glauconite, while the upper beds are paler and become finer.[6] The remainder of the Lower Cretaceous beds consist of a very varied series of sedimentary rocks with much lateral variation of facies. The oolitic ironstone of the Claxby Beds near Nettleton grades southwards, until it becomes the Hundleby Clay near Spilsby. The Tealby Beds, dark grey, green and pale clays and shales, are divided north of Alford by the impure yellowish-coloured Tealby Limestone Bed. The Fulletby Beds comprise mainly clays grading into a harder, sandy layer of 'Roach'. Known only from boreholes, the Skegness Clay and Sutterby Marl rarely exceed four metres in combined thickness before dying out north of Binbrook. Overstepping them to the northwest, the Carstone consists of fine glauconitic sands with clays that grade upwards into coarser sands with pebbles, becoming finer and thinner northwards until they lie unconformably upon the Kimmeridge Clays to the north of Caistor. The Red Chalk (or Hunstanton Red Rock), although only four metres thick at maximum, and often less than two metres, is one of the most visually obvious beds in the Wolds.

During the Upper Cretaceous, the 'Northern Province' sea deposited chalk, overlapping further than the previous beds. With a maximum thickness of nearly 100 metres near Louth, the chalk commences with the Ferriby Chalk Formation (Lower Chalk), comprising a hard grey chalk with several 'pink' bands, capped by the green-grey Plenus Marl. A darker grey chalk then gives way upwards to a pure white chalk in the Welton Formation (Middle Chalk).[7] Towards the end of the Upper Cretaceous the entire area was lightly faulted and gently uplifted above sea level, before being weathered and eroded during the Tertiary and Quaternary periods to form the present-day landscape.

Notes and further details on page 136.

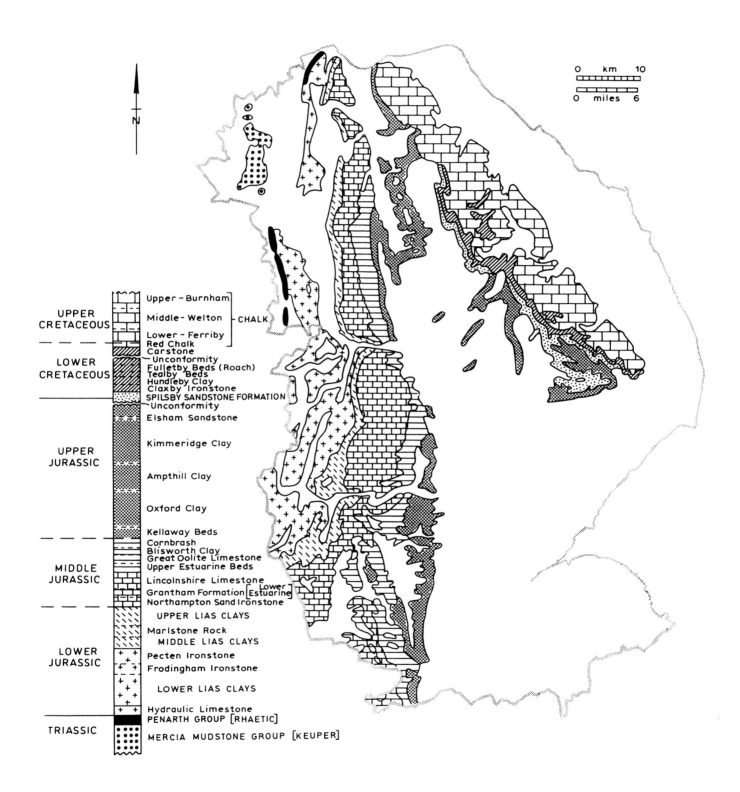

UPPER
CRETACEOUS

Upper - Burnham ⎤
Middle - Welton ⎬ CHALK
Lower - Ferriby ⎦
Red Chalk

LOWER
CRETACEOUS

Carstone
Unconformity
Fulletby Beds (Roach)
Tealby Beds
Hundleby Clay
Claxby Ironstone
SPILSBY SANDSTONE FORMATION
Unconformity

Elsham Sandstone

UPPER
JURASSIC

Kimmeridge Clay

Ampthill Clay

Oxford Clay

Kellaway Beds
Cornbrash
Blisworth Clay
Great Oolite Limestone
Upper Estuarine Beds

MIDDLE
JURASSIC

Lincolnshire Limestone
Grantham Formation ⎡Lower⎤
                   ⎣Estuarine⎦
Northampton Sand Ironstone

UPPER LIAS CLAYS

Marlstone Rock
MIDDLE LIAS CLAYS

LOWER
JURASSIC

Pecten Ironstone
Frodingham Ironstone

LOWER LIAS CLAYS

Hydraulic Limestone
PENARTH GROUP [RHAETIC]

TRIASSIC

MERCIA MUDSTONE GROUP [KEUPER]

0   km   10
0   miles   6

N

DRIFT GEOLOGY

John Aram

The 'drift' deposits of the county include all sediments formed and deposited during the last few millions of years since the end of the Tertiary period. These deposits mainly originated during the Pleistocene ice ages and warmer inter-glacial times when melting ice-caps caused a widespread rise in sea-levels. A chronological sequence cannot be determined in these deposits since they tend to be localised in occurrence and only rarely have contacts with other drift deposits. The major exception is the time boundary provided by the discontinuous sheet of Anglian till (boulder clay), representing a time when the entire region was covered by a major ice-sheet. Some deposits can be seen to pre-date this event by lying beneath the till, but most deposits overlie and therefore post-date it.

The subsequent Devensian ice-sheet reached the northern and eastern margins of the county only, limiting its value for correlation purposes. Since each ice advance tends to remove or rework all pre-existing unlithified deposits, there are further difficulties of correlation with glacial deposits possibly containing derived material from earlier glaciations. Conflicting 'evidence' has helped to create uncertainties in the glacial history of the county; especially since their solution must link into the glacial histories of adjacent regions.

Till (boulder clay) consists of a mixture of clays and rock fragments of varied sizes deposited by an ice-sheet during the Anglian or Devensian glaciations. Dependent upon the nature of the bedrock over which the glacial-ice moved, the relative proportions of the main components may vary from a very stony mixture to a massive clay. Where the eroded clay bedrock has a distinctive colour it often forms the predominant colour of the till.[1] Such colouring may similarly be given by the rock fragments if they are particularly abundant or of a distinctive lithology. Tills rich in chalk clasts are recognised as pale 'chalky till' across large areas of the county. Abundant rock fragments of a distinctive lithology, such as Red Chalk or Spilsby Sandstone, may be used to trace the general directions of ice movement in an area. Less common rock types ('erratics') found in tills from Lincolnshire may help to identify possible distant source areas for the glacial ice.[2] Such rocks may have been reworked from earlier deposits, hence any conclusions must be very tentative. Glacial deposits may include not only well-compacted basal (lodgement) till but englacial and supra-glacial materials also. Where melt-water was abundant beneath, within or upon the ice, tills may contain irregular 'sand' beds and lenses within the till mass.[3]

The **sand and gravel** deposits indicated have many different origins, substantial variations occurring in many cases within an individual deposit. Isolated patches lying on top of tills may be the products of sub-aerial weathering removing finer material from tills, or the weathering-out of coarser deposits within tills referred to above.[4] Close to modern ice-sheets, turbulent melt-water streams carry away large quantities of clays, silt and sands while gravel, pebbles and boulders may be moved more slowly, until deposited in sediments downstream. 'Braided channels' are a feature of such sediment-loaded rivers, the distinctive sedimentary structures being seen in fluvio-glacial sands and gravel deposits throughout the county. When followed downstream fluvio-glacial deposits usually grade into normal fluvial deposits as the glacial influence on flow patterns and sediment supply decreases. At a fixed location a similar sequence vertically may be produced by the progressive retreat of an ice-front. The terraces of the rivers Trent and Witham may reflect such ice retreats and advances, with varying availability of water and sediment combined with changes in their outfall level. Deposits in the floors of the rivers Bain and Slea and along the border of the Fens may be related to similar events. It has been suggested that they also contain marine beach deposits related to an inter-glacial high sea level. They could also represent the kame terrace shoreline of a pro-glacial lake trapped between glacial ice in the Wash and the dip slope of the Middle Jurassic strata. Such a lake would have experienced seasonal freezing of its surface, allowing fine clay particles to settle, forming distinctive seasonal couplets of laminated deposits (varve clays).[5]

Deposits of **peat** were formerly more extensive in the county than the present map would suggest; a combination of draining, deep ploughing and modern farming methods have, through oxidation and bacterial action, reduced areas where the deposits were thinnest and closest to the surface. Conditions for peat formation in lowland areas are related to waterlogged ground conditions, which may themselves be linked to impeded drainage due to topographic barriers or fluctuating sea levels. The causes and dates of origin of each area of peat are therefore likely to be different.

The areas of **alluvium,** predominantly consisting of clays and silts, occupy the lowest-lying parts of the county. They originated in flood waters of different types, some from rivers with very low gradients that broke their banks and flooded over extensive flood-plains, others related to marine flooding following exceptional storms that both built up and destroyed banks of fine silts and carried finer clay particles inland to areas where they met 'land-water' draining towards the sea.

Fine to medium blown sands: those well away from the present-day coastline originated during cold climatic conditions when lack of vegetation and soil cover allowed the wind selectively to erode and deposit sands a short distance away from their source. Areas of glacial outwash, river deposits and soft, easily weathered, sandstones, such as the Spilsby Sandstone, were particularly liable to such processes. Coastal sand-dunes were formed by selective wind action across very wide low-angle sand beaches where the finer grades of sand are blown landwards until they are trapped by vegetation on the rise over the dune ridge. The 'Old Dunes' at Gibraltar Point show that the shoreline has been accreting at this point for over a century, building new dune ridges progressively further seawards.

Notes and further details on page 136.

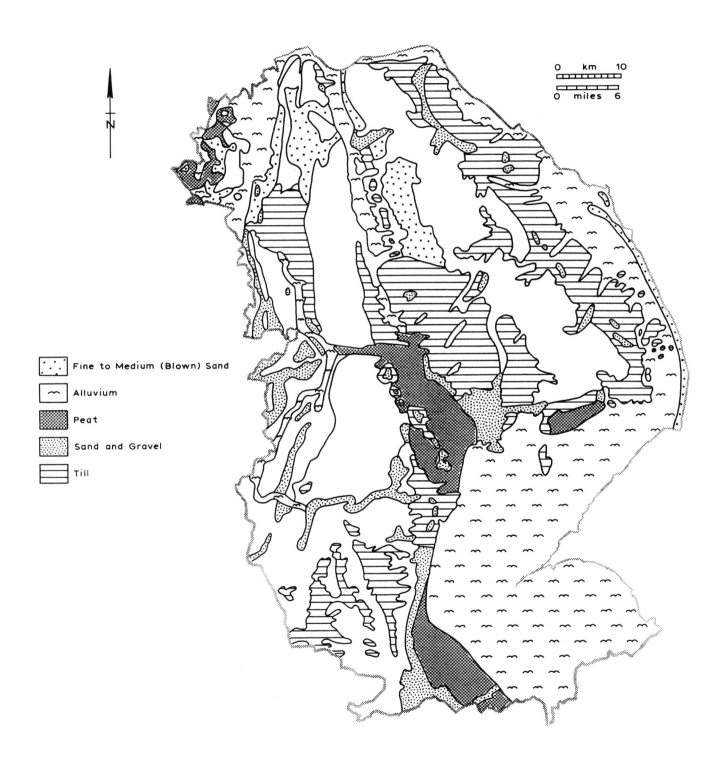

Fine to Medium (Blown) Sand

Alluvium

Peat

Sand and Gravel

Till

0   km   10

0   miles   6

N

7

NATURAL REGIONS

David Robinson

With its long coastline, Lincolnshire forms a somewhat blunted peninsula. Three-quarters of the land is below 30m., yet Normanby Top at 170m. in the Wolds is the highest point in eastern England. There are two lines of hills–the mainly chalk Wolds and the limestone Heath, between which is a clay vale broadening southwards to the peat- and silt-filled depression of the fens. To the west lie the Trent vale and the Isle of Axholme, while to the east is the Lincolnshire Marsh fringed by a sand-dune and saltmarsh coastline.

The Isle of Axholme includes low flat-topped hills of red Keuper Marl, with peatlands and patchy blown sand on the west and to the east the carr lands of the River Trent where warping drains from the tidal river were used to spread silt. Drainage was started in the 17th and completed in the 19th century.

The meandering Trent flows in a broad vale of alluvium, fronted on the east by low hills culminating in the impressive Burton Cliff (61m.), overlooking the Trent Falls. South of Gainsborough are low hills with a bluff of Keuper Marl overlooking the Trent, and the wide clayfilled Till valley draining south-east. West of Lincoln are expanses of much-quarried sands and gravels, south of which is the upper course of the Witham with its tributary the Brant, both flowing on clays.

The Lincoln Heath is capped by oolitic limestone, varying in height from nearly 77m. north of Lincoln to between 123m. and 154m. on the Kesteven uplands. The hills narrow from fifteen miles wide in the south to less than three miles in places north of Lincoln, with a steep west-facing escarpment and a gentle dip slope to the east. They are cut by the distinctive Lincoln Gap and, at a higher level, the Ancaster Gap with its infill of river gravels. Clays form the lower part of the scarp slope, with the Frodingham Ironstone east and north of Scunthorpe. Here is also an area of cover sands with warrens, heathland and woodland.

The hills between Kirton and Lincoln are dry with many dry valleys in the dip slope between Lincoln and Ancaster. The pattern of straight roads and hedges tells the story of late 18th- and early 19th-century enclosure from trackless heath and rabbit warrens. The Kesteven Uplands have an extensive cover of glacial boulder clay with remnants of natural woodland, and are dissected by the north-flowing Witham and the south-flowing Glen and Eden. The Marlstone Ironstone forms a secondary escarpment to the west of Grantham, and the Northampton Sands Ironstone was quarried between Colsterworth and Grantham.

Where the Clay Vale of mid-Lincolnshire narrows markedly to the north, the River Ancholme was straightened and the wet carr lands drained in the 17th and 19th centuries. The low hills, on which stand villages like Howsham and the Kelseys, are capped by boulder clay. Cover sands are banked against the Wolds north of Caistor and spread south along the scarp foot with conifer plantations in the Market Rasen area. From the valley of the Barlings Eau an undulating boulder clay cover extends southeast, with ancient woodlands in the Bardney Forest. The woods and heathy moors of the Woodhall-Coningsby area are on sands and flinty gravels washed down from the Wolds by glacial melt waters.

The extension of the Fens towards Lincoln, bounded by the Witham and the Roman Car Dyke, is predominantly of peat. The other major areas of peat are south from Deeping Fen and in the East Fen. Gravels line the fen edge south from Potterhanworth, with quarrying in the south at Langtoft and Tallington. The rest of the Fens is divided into alluvial and finer silt soils, the latter in the east nearer the Wash, particularly the Townlands, the silt bank of varying width on which the older settlements stand and which separates the drained fen from land won from the sea. The most extensive saltmarsh reclamations in the last three centuries were between Skegness and Wrangle, round the former Bicker Haven and between the Welland and Nene estuaries.

The two main phases of drainage were in the 17th and 18th centuries, but it was not until the early 19th century that the Lindsey Fens were completely drained and brought under cultivation. Today nothing is left of the natural fenland. The lighter silts double crop for vegetables, and bulbs and flowers predominate round Spalding.

The Wolds, capped by chalk, rise to a plateau of about 123m., with a simple west-facing escarpment in the north and an eastern margin truncated by a former sea cliff. The extensive Brocklesby estate woodlands occur on the dip slope. In the central Wolds, the headwaters of the Waithe Beck system have cut back in steep-sided valleys, and the Nettleton Beck and River Rase have cut deeply into the western escarpment. In the southern Wolds the escarpment turns east and the chalk outcrop narrows towards Candlesby. The River Bain rises near Ludford and flows south through sandstones and clays, while the River Lymn tumbles through the spectacular New England gorge into a valley surrounded by a wide ledge of Spilsby Sandstone.

The Lincolnshire Marsh is divided into the undulating boulder clay Middle Marsh, and the flat Outmarsh of marine silts with occasional hummocks of boulder clay around Hogsthorpe. Along the edge of the Middle Marsh from Tetney to Barton on Humber are artesian blow wells where lenses of sand allow water from the chalk to reach the surface.

Before the stormy 13th century the Lincolnshire coast was protected by offshore islands and gravel shoals. Their final destruction provided the basis for the present sand-dune system, best seen in the North Somercotes Warren. Between Mablethorpe and Skegness the coastline has retreated and since the disastrous storm-flood of 1953 is now protected by massive sea walls. Narrow saltmarshes fringe the Humber estuary, widening into 'fitties' towards Donna Nook. Between there and Theddlethorpe is a complex of dune, marsh and wide sandy beaches, with a similar complex at Gibraltar Point built largely by southward longshore drift. The Wash coast is fringed by saltings, at their widest between the Welland and Nene outfalls.

Notes and further details on page 136.

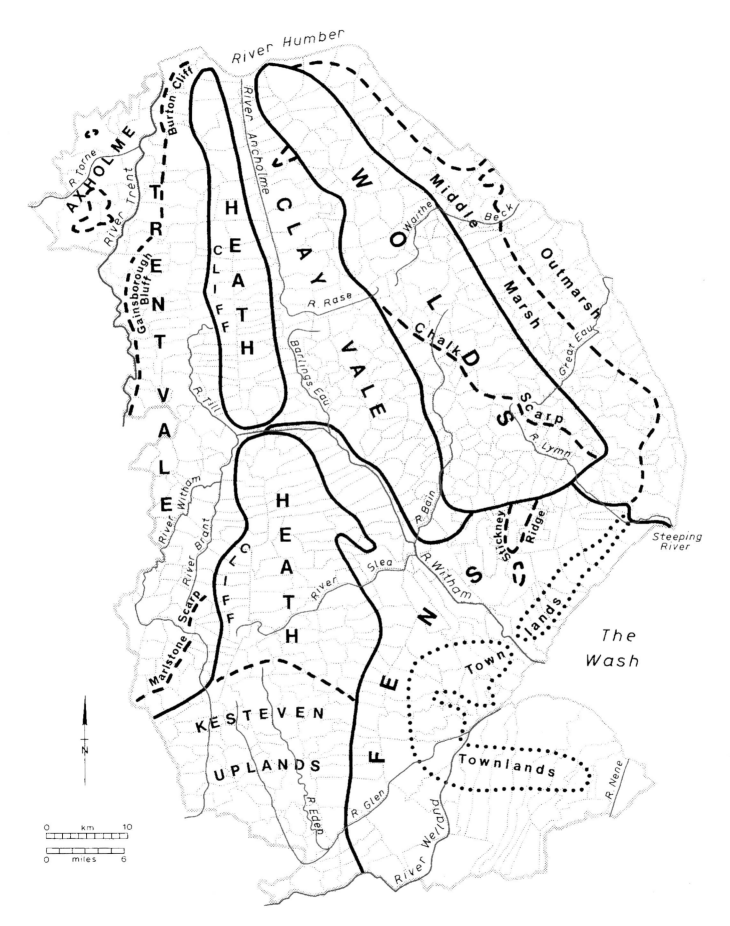

River Humber

AXHOLME

R. Torne

River Trent

Burton Cliff

Gainsborough Bluff

TRENT VALE

CLIFF HEATH

River Ancholme

CLAY VALE

WOLDS

Middle Marsh

Beck

Outmarsh

R. Rase

R. Barlings Eau

Chalk

Scarp

Great Eau

R. Lymn

R. Till

River Witham

River Brant

Scarp

Marlstone

CLIFF

HEATH

River Slea

River

R. Bain

R. Witham

FENS

Stickney

Ridge

Scrublands

Steeping River

The Wash

KESTEVEN

UPLANDS

F E N

Town

Townlands

R. Eden

R. Glen

River Welland

R. Nene

0   km   10

0   miles   6

9

The Beginnings of Farming: The Neolithic Period   *Jeffrey May*

The fertile soils of Lincolnshire encouraged the development of farming at an early date, probably no later than *c.*4000 BC. The earliest farming settlements were probably small and few, and are consequently difficult to find. The earliest site with structures so far found is at Tattershall Thorpe, where excavation revealed traces in the subsoil of a wooden building, square in plan. Pits and hollows containing earlier Neolithic pottery and flint artefacts from Dragonby, Little Gonerby and Tallington, however, show that Neolithic habitation sites were widespread in the county, and the distribution of stone axeheads suggests that forest clearance was taking place almost everywhere.

It is not at all certain whether farming was introduced by immigrants, or was developed gradually by hunter-gatherer communities during the later years of the Mesolithic period, or both. Early Neolithic pottery in Lincolnshire certainly conforms 'to wider British or even continental European traditions, and the essential plants and animals such as wheat and barley, sheep and goats, being near Eastern or south-east European species, must have come from abroad. Other early farm animals such as cattle and pigs, however, were native to Britain, and it is by no means certain whether these species were domesticated anew. Yet apart from axeheads, there is little sign in Lincolnshire of exotic objects such as might have been brought by trade, and which would clearly demonstrate regular contacts with a wider world.

Lincolnshire's Neolithic communities also followed the western European tradition of multiple burial in massive earthwork monuments known as long barrows. These barrows have been recognised as a prominent feature of Neolithic Lincolnshire since they were first mapped and excavated in the 1930s. Their frequent occurrence on the higher ground of the Wolds initially led to the presumption that settlement was concentrated in this area, despite thinner and poorer soils. Detailed study of long barrows at Skendleby, however, suggests that they were sited where they could be seen on the skyline from the nearby valley floor, and it is here that accompanying settlement is likely to be found.

The long barrows often seem to be grouped in pairs. Beneath the earth and rubble mounds are substantial timber structures, pits and other features. Burials were by inhumation, and multiple disarticulated skeletons and parts of skeletons hint at practices which attached little significance or respect for the individual deceased in the manner of later ages. Perhaps the burials were in some way special, sacrificial or symbolic, and should not necessarily be taken as examples of the normal method of disposal of the dead.

Later in the Neolithic period, ceremonial centres or henge monuments were built, and one such at West Ashby, near Horncastle, became the site of an elaborate funerary structure in the ensuing Bronze Age. The West Ashby monument was a small oval ditch with an entrance facing northeast. Simple though it is, the form relates West Ashby to ceremonial sites found widely in Britain, of which Stonehenge and Avebury are the most famous examples. Another possible henge monument is at Stainsby, on the Wolds, again with an entrance facing northeast. No doubt others exist beneath later barrow burials.

During the later part of the Neolithic period, contemporary with the West Ashby henge monument or only a little later, individual burials were often placed beneath round barrows and accompanied by distinctive pottery beakers, flint implements and the earliest metal objects of copper and sometimes gold. One of these burials was excavated at Tallington, in the Welland valley, while others are known from the Wolds. Settlements of the later Neolithic period are as rare as earlier ones, and at present are best represented by collections of pottery fragments: from sites on the sandy soils of Risby Warren, Dragonby and elsewhere around Scunthorpe. Excavations have revealed pits in a few cases, but no dwelling houses or other structures are yet known.

The commonest artefacts from Neolithic Lincolnshire are stone axeheads. Found in considerable numbers both in flint and volcanic rock their distribution shows Neolithic activity in most areas of the county. Even voids in the distribution, such as are to be seen in the fens, may merely result from the masking of Neolithic land surfaces and artefacts by the later deposit of silts or peat growth. If stone axes were used for forest clearance in connection with farming, it would seem that great tracts of land were already opened up and settled by *c.*2500 BC, in the river valleys as well as on higher ground, and that, given time, heavy soils presented no insuperable problems for the simple ards likely to have been used for ploughing. It is no longer possible to argue, as some once did, that Neolithic settlement was largely confined to upland areas such as the Wolds where the long barrows are most frequent.

The axeheads reveal another important aspect of Neolithic Lincolnshire. Those of flint were seldom if ever made of local rock, which is generally unsuitable for making large stone tools, but are likely to have come from East Anglia or elsewhere in southern Britain. More easily identified petrologically are the axeheads of volcanic rock, many of which came from Great Langdale in Cumbria, a distance of 200 or more kilometres from Lincolnshire. Trading on a regular and considerable scale seems to be the obvious explanation for their presence, although other means of dispersal of the axeheads can also be imagined, while centres of redistribution have been suggested on the Lincolnshire Wolds. River valley routes across the Pennines would have been possible, and the discovery of unworn Great Langdale axeheads in the river Trent in Nottinghamshire suggests that boats as well as land transport were commonly available in the region.

Notes and further details on page 136.

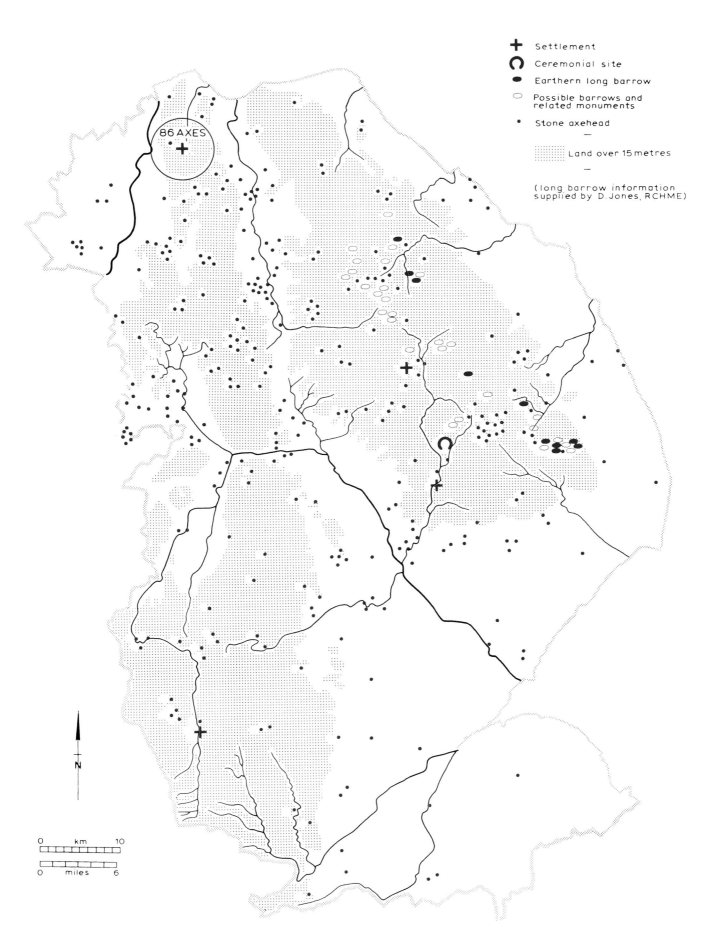

Settlement
Ceremonial site
Earthern long barrow
Possible barrows and
related monuments
Stone axehead
—
Land over 15 metres
—

(long barrow information
supplied by D. Jones, RCHME)

86 AXES

0   km   10

0   miles   6

N

11

For more than three thousand years after the beginnings of farming, Neolithic, Bronze Age and Iron Age communities in Lincolnshire cleared woodlands and wastes for agriculture and for stock grazing. By the later Iron Age, the landscape could have been almost as open as it is today, and the population as numerous as at any time in the Middle Ages. Society had become highly stratified, with kings, lesser nobility, warriors, priests or druids, traders, craftsmen and humbler folk all integrated into complex economic and social systems. We can also infer well-developed political, legal, ceremonial and religious systems, far more advanced than might be supposed from the derogatory term 'barbarian' so often used by the conquering Romans about other peoples.

Lincolnshire formed part of a vast territory stretching from the Humber to the river Nene, whose people were collectively known as the Corieltauvi, and whose principal centres, according to the Greek geographer Ptolemy, were Lindon (Lincoln) and Ratae (Leicester). Archaeology enables us to fill in more detail, and to identify other possible major settlements, whose distribution suggests a regular pattern of smaller districts and subordinate villages and farms. Excavation of one such major settlement at Dragonby revealed dense occupation and a rich and varied material culture, with finely-made pottery, metalwork and evidence for such crafts as weaving.

Unlike many areas of Iron Age Britain, Lincolnshire saw very few major fortified sites. A ploughed-out 'hillfort', dating early in the Iron Age, was found recently at Tattershall Thorpe but no others are known in Lindsey (unless the small enclosure of Yarborough Camp near Kirmington belongs to this period). In Kesteven, a few small undated forts such as Honington Camp may belong to the Iron Age, but the region has nothing like the vast fortresses that characterise Wessex or the Welsh Marches. It is hard to believe that the Corieltauvi were less troubled by war. More likely, political control may have been more unified, or chariot fighting tactics favoured mobile warfare rather than static defences. Alternatively, the region may have been less disturbed in the late Iron Age by the aggressively expanding economic influence and military power of Rome.

The heartland of Corieltauvian wealth and power lay in Lindsey, although settlements at Sleaford and Ancaster show that wealth extended southwards into Kesteven. Towards the end of the period, Sleaford may have been a key site for coastal and overseas trading, since much of what is now Holland was marshland penetrated by creeks, or open sea, allowing ships to reach places now far inland. Other natural points of entry along the Lincolnshire coast could also have been used, although evidence at present is limited to Grimsby, at the mouth of the river Freshney. Boats could also have penetrated far up the Witham, perhaps to Fiskerton, where a massive timber causeway would have facilitated unloading and distribution. The river Humber, too, allowed access to such settlements as South Ferriby and Old Winteringham, while the western districts could have been reached from stathers along the river Trent.

We can infer that salt, made in quantity along the coast near Ingoldmells and by the marshy creeks around Wrangle, Heckington and Helpringham, was an important commodity for trade, together with metalwork, animals and animal products. Imports included fine quality pottery, metalwork and occasionally more exotic items such as coral for ornamenting bronzes, and wine or other luxuries from Spain. Trade may have been stimulated by the adoption of coinage in the first century BC. A regular series of issues in gold and silver testifies to prosperity and economic stability, as well as to considerable skill in engraving and metal technology. From the coins, too, we can learn the names of rulers, otherwise unknown to history.

Only kings or aristocrats would have owned such splendid objects as the coral-ornamented shield from the river Witham, or the swords with their decorated scabbards from the Witham and Trent. Gold necklets or torcs were probably symbols of rank and power, and two of Britain's finest come from Ulceby, near Kirmington. Horse-gear and chariot fittings made of copper alloy are known from many places in the county, and mould fragments from a settlement at Grimsby give insight into how such things were made. Feasting among the wealthy is attested by a copper alloy spout in the form of a bull's head from a bowl probably for straining wine, found at Kirmington.

It may be no coincidence that the richest settlements are all on or near high ground, or are found in locations favourable for trading. We might imagine an aristocracy primarily concerned with horse- or cattle-raising on the hills of the Wolds and Cliff. Supporting them would be an underclass of agriculturalists whose smaller and poorer settlements are now being recognised, defended as at Colsterworth, undefended as at Ancaster Quarry. The lesser folk grew corn and other crops and kept livestock, living only a little above subsistence level.

Temple sites are more difficult to recognise, although there were possibly two on the Wolds. For the rest, we can only surmise from later Romano-British evidence, such as the carved stone most probably from a temple at Ancaster recording a dedication to a Celtic god, Viridius by a Celt called Trenicus. More puzzling is the near-complete absence of Iron Age burials in Lincolnshire, and we have to assume that the dead were cremated and their ashes scattered, or that there was some other method of above-ground disposal.

It was evidently a prosperous land that attracted the Romans in c.AD 45, when the Ninth Legion undertook the conquest of the Corieltauvi. No match for the power that faced them, and with territory unsuitable for prolonged defence or guerrilla warfare, the Corieltauvi were over-run. The aristocracy either adapted or fled; lesser folk no doubt survived more easily. Townships, temples, farms and industries survived too, to form the basis of our map of Roman Lincolnshire.

Notes and further details on page 137.

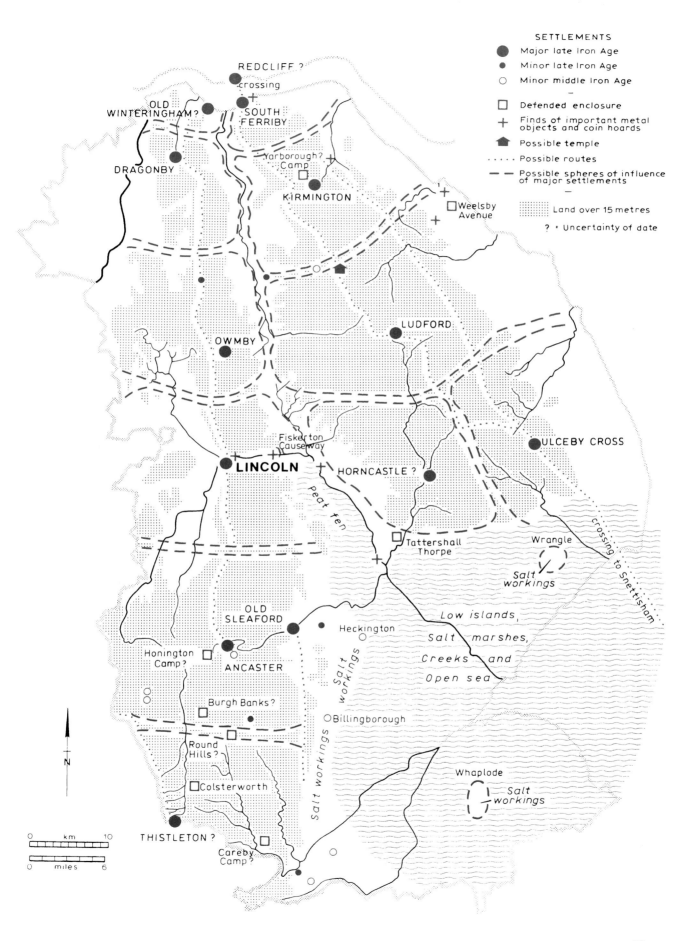

SETTLEMENTS

Major late Iron Age

Minor late Iron Age

Minor middle Iron Age

Defended enclosure

Finds of important metal objects and coin hoards

Possible temple

Possible routes

Possible spheres of influence of major settlements

Land over 15 metres

? = Uncertainty of date

REDCLIFF?
crossing
OLD WINTERINGHAM?
SOUTH FERRIBY
Yarborough? Camp
DRAGONBY
KIRMINGTON
Weelsby Avenue
LUDFORD
OWMBY
ULCEBY CROSS
Fiskerton Causeway
LINCOLN
HORNCASTLE?
Peat fen
Tattershall Thorpe
Wrangle
Salt workings
crossing to Snettisham
Low islands,
Salt marshes,
Creeks and
Open sea
OLD SLEAFORD
Heckington
Honington Camp?
ANCASTER
Burgh Banks?
Salt workings
Billingborough
Round Hills?
Colsterworth
Whaplode
Salt workings
N
km   10
miles   6
THISTLETON?
Careby Camp?

13

7 ROMAN LINCOLNSHIRE

Ben Whitwell

Iron Age Background: It is now clear that a number of the Roman towns in Lincolnshire, such as Old Winteringham, Dragonby, Kirmington, Owmby, Ancaster, Sleaford and Sapperton, started in the Iron Age. In the countryside, too, both villas and humbler settlements can be seen to have been preceded by Iron Age occupation; at Winterton Roman villa there is evidence for Iron Age hut-circles and field systems. There is, therefore, growing evidence of a continuum of occupation from the Iron Age into the Romano-British period. The topography of Lincolnshire was considerably different from the present day; there was a major inlet at the Wash, and the Witham and Ancholme valleys and the Isle of Axholme were areas of marshland with island occupation.

Roman Military Conquest: The way in which the Roman forts were placed to control and subjugate the Iron Age population can perhaps best be seen at Kirmington, where a major Iron Age settlement has a double-ditched fort superimposed upon it. This in turn was succeeded by a Roman civilian settlement. A similar sequence can be seen at Ancaster, but not at the majority of Lincolnshire's small towns. Some sites, such as Owmby, have considerable evidence of Iron Age occupation and subsequent Roman civilian occupation, but none for a military fort between these two phases. So far there is little evidence of a heavy military presence throughout the county. Lincoln itself, both as a legionary fortress and subsequently as the only chartered town in the county area, must have dwarfed in size and splendour the smaller Roman towns.

Small towns: These were generally composed of strip buildings with their narrow end onto the road. Where excavated, these buildings are generally found to be a combination of shop front and living quarters behind. These towns also had a hinterland of subsidiary settlement in the form of farms and villas; outlying irregular fields and enclosures may often have served the preceding Iron Age settlements and continued in use until the Roman period. Some of these small towns such as those on the Wolds at South Ferriby, Kirmington, Caistor, Ludford and Horncastle have no known Roman roads associated with them. A few of them such as Caistor, Horncastle and Ancaster had stone defensive walls which appear to have been built in the late Roman period to defend a small part of the preceding open settlements.

Rural Settlement: Major stone-built villas, with their characteristically regular layout, occur widely on the limestone uplands and the chalk Wolds. Their distribution reflects the availability of building material and in some cases the proximity of industrial raw materials. It is now clear that there were many more rural settlements, of less regular forms, on the uplands than was previously suspected. Some types of distinctive rural settlement recognised from aerial photography can be seen to repeat themselves throughout the county area, such as the so-called ladder settlements, but many other different forms of farmsteads represented have yet to be classified in detail.

Communications: The major route through Lincolnshire was Ermine Street which linked London with the military north, coming up to Lincoln and proceeding on to the Humber at Winteringham. The Fosseway met Ermine Street south of Lincoln, continuing southwest to Ilchester in Somerset and beyond. These and other major routes, laid out during the conquest period, were metalled, but there must have been many minor roads and tracks which remained unmetalled. For instance, Caistor High Street, prehistoric in origin, continued to serve the Roman settlements along the western edge of the Wolds and formed a link between South Ferriby on the Humber and Horncastle, close to the Roman coastline of the Wash. The many rural sites would also have required tracks to connect them to their market centres. Waterways, such as the Trent, the Ancholme, the Witham and the Slea, would also have been used extensively for transport and trade.

Trade: There is no convincing evidence for the large-scale exploitation of ironstone within the county, though numerous discoveries of slag in the Scunthorpe region and around Grantham suggest at least many small-scale production sites. The extraction of salt from sea water was a major industry and salted meat and fish would have been extensively traded. Pottery was produced at kilns throughout the county. Many of these were on a small scale, but some larger scale industries are indicated to the southwest of Lincoln, at Swanpool for instance, and on the edge of the Wolds in the area of Walesby. Pottery was also imported and fragments of amphorae, most usually of Spanish origin, have been found at many rural sites as well as in the small towns. These indicate trade in wine and other materials such as fish sauce which were transported from their Mediterranean origins. Samian ware, imported from production sites in France and Germany, is also widely found.

The End of the Roman Period: Some of the small Roman towns of Lincolnshire such as Ancaster and Caistor have Anglo-Saxon cemeteries close by. It has been suggested in the past that these may represent the burial grounds of settlers, brought in during the late Roman and early sub-Roman period to defend those towns and their surrounding areas from further incursions of their own people. However, where the towns have been extensively excavated, as at Hibaldstow, the picture that emerges is one of gradual dereliction with isolated buildings being burnt down but others continuing into the early fifth century. At a number of Roman rural sites, Anglian pottery has now been found. It is too early to assess the significance and dating of this pottery to decide whether it represents contemporary or post-Roman reoccupation of these sites. Several more cemetery sites are suspected from surface finds. The evidence suggests a much more extensive Anglian occupation of Lincolnshire than had previously been suspected, but how this relates to late and sub-Roman settlement in the area is as yet impossible to assess. It provides an exciting prospect for future research in the county.

Notes and further details on page 137.

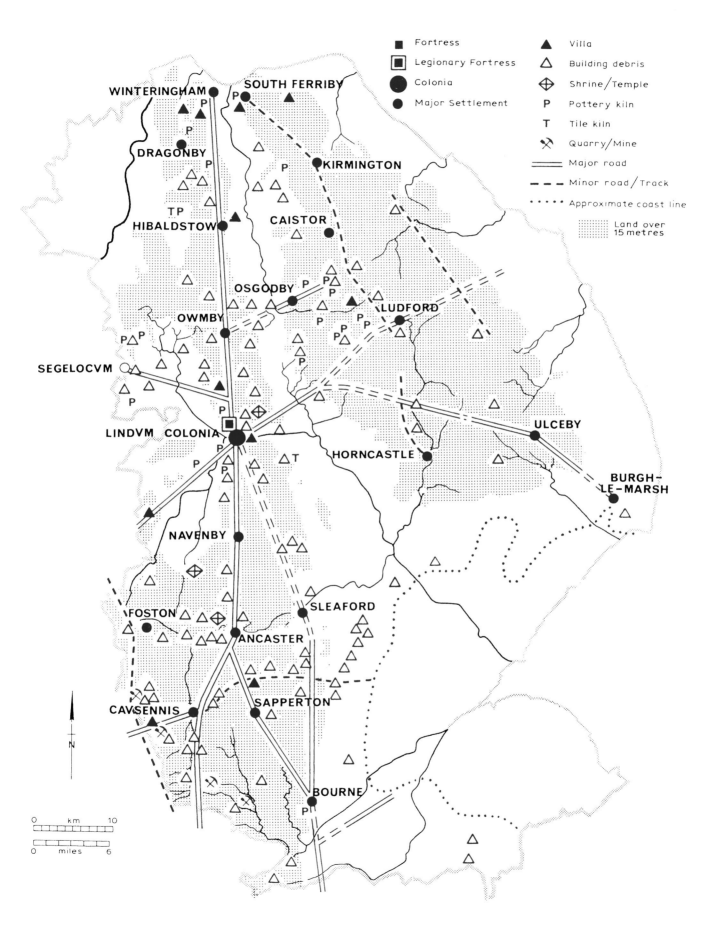

Fortress
Legionary Fortress
Colonia
Major Settlement

Villa
Building debris
Shrine/Temple
P Pottery kiln
T Tile kiln
Quarry/Mine
Major road
Minor road/Track
Approximate coast line
Land over 15 metres

WINTERINGHAM
SOUTH FERRIBY
DRAGONBY
KIRMINGTON
HIBALDSTOW
CAISTOR
OSGODBY
OWMBY
LUDFORD
SEGELOCVM
ULCEBY
LINDVM COLONIA
HORNCASTLE
BURGH-LE-MARSH
NAVENBY
FOSTON
SLEAFORD
ANCASTER
CAVSENNIS
SAPPERTON
BOURNE

0 km 10
0 miles 6

N

ROMAN LINCOLN

Michael J. Jones

Lincoln's geographical position and topography afforded an opportunity for settlement whose strategic potential was realised by the Roman army in the mid-first century AD. The site's location at the junction of the rivers Till and Witham at a gap in the Jurassic Ridge—itself a natural north-south routeway—had already attracted an Iron Age community on the banks of the Brayford Pool by the first century BC.

The army built its fortress on the hilltop to the north of the river at some date, still uncertain, in the Neronian period (AD 54-68), and improved the existing communications by constructing new roads. For a decade or so, about 5,000 soldiers of *Legio IX Hispana* occupied the site, before being replaced in 71 by *Legio II Adiutrix*. Following the pacification of the local tribe—the Corieltauvi—and the army's advance northwards in *c.*AD 78, the former fortress was designated a *colonia,* a self-governing community made up partly of discharged legionaries. The new city was provided with a range of public works and appears to have prospered, expanding in all directions but particularly to the south along Ermine Street. This process took place mainly during the second century AD.

The earth ramparts of the former timber fortress were fronted in stone, and its grid system of streets partly continued. Where barracks and granaries had once stood, temples, baths, the forum and probably a theatre rose, surrounded by domestic and commercial establishments. Part of the impressive forum-basilica—the civic centre—was uncovered in excavations in 1978-79; it had replaced the headquarters building of the fortress. Its plan, as so far established, is of more than usual interest for Britain, and may reflect continental design influence. The north wall of the basilica is partly represented by the so-called Mint Wall, still standing *c.*5 metres high, while its frontage on to the main street was an impressive colonnade. Part of the east range as excavated is exposed for public view. The baths were revealed in 1956-58 in the north-east part of the city. Roman Lincoln is famous for its aqueduct, although the source and workings of the system are not perfectly understood; drains and sewers are also known.

The hillside to the south was being developed by the early second century. It contained a number of public monuments, including a fountain and baths, along its main north-south street which had to be stepped up the steeper slope, while wheeled vehicles took a diagonal route. Mainly, however, it was used for private houses. Remains of several have come to light, dating primarily from the late second to the fourth centuries, and heating systems and mosaic floors were a commonplace. Fragments of architectural marble from several sites around the Mediterranean have turned up on the sites of public, private and commercial properties.

This lower area was also subsequently provided with walls, extending down almost to the river, approximately forty metres north of the present course; reclamation since the Roman period has narrowed it to the appearance of a canal. No major wharves have yet been identified. The enlarged enclosure covered almost 100 acres (*c.*40 hectares), more than doubling its original size. Gate structures have survived comparatively well, and some are still visible, but others remain problematic.

The low-lying land south of the river became an extensive commercial suburb, with ribbon development being preceded by landfill operations. Similar commercial establishments—long, narrow 'traders' houses'—are known from other extra-mural sites, but here to the south they have been found at several different locations, up to one kilometre south of the south gate. Yet it is difficult, if not impossible, to identify the functions of the associated workshops. Remains of ironworking are apparent at some of the sites. The cemeteries, too, occupied much space outside the walls, in some cases extending for several hundred metres along main routes. Land on the urban fringes was exploited for mineral resources and industrial activity sometimes took place in proximity. Pottery kilns are known to the southwest, northwest, east and later particularly in the Swanpool-Boultham area. Pottery became a major industry in the fourth century.

That period saw Lincoln's status being raised to that of a provincial capital, as Britain was subdivided into four. The injection of new officials and the workings of the taxation system helped to maintain the city's prosperity until the last quarter of the century. The walls were refurbished and private houses developed on a grand scale, while some public works began to decay. A church was built in the forum courtyard, possibly in the fifth century, and may have been that of the bishop. Its site appears to have continued as a Christian centre, while the rest of the town, already depopulated, was largely deserted, and its street system was lost in the next few centuries.

Notes and further details on page 137.

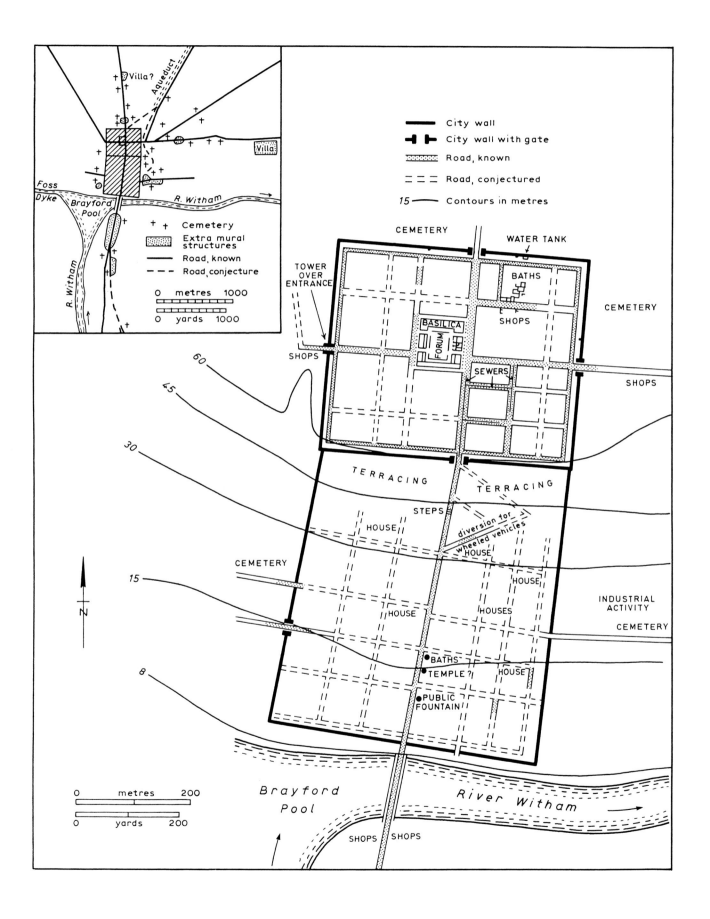

City wall
City wall with gate
Road, known
Road, conjectured
15 —— Contours in metres

CEMETERY   WATER TANK

TOWER OVER ENTRANCE   BATHS

CEMETERY

BASILICA FORUM   SHOPS

SHOPS

SEWERS   SHOPS

60
45
30   TERRACING   TERRACING

STEPS   diversion for wheeled vehicles

HOUSE   HOUSE

15   CEMETERY   HOUSE

8   HOUSE   HOUSES   INDUSTRIAL ACTIVITY

N   BATHS   CEMETERY
          TEMPLE?   HOUSE

          PUBLIC FOUNTAIN

metres 200
yards 200

Brayford Pool   River Witham

SHOPS SHOPS

Villa?   Aqueduct

Villa

Foss Dyke   Brayford Pool   R. Witham

R. Witham

+ + Cemetery
Extra mural structures
Road, known
Road, conjecture

0 metres 1000
0 yards 1000

17

IRON AGE AND ROMAN COASTS AROUND THE WASH

Brian Simmons

I: The Background

To attempt a reconstruction of coastal change for relatively ancient times is a task which is peculiarly difficult and complex. In essence it is an interdisciplinary pursuit, for it should incorporate a wide knowledge of a variety of academic pursuits. In order to achieve a realistic result the dynamics of the solid earth, the world oceans and the atmosphere have to be taken into consideration. The maps reproduced here cannot pretend to have been based on all the information which is available from geomorphologists, hydrographers, geophysicists, oceanographers and climatologists, either worldwide or on a regional basis.

These maps are, therefore, the products of a limited knowledge of some of those disciplines but are, more importantly, the result of eliciting information from experts in their various fields. There is inevitably a tendency towards an archaeological bias although it is hoped that this bias is not a strong one. Nevertheless, the purpose of the maps is an attempt to answer some basic questions of the type which will always intrigue the archaeologist and, indeed, the anthropologist too. Before discussing those questions it may be realistic to mention the use of the terms 'coast' and 'coastlines' in the context in which they are applied in these maps. It is comparatively simple to draw a line on a map and declare that here or there was the coast at a particular moment. The image that is portrayed is one of a strict division between land and water. Nothing could be further from the truth, and particularly so in the wild and ever-changing marshes found around the Wash. Observers of these marshes today in, say, Frampton and Freiston will soon discover that the sea does not come up to one particular place and no further. Even if the coastlines depicted on the maps are accurate–they are, of course, open to an element of doubt–some latitude must be allowed for variations in seasonal tides. Often the variations mean that in a low-lying area such as the Lincolnshire fens large tracts of land can be under water at one time of the year and, conversely, can be fairly dry at another.

There has been considerable archaeological fieldwork done in the Lincolnshire fens and adjacent areas over the past forty years or so. Many hundreds, if not thousands, of new sites have been found, the great preponderance of these being Roman and, to a lesser extent, Iron Age. The most recent of this fieldwork, the Fenland Survey, discovered a further 500 Roman sites alone, in an area which covered only thirty per cent of the Lincolnshire silt fens. There were in addition 100 Iron Age sites found during this Survey. If these new Iron Age and Roman sites are added to those already known, the occupation of some parts of the Fens and Marshes becomes complex. Other parts are empty of settlement, or so it would seem at first glance.

Distribution maps can be notoriously misleading. Sometimes they proclaim not a true distribution of this or that specific which the researcher is considering but the distribution of the fieldworker's predilection for one tract of land and not another, or for one type of site and not another. Care has to be exercised in order not to misinterpret the information. Having stated a note of caution, the fact remains that during the Iron Age the fens of Lincolnshire were only occupied in a minor way. However, along the western fen-edge there is a clear group of sites of this period.

Within two centuries the settlement patterns were to change dramatically. It has been claimed that within the Roman period the fens were more populous than at any other time. The causes of this seemingly sudden turn of events will be discussed shortly, but the enigmatic question remains of why the fens appear to have been more attractive in one cultural period and not before or after. What occurrence, or set of occurrences, had come about to cause the land to be used and settled at one period rather than another?

To start with, the modern researcher tends to examine the land as it is at the present moment. The arrangement of contours, the natural drainage system, the land and the sea will appear to have remained unchanged. Workers in other disciplines have observed from the geological record and elsewhere a remarkable phenomenon in the movement of sea since the last Ice Age, say over the past eight millennia. This record has been pieced together painstakingly in many places around the North Atlantic, and not only in Britain. The sea-level at that time eight thousand years ago would seem to have been thirty metres below the present one. As far as Britain is concerned, the modern mean sea-level is referred to as an Ordnance Datum Newlyn (ODN).

The sea rose gradually over the next six thousand years, but not consistently so. If the rise of the sea-level is seen as a graph, the sea rose as an irregular curve on that graph until, at the beginning of the Iron Age (somewhere around 500 BC–the date cannot be precise), the sea-level was actually higher than that of today. Within about five or six hundred years the sea began to regress until by AD 100, or shortly after, more land was available than at any other time since before the Iron Age. There are many reasons which govern the rise and fall in sea-level; changing climatic conditions, the melting of the ice-cap at the poles, tectonic movements, and so on. As far as the land around the Wash is concerned, a very slight rise in sea-level can cause immediate problems. As land in the fens and marshes is rarely above seven or eight metres ODN, a difference in sea-level results in either more or less land for use and settlement. Thus, in theory, in the early Iron Age a change was starting to happen in the land around the Wash.

Iron Age Coast

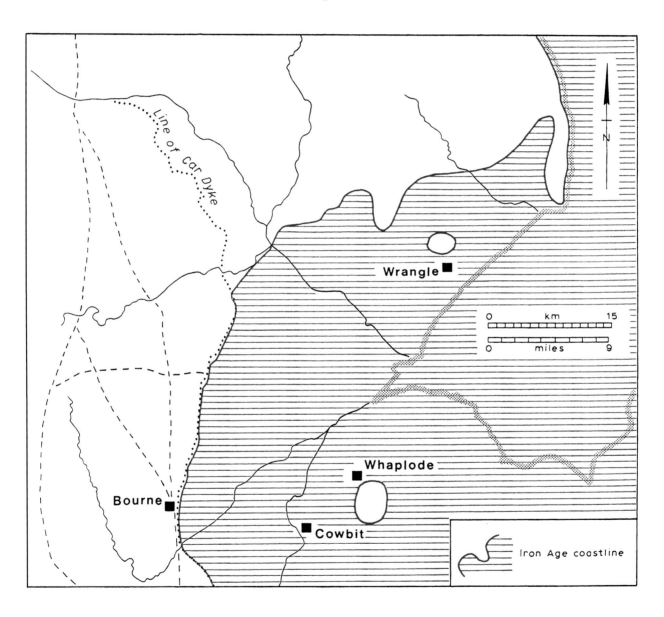

II: Archaeology

The mapping of ancient coasts depends in part on the retrieval of physical evidence. The principles of archaeological fieldwork are well-established–the use of aerial photography, soil type recognition, geophysical prospecting, and the careful recording of surface artefacts are all parts of this process, together with the noting of man-made features associated with concentrations of artefacts. When the information is plotted onto maps, certain patterns begin to emerge. Overall, an initial generalisation is observed for the Wash lands: there are no finds for the Neolithic period and the only Bronze Age discoveries are barrow cemeteries in the peat fens. Nothing is known of the prehistory of the silt fens, perhaps because these ancient landscapes have been buried by later alluvial deposits.

Once we move into proto- and historic periods the scene changes. Iron Age sites are seen along the western fen-edge, on a strip of land immediately to the east of the gravels on which lies the long run of modern villages stretching from the Kymes in the north to Bourne in the south. These Iron Age sites appear to reflect the later course of the Roman Car Dyke. There are other minor but important groupings of occupation deep into the fens, principally in Wrangle, Whaplode and Cowbit. As in the succeeding Roman period, there is no evidence of land use or settlement in the peat fens.

A remarkable change occurred after the Roman conquest, mainly in the second century AD. Occupation proliferated throughout the silt fens. Some of these sites are extensive, covering one hundred acres (40 ha) or more. The nature of land use and occupation during the Roman period is difficult to determine, for little or no extensive archaeological excavations have taken place. Nevertheless, an image can be produced of life and activity in this salt-affected landscape. To start with, any idea of exotic, wealthy Roman habitations should be discounted. There is no evidence to suggest towns and villas in these Roman fens, nor is there any record of extensive road systems or a military presence. More importantly, the archaeological information retrieved from the area so far suggests no large-scale cereal farming, as many historians would have us believe. It is more likely that the economy of the Roman fenlands depended on more mundane industries which were possibly of a seasonal nature.

In order to emphasise this picture, a comparison of the Roman and Iron Age coasts indicates some new Roman land between the Car Dyke and the *Midfendic,* together with a series of low-lying offshore islands. The very nature of this landscape is one of marsh or proto-marsh, which was infested by saltwater creeks. Salt is anathema to the successful growing of cereals. A more realistic reason for the many settlements in this Roman reclaimed land would be the production of salt (for which there is abundant evidence) together with pursuits related to salt; the preservation of meat, fowl and fish (including molluscs), and the tanning of leather may be inferred. If this is so, then some cattle ranching as well as fishing and wild fowling could have been of importance. Other trades and crafts may have been undertaken during the Roman period and, perhaps, also in the earlier Iron Age; basket making, turf cutting and the collecting of feathers (for quilts and pillows) spring to mind.

The many Roman occupation sites suggest a low level of subsistence. Although these sites have yielded large quantities of potsherds gathered from intensive programmes of archaeological field survey, there are very few artefacts indicating any degree of wealth. Unlike many other Roman sites, there are few coins and other metalwork from the Roman fens, nor are there mosaics, wall plaster or tiles, those indicators of Romanisation throughout the Empire. Instead, we should consider that the people living here at that time were British with a veneer of things Roman touching on their daily lives– the so-called Native Settlements. From the evidence to date, the thrust of Roman occupation would appear to have commenced in the reign of Hadrian (AD 117-138), an Emperor who is known to have enticed settlers to inhospitable areas with the promise of rent-free land for five years.

By about AD 375 weather and sea-level once again mitigated against the safe occupation of the fens. Added to these hazards was another–the increasing attention given to the east coast of Britain by incoming Anglo-Saxon tribes. Abandonment of the Roman fens was almost complete, or so it would appear; the fens were not to be reoccupied for another hundred years or more and even then only in isolated pockets.

The end of the period is interesting from another point of view. The defence of the coast against the Saxon invader from Norfolk southwards and along the south coast is attested through the series of military positions known as the Forts of the Saxon Shore. Some of these were in position by AD 300, others may have been introduced afterwards. In the fourth century further military installations were built: the signal stations of the Yorkshire coast as well as the forts in the west. These improvements appear to leave a large gap along the coast of Lincolnshire. But is this so? The modern coastline is silent on the subject, but important sites in Burgh le Marsh, South Kyme, Billingborough and Bourne could be the key to understanding the defence against Saxon incursions. It would also give a greater realism to the strengthening of the town defences in Horncastle at this time. As with many other topics in the Iron Age and Roman occupation of the fens, much more research is needed before this and other questions can be answered.

The Roman Coast

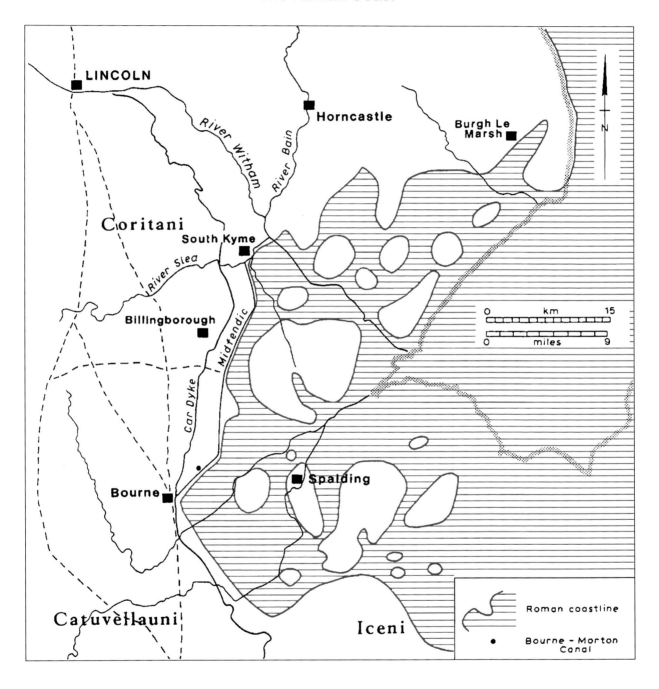

LINCOLN

Horncastle

Burgh Le
Marsh

River Witham

River Bain

Coritani

South Kyme

River Slea

Billingborough

Midfendic

Car Dyke

Bourne

Spalding

Catuvellauni

Iceni

0 km 15

0 miles 9

N

Roman coastline

Bourne - Morton
Canal

11 LINCOLNSHIRE IN THE ANGLO-SAXON PERIOD, *c.*450-1066 *Alan Vince*

Excavation on many Romano-British settlements, both rural and urban, has shown that they underwent a drastic decline in population, often amounting to a total abandonment, in the early fifth century. The only evidence for the distribution of settlement in the fifth to seventh centuries comes from archaeology and is by no means clear. There are, for example, a few finds of decorative metalwork from late Roman settlements which suggest that people of Germanic origin were present in the fourth and early fifth centuries, although their numbers cannot he estimated. By the late fifth century, however, there were several large cemeteries in the county in which cremation was the standard rite. Opinions vary as to the significance of the cemeteries, of which a dozen are known at present. Either they were serving only a small proportion of the population of the county or the population was much smaller in the late fifth and sixth centuries than it had been a century before. The discovery of a cemetery on the site of the church of St Paul in the Bail, Lincoln, which includes burials dated by radiocarbon to the sixth to seventh centuries, but where the burial rite was unaccompanied inhumation, suggests that the former interpretation may be the right one. In this case we can postulate that a British population (that is, the descendants of the Romano-British inhabitants) continued to live in Lincolnshire side by side with immigrants from the area of present-day Germany, Denmark and Holland.

Later in the sixth century, inhumation cemeteries are found in which the dead were buried fully clothed and accompanied by grave goods, such as pots and weapons. In contrast to the cremation cemeteries, these inhumation cemeteries are small and are sometimes found close together. This suggests that many more remain to be found and that by the later sixth century Anglo-Saxon communities were widespread and buried their dead in cemeteries adjacent to their settlements.[1] The location of these settlements is very poorly understood and at present is known only through finds of potsherds and other debris discovered by fieldwalking. A systematic fieldwalking survey of parts of the fens provides the best evidence for the density of settlement. However, a survey of pottery collections housed in the City and County Museum, Lincoln, suggests that away from the fens settlement was restricted to the lighter soils, sands and gravels and the limestone uplands. The heavy soils of the Trent valley and the Vale of Ancholme, for example, have not produced evidence for early Anglo-Saxon settlement.

The first documentary references to the area occur in Bede's *Ecclesiastical History* and show that by the 620s the northern part of the modern county, Lindsey, was a separate political unit, although it was subservient first to Northumbria and then to Mercia. The majority of the documentary evidence for the later seventh, eighth and early ninth centuries refers to the Church and a number of sites have been identified as those of early Christian centres. The nature of these sites–their size, their internal layout and their relationship with secular settlement–remains to be determined. It is also unlikely that we know the total number of such sites. Settlements have again been identified mainly through pottery scatters, with the exception of a high-status site at Flixborough. These pottery scatters sometimes occur on sites occupied in the early Anglo-Saxon period but sometimes represent apparently new settlements, as at Flixborough. Finds of Ipswich-type ware along the coast, from the south bank of the Humber to the fens, indicate some sort of coastal trade by this period although inland sites, for example along Lincoln Edge, were supplied almost entirely with locally-produced pottery.

From the late ninth century onwards there is evidence for extensive Scandinavian influence in the county. This is shown by place-names, the names of individuals recorded in documents, the names of moneyers marked on coins produced at the Lincoln mint (in existence by the early 10th century), and in the material culture. This body of data confirms the historical record that Lincolnshire was within that part of Mercia ceded to the Viking army in 874 following the defeat of the Mercian king, Burgred, at Repton. Opinions vary as to the relative contributions of Anglo-Saxon and Scandinavian peoples to the population of the county. At one extreme it is argued that there was a change of political overlordship which imposed a Scandinavian culture upon an Anglo-Saxon population while at the other extreme is the suggestion that there was an extensive immigration from Denmark over a considerable period of time from *c.*874 until the English recapture of the county *c.*920. It was not until the middle of the 10th century, with the defeat of Eric Bloodaxe, that English control of Lincolnshire was finally established; even after this, popular feeling seems to have been with the Danes. In 993 an army mustered to fight the Vikings, who were ravaging the lands beside the Humber mouth, failed to engage because, according to Florence of Worcester, 'they were Danes on their father's side'. Twenty years later, Swein of Denmark landed at Gainsborough in preparation for an assault on the English and, having received the submission of Northumbria and Lindsey, marched south leaving the area under the control of his son, Cnut.

The archaeological evidence suggests that many of the nucleated villages of Lincolnshire came into existence early in the Anglo-Scandinavian period. The parish division of the county seems to reflect a pattern of landholding established at the latest by the end of the 10th century but whether this pattern was imposed from scratch in the late ninth century or was developed from a pre-Viking situation is unknown. Domesday Book, however, records that certain estates, which at the time of the Domesday survey were held by separate landholders, still had connections with a central vill. It has been suggested that these sokes originated in the pre-Viking period and reflect an earlier system of administration. The county of Lincolnshire with what approaches its historic boundaries seems to have been in existence by the early 11th century. Before that it is thought that the area was administered as two units based respectively on Lincoln and Stamford.

Notes and further details on page 137.

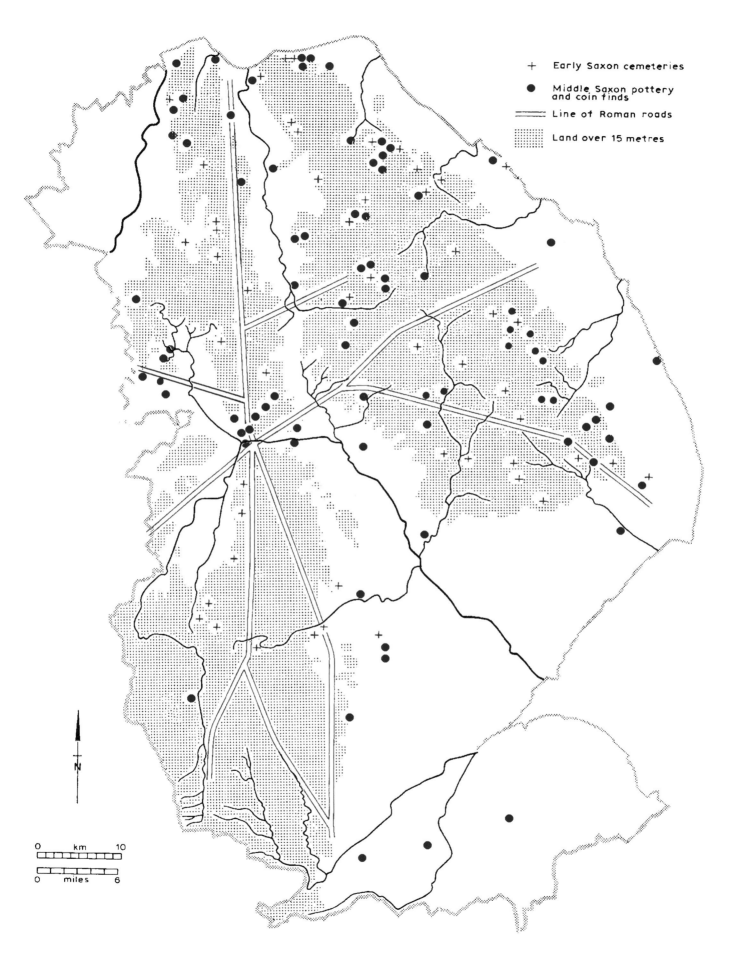

Early Saxon cemeteries

Middle Saxon pottery
and coin finds

Line of Roman roads

Land over 15 metres

0   km   10

0   miles   6

23

The six centuries from the end of the Roman administration in Britain until the Norman Conquest, being poorly served by the historical sources, understandably represent Lincoln's 'dark ages'. Although recent archaeological research has added to our knowledge, especially of the 10th and 11th centuries, much of the period remains intractable.

Archaeologists divide this formative period of English history into three: early (to *c.*650), middle (to *c.*850) and late Saxon. For several centuries from *c.*400 it is clear that Lincoln was no longer the centre of a large population: urban settlements were unnecessary to and unsupportable by the changed social and economic systems of the Anglo-Saxons. Nevertheless, some form of occupation continued, as evidenced by the Christian burial ground on the site of the Roman forum which was possibly associated with an adjacent church. It may have been a royal as well as an ecclesiastical centre; although there can be no certainty, Lincoln remains the strongest candidate for the capital of Lindsey. While the Roman street-grid fell into disuse, the strong fortifications, the survival of roads leading to the walled enclosure, and the presence of the river would all have contributed to creating a sense of place. Recent analysis has shown that, contrary to earlier ideas, there is pagan Saxon pottery from sites in Lincoln, indicating some form of settlement, however small. New lanes were formed, linking Roman gates and sometimes running diagonally to the former Roman grid.

We cannot yet tell how soon Anglo-Saxons took over political control, or whether, as seems possible, a British enclave survived for some time. Bede's account of the visit of Bishop Paulinus in *c.*627-9, when he met and converted the 'prefect of the city', Blecca, suggests the existence of some form of political organisation—perhaps even that representing the headquarters of the Kingdom of Lindsey. The stone church built by Paulinus was ruinous a century later, according to Bede. Its location is uncertain; its identification with that found in the forum is no longer considered likely on the grounds of both the evidence for timber construction and the dating of adjacent burials. A significant grave in the sequence here contained a seventh-century hanging bowl and was buried within a stone chapel. It presumably belonged to an important ecclesiastic, whose remains were subsequently translated to another site.

Otherwise the seventh and eighth centuries remain a mystery. Lincoln yields up no early coinage. Nor has it yet produced evidence for a 'wic', or trading settlement, as has come to light at several ports and other historic towns. Any such focus might lie, as at London and York, further upstream or downstream of the walled area, if it existed at all. The suggestion by Bassett that the southern suburb of Wigford originated in this way, and actually contained the royal palace of Lindsey, receives no support from archaeology as yet. Rather, among the modest quantities of Middle Saxon pottery found, the highest concentration was derived from the grounds of the Lawn, west of the upper city, near to the site of the medieval church of St Bartholomew. Presumably a farmstead or a market is indicated.

A dispersed hoard of the late ninth century found at the site of St Paul in the Bail may point to a growing economy in that period. The Viking settlement which followed clearly had a major effect on the city and coincided with a period of urban revival. We know that Lincoln was a mint and a town of national importance by the mid-10th century. Archaeology now suggests that reoccupation began by 900, that its growth was fast and continued up to and beyond the Norman Conquest.

Only since the 1970s have the slight traces left by timber buildings of this period been recognised, but now they are known from several sites. In particular the site at Flaxengate yielded a long sequence, showing increasing structural refinement and including both houses and workshops. They were laid out along a new north-south street parallel to the Roman Ermine Street whose line roughly survived nearby. Later a new east-west street was constructed to link the two. More recently, the detailed study of pottery types from excavations has also allowed us to articulate the town's growth, initially to be seen in the south-east part of the lower walled city and towards the river, subsequently across the river to Wigford and only later in the 10th century into the Upper City, which may have remained a royal enclave, or reserved area, until that date. The suburbs to the east and west of the city show some growth from the 11th century.

The Mint lay in the lower city. The names of the moneyers of the late 10th century suggest a mix of Anglo-Saxons and Scandinavians, and the artefacts recovered from recent investigations are also witness to trade with the Scandinavian world. Several sites have yielded evidence for industrial activity, notably copper- and glass-working, but other materials are represented, including bone, antler, silver and jet. Some reclamation took place on the waterfront to facilitate this renewal of large-scale trading, while traces of fishtraps and fish farms are found on the east side of Brayford Pool.

Many of the city's parishes originated in this period. Investigations at St Mark's in Wigford indicated a mid-10th-century date for the earliest church and graves, roughly the same as the conversion of the former chapel at St Paul in the Bail into a parish church. These original parishes were small and often proprietary; later, parish creation was made more difficult but forty or so churches were in being by 1100.

By the Norman Conquest, the town was again flourishing and populous, its inhabitants numbering more than 5,000, according to estimates based on the Domesday Survey.

Notes and further details on page 138.

Late Anglo-Saxon Lincoln: *c*.1000

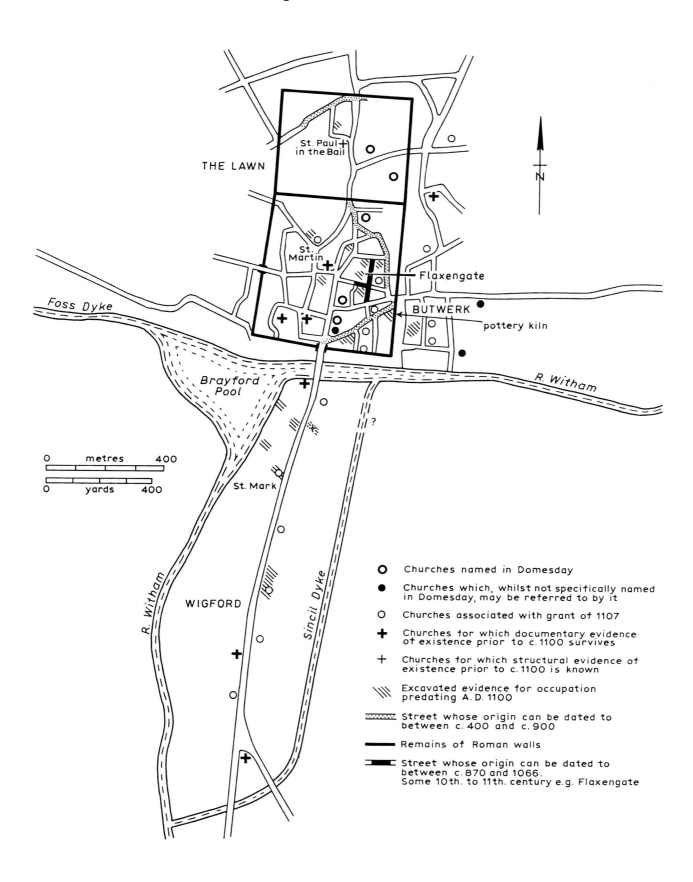

THE LAWN

St. Paul in the Bail

St. Martin

Flaxengate

BUTWERK

pottery kiln

Foss Dyke

Brayford Pool

R. Witham

R. Witham

St. Mark

WIGFORD

Sincil Dyke

N

metres	400
yards	400

O	Churches named in Domesday
●	Churches which, whilst not specifically named in Domesday, may be referred to by it
○	Churches associated with grant of 1107
✚	Churches for which documentary evidence of existence prior to c.1100 survives
+	Churches for which structural evidence of existence prior to c.1100 is known
\\\	Excavated evidence for occupation predating A.D. 1100
	Street whose origin can be dated to between c.400 and c.900
▬	Remains of Roman walls
▬	Street whose origin can be dated to between c.870 and 1066. Some 10th. to 11th. century e.g. Flaxengate

I: Iron Age and Roman

The extensive salt marshes which bordered east Lincolnshire in the Iron Age and Roman periods were the setting for one of the county's more significant early industries, that of salt production. Remains of the process, in the form of its distinctive fired-clay industrial waste, have been known since at least the 19th century, although the association of this material with the production of salt was not made until well into the 20th century.

Many of the initial discoveries of salterns were made on beaches in the Ingoldmells area, where storms and tidal action occasionally remove the protective layer of sand and offer a fleeting glimpse of the underlying vestiges of the Iron Age and Roman wetlands. On one such occasion, at the turn of the 20th century, S. Maudson Grant discovered a circular wall, 4.5 metres in diameter and 20 cm. high, composed of fragments of rough-baked pottery and burnt clay. From the domestic pottery he collected, an Iron Age date can be inferred for the site. Although other sites have since been discovered under similar circumstances (for example, by H.H. Swinnerton in 1932 and by F.T. Baker in 1952), Grant's site remains one of the most complete so far seen.

Pottery and 'briquetage', the overall name used for fired-clay debris from the sites, have also been discovered inland from Ingoldmells, notably in Orby, Addlethorpe and Hogsthorpe. Many of these sites are buried by up to three metres of post-Roman alluvial deposits and most have been discovered during commercial excavations such as dyke cutting; surveys conducted by Betty Kirkham have ensured that these sites are recorded. The findspots from the Hogsthorpe area shown on the map are chiefly the result of Kirkham's investigations. Whether a similar pattern would follow correspondingly intense fieldwork in the remaining marshland to the north and south is uncertain. However, if the hummocky nature of the boulder clay underlying the flood deposits is unique to that particular area of the marshland this may have especially suited the salt makers.

The majority of Iron Age and Roman salterns on the map lie around the inner edge of the fenland basin. Most of these sites have been damaged by intensive arable agriculture and their remains have been found during fieldwalking, notably by Sylvia Hallam, the Car Dyke Research Group and the Fenland Survey. In a report on the Fenland Survey, the authors have suggested that the salt making sites were positioned on the 'quiet water', inland edges of the saltmarshes. In these areas the flow of saline water is most controllable, and the material requirements of the industry, clay to make the 'briquetage' and fuel to aid the evaporating process is to hand. Due to the overflowing of freshwater streams entering the fenland a band of peat was formed around the landward edge of the tidal marshes; this would have provided an abundant source of fuel for the salt makers.

The Iron Age and Roman marshes were often much wider than their modern counterparts. Extensive creek systems pierced the otherwise stable and habitable marshland. As a result settlement took place to the east of the salterns in the Roman period and, to a lesser extent, in the Iron Age. The Roman marshes were at least 10 km. wide in the Billingborough/Quadring area and settlement sites extended over that distance. The extent of the marshes would, of course, have varied from area to area. Nevertheless, a similar pattern of salterns, around the inland edges of occupied marsh land but near to the peat, was recorded in Wrangle during the Fenland Survey. Here domestic sites were found close to the modern coast at little more than a metre above the present sea level, and it is very likely that part of the Roman marsh and its settlements have since been inundated and eroded by the sea. A similar series of events is likely to have taken place around Ingoldmells, the recorded sites being on the inland edge of marshes that are now lost to the sea.

In the absence of a completed modern excavation on an Iron Age or Roman saltern, the method of extracting and processing salt in Lincolnshire is unclear. Tens of thousands of pieces of briquetage have been collected although little has been recovered intact. Fragments of clay troughs feature heavily among the Lincolnshire debris. A fragmentary fired clay trough from Ingoldmells has been reconstructed. It is some 71 cm. long, 9 cm. deep and 23 cm. broad at one end, tapering to 16 cm. at the other. Significantly this trough has marks on the underside indicating it was once subjected to heat or fire, presumably in an evaporating process. A 'clean' circular mark suggested the trough had rested on a support. Such items, otherwise known as handbricks, props or pedestals, are commonly found on saltern sites from both the Iron Age and Roman periods. In the south-western fenland region it has been noted that supports on the Iron Age sites are invariably shorter than those of the Roman period. Other than that, the chief difference between Iron Age and Roman briquetage is that more 'bridging pieces' appear on Iron Age sites. These are simple, hand-moulded pieces of clay which were apparently used to stabilise parallel troughs, by bridging or connecting them.

There is scant evidence for precise dates of Lincolnshire's salterns. The three radiocarbon dates, from Billingborough, Hogsthorpe and Helpringham, are all Iron Age. Domestic pottery found on Iron Age salterns in the south-western Fens is of a type in use *c.*400-150 BC. Precise dating of the Roman salt industry in Lincolnshire has yet to be achieved. A termination date early in the Roman period has been suggested for saltern sites in both Essex and Sussex. However, in Norfolk, a second or third century AD date has been linked to salt production at Denver.

In addition to the possible uses of salt as a currency or medium of exchange, there would have existed a marked need for salt in the fenland region, both for the general domestic uses of the local communities and, through the preservation of meat and fish, to make the abundant fen produce available for sale to the wider population. Salt is also essential in the preservation of hides.

Notes and further details on page 138.

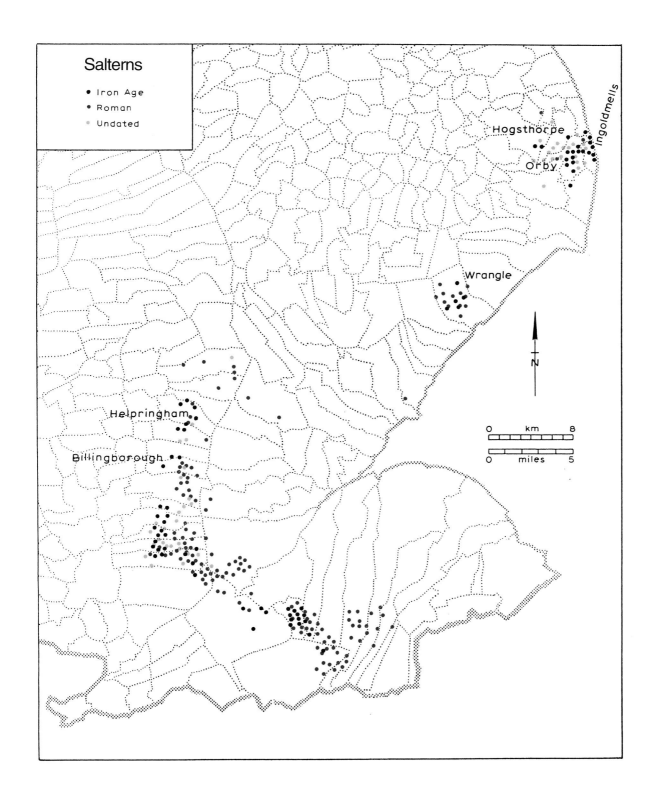

II: Saxon and Medieval

The salt-making industry was, as has been demonstrated, already well-established on the Lincolnshire coast by the Roman period. Whether, or in what way, it survived in the years following the breakdown of Roman administration is not yet known, yet Domesday Book shows that it was equally well-established in 1086, and a site of about this date has been recorded near Bicker. What had happened in the intervening years? It is hard to believe that such an important commodity went out of use, but it may be that new methods of production came into being which left no recognisable physical remains. Despite the recent increase in information on Early and Middle Saxon settlement in the fenland, the locations of contemporary salt-making have yet to be identified. No comparable fieldwork has been carried out in search of Saxon sites in the Lindsey marshland.

The map of medieval saltern sites is inevitably a composite one, showing only the approximate position of sites of different dates spread over seven centuries, from the time of the earliest written or archaeological record to the early 1600s. In 1086 salt-making sites or salterns were listed in various places all the way up the Lincolnshire coast. Mysteriously, several belonged to villages well away from the sea, for example to Maidenwell and Fotherby, and it has to be concluded that these places possessed holdings in the marsh to the east. Sites mentioned in 1086 are shown as open circles on the map, and where a precise number of sites was stated, this is given within the circle. Later medieval salterns are shown as stippled areas, since it is not possible to know their operational dates. The two sites excavated in recent years, at Quadring and Wainfleet, are indicated by a triangular symbol.

What the map cannot show in detail is how the landscape changed over the years, in particular the coastline. As the marsh accumulated, the salt makers moved to remain near the salt water, their basic raw material. Steady accretion occurred on the coast from Boston northwards to Wainfleet and in the Marshchapel Somercotes area, and the progress of land reclamation can be traced by noting the series of successive sea banks. On the south side of the Wash there were more extensive marine deposits, and greater enclosures made at any one time.

All along the coast, estuaries or havens, for example Saltfleet, Wainfleet, Wrangle and Fleet, gradually silted up and were eventually almost completely closed off. Bicker Haven dwindled down to one small channel, and salt-making sites near the village of Bicker are now up to 15km from the sea. Further north they cluster outside the successive medieval sea banks.

Methods of manufacture were different from those used in Roman and pre-Roman times and have left quite different traces on and in the ground. The most obvious evidence is that of the wholly artificial mound built up chiefly from waste soil left by the salt makers. Groups of these mounds can be seen in many areas of former medieval shoreline such as Gedney Dyke, Holbeach Hurn, Wrangle and Friskney Tofts, Grainthorpe and Marshchapel. Examples are generally close to an early sea bank. The mounds are all the more striking since they lie in an otherwise flat landscape of marsh or former marsh.

Medieval and later documents give information not only on the location of sites but also on the appearance and equipment, and much has been learnt about the process. Some of this has been corroborated by modern excavation. The actual equipment and technology involved in the process is documented nationally in accounts from as late as the 17th and 18th century. The three main phases of activity were collection, filtration and evaporation. Initially salt-impregnated mud was scraped up after high tides, since it then has a higher saline content than seawater itself. It was stored under cover until required, when the salt was washed out of it. This filtration process required the silt to be placed in a trough lined with turves and washed through with fresh water. This dissolved soluble and undesirable salts present, such as potassium chloride (better known to us as Epsom salts). The resulting solution was channelled into a succession of barrels and vats where any remaining sediment settled. The brine was evaporated by boiling in lead pans (which apparently had no adverse effect on the salt) over pairs of long narrow clay-built hearths fuelled by steady peat fires. The remains of fuel ash, hearths and burning contribute a variety of dark brown and red hues to the soil, especially when a site has been ploughed deeper than normal. Seen from the air, these colours, together with that of the pale discarded silt, are quite striking and can often help to identify a former site where no spoil heap now remains.

The salters' buildings were made of locally available materials, light timber with mud walls and reed thatch. Excavations at Quadring and Wainfleet have revealed hearths and remains of the clay linings to some of the long-perished wooden containers and of turves used in the filtering. Observations on late Saxon salterns cut through by ditches between Bicker and Donington have shown that the same types of container had been in use since before 1086.

Salt-makers rented their salt-making areas, and often a grant of peat-digging rights accompanied a lease. The operations were carried out only during the summer months and rentals show that payments to landlords in the form of salt were made at Midsummer and Michaelmas only. However, the saltboilers were also smallholders and had other means of subsistence to keep them through the remainder of the year. Inventories from 16th-century Lindsey detail property including vessels and implements in use on site as well as stock such as geese and sheep.

The Lincolnshire industry died out around the early 1600s, earlier than in some parts of Britain where it carried on into the 18th century. One of the principal reasons for the decline was the importation of cleaner, whiter, sun-evaporated salt from the Bay of Biscay.

Notes and further details on page 138.

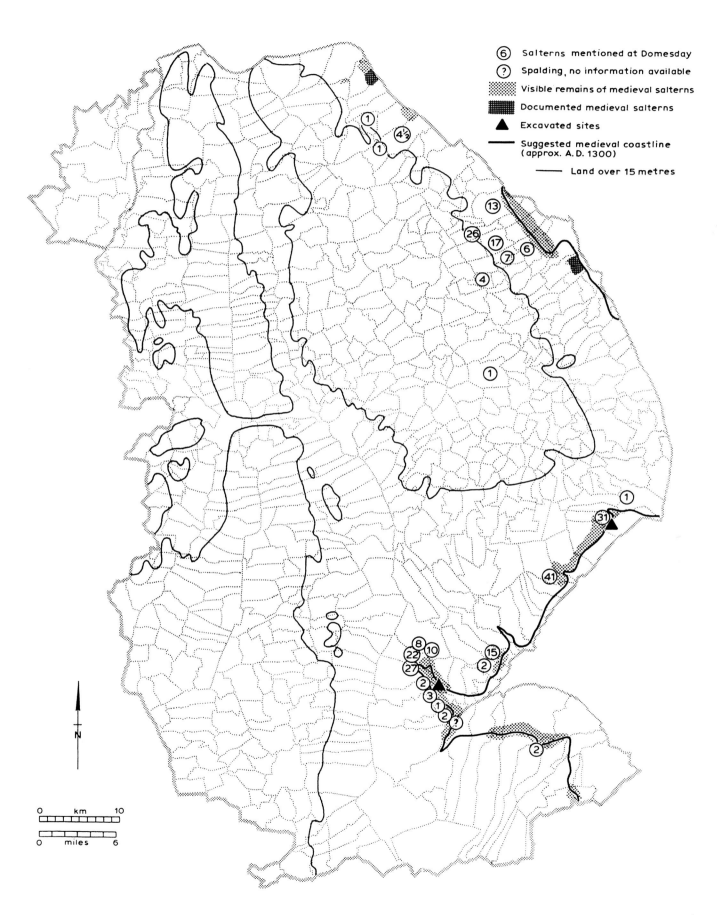

- ⑥ Salterns mentioned at Domesday
- ⑦ Spalding, no information available
- ▓ Visible remains of medieval salterns
- ■ Documented medieval salterns
- ▲ Excavated sites
- ── Suggested medieval coastline (approx. A.D. 1300)
- ── Land over 15 metres

0 km 10

0 miles 6

N

29

THE DISTRIBUTION OF SILVER STREET KILN-TYPE POTTERY   *Jane Young*

During the second half of the ninth century large areas of the country were subjected to a series of raids and incursions by Viking invaders. Settlement followed and urban-based communities grew up, those in the East Midlands being centred on Derby, Leicester, Lincoln, Nottingham and Stainford. All of these centres except Derby have been shown by finds of kilns or wasters to have been producing pottery by the 10th century.[1] The high-quality wheel-thrown pottery produced in these centres was in direct contrast to the often crude handmade wares made during the preceding Anglo-Saxon period. Within the area this development is unlikely to have been the result of new impetus being given to existing local industries, but is more likely to have come from imported ideas and craftsmen. Certainly at both Lincoln and Stamford the introduction of these technologically superior pottery types was sudden, with no evidence at all for a transitional stage between Anglo-Saxon and late Saxon types.

Archaeological evidence shows that in Lincoln several of these local pottery industries were established by the late ninth century. The earliest dating at present relies on evidence from the Flaxengate site[2] where local wheel-thrown sand- and shell-tempered wares were found in deposits dating to before the construction of the earliest timber buildings in the late ninth or early 10th century.

In 1973 excavations at Silver Street[3] in Lincoln revealed the remains of three kilns producing shell-tempered pottery. Substantial amounts of this pottery including wasters were found, indicating large-scale production. To date 89,546 sherds of this pottery have been recovered from Lincoln and its environs. The largest of the kilns was of unusual size, at least 5.9 by 1.5 metres internally, a capacity as yet unparalleled. The firing technique used was a relatively simple one, in which both the vessels and the fuel would have been stacked together in the manner of a bonfire. By analogy with the pottery from other sites the kilns at Silver Street can be dated to the mid- to late 10th century. The pottery itself is generally oxidised and varies in colour from light red to reddish-yellow. Shell inclusions are visible as small white specks on the surface. The manufacture of the ware is of a very high standard. Vessels are consistently well-thrown and even the handles and spouts are made on the wheel. Use is made of templates to standardise the vessel and rim shapes.

The main decoration consists of diamond or square roller stamping in bands on the rim and shoulder of the pots, although use is also made of finger-pressed strips and of bosses. A few vessels are even glazed. The range of forms is quite diverse. Jars were the main form produced and these were made in varying sizes from very small (*c.*5 cm. rim diameter), possibly used as cups, to very large ones (up to 30 cm. rim diameter) used for storage. The medium-sized jars were used for a variety of purposes including cooking, industrial use and storage. These jars were adapted for use as pitchers by the addition of a tubular spout and one or more handles. Wide-mouthed jars were made, possibly for table use as they are always highly decorated. Other jars were made with pouring lips. Bowls and dishes seem to have been made in every shape and size, very small ones for use as glass crucibles, small highly-decorated ones for table use, spouted and lugged ones for cooking, and some intended for use upside-down as bakers. Other forms such as lamps, pedestal cups, costrels, lids and decorated necked pitchers copying continental examples were also produced. This industry flourished in Lincoln from the late ninth to the late 10th centuries. At present no evidence can be found to explain its demise in the late 10th to early 11th centuries.

Ceramic distribution maps are commonly used to show trade and commerce. Pottery is the one artefact that is found on almost all medieval sites; it is readily broken in use but is almost imperishable under most conditions. As the result of research undertaken during the past three years as part of the East Midlands Anglo-Saxon Pottery Project,[4] identified findspots of Silver Street kiln-type pottery have dramatically increased. Detailed study of the fabric has shown no evidence for its being manufactured elsewhere. There is always some difficulty interpreting ceramic plots. Although they may to some degree reflect commercial, economic and social links, they can tell us little unless we are aware of all the factors involved. At first glance the distribution map for the Silver Street pottery appears to show that findspots are commonest to the north and east of Lincoln. This pattern, however, is only a reflection of the intensive fieldwalking in these areas done by Eleanor and Rex Russell in the 1960s and 1970s. The apparent gaps in the extreme north and to the south of Lincoln reflect the large amount of pottery from these areas still awaiting examination. Nor is it possible to show the various phases of settlement that must have taken place within the *c.*130 years that the Silver Street kiln-type pottery was produced. In effect this map can only give an indication of the overall spread of the Silver Street material and of settlement during the late ninth to the late 10th centuries.

It is to be expected that a distribution plot at this period would show a concentration near the production site, then intra-urban occurrences with a small number of other findspots. The patterning evident in the Silver Street pottery, however, does not follow this theory, but indicates a wide distribution network well into the rural hinterland and beyond. Outside the county, the pottery is found at York and Beverley, at Nottingham, Newark, Collingham and Thurgarton, at Leicester and South Croxton, and at Tamworth. Such finds are too numerous to be accounted for by simple exchange methods and suggest marketing by a middleman. The most interesting find is of a complete jar found in a grave at Birka in Sweden.[5] All the evidence from both the pottery itself and its distribution points towards industrial specialisation by a group of potters who had access to an increasing population and the means effectively to market their goods.

Notes and further details on page 138.

30

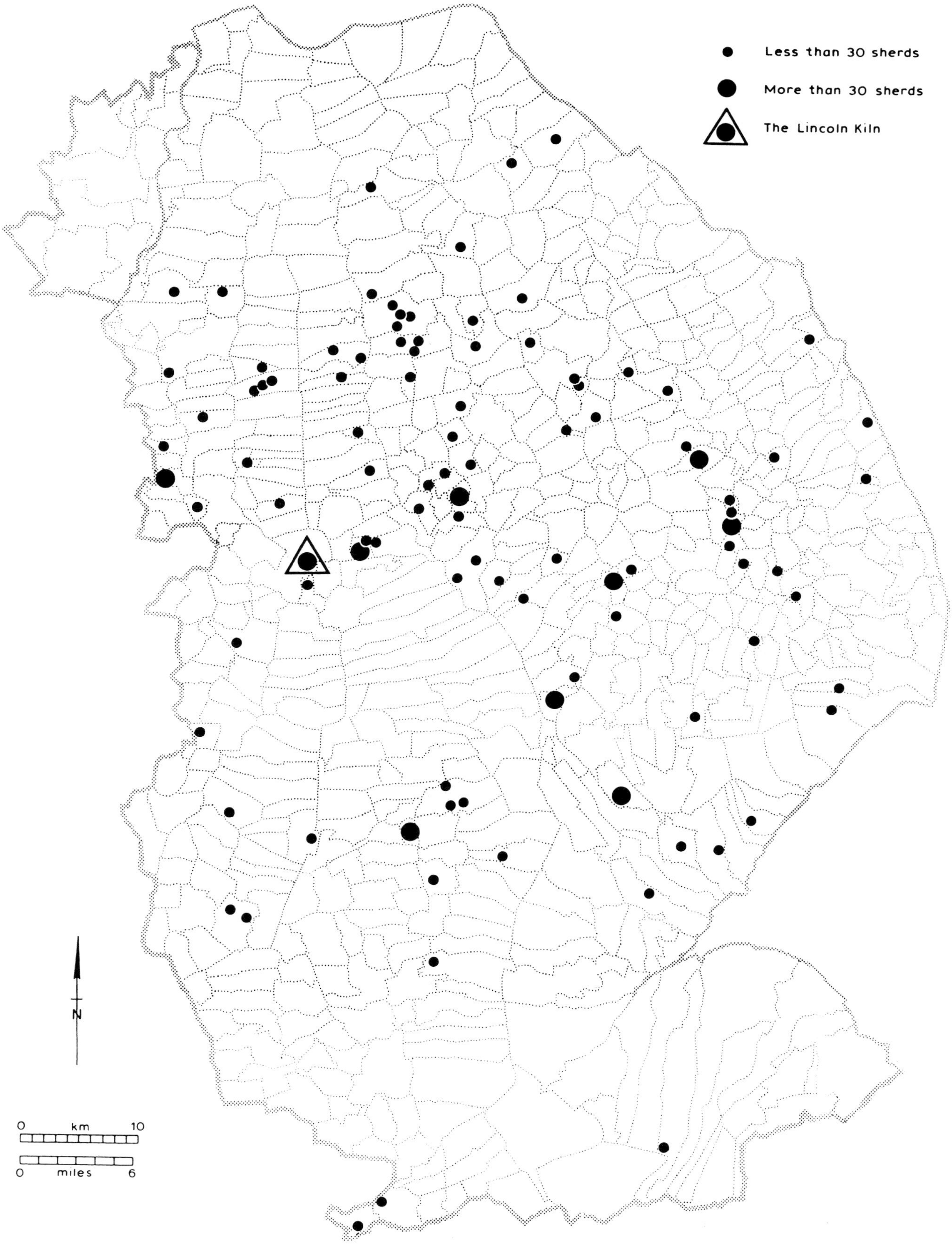
Less than 30 sherds
More than 30 sherds
The Lincoln Kiln
N
0 km 10
0 miles 6

Michael J. Jones

The thriving town which had developed during the two centuries preceding the Norman Conquest was just the sort of place to attract attention from the new rulers. As William returned from the North, a castle was erected in 1068 in a dominant location, the south-west quarter of the upper Roman city, its earthern, bank mounded over parts of the Roman south and west walls. Within half a century it had been rebuilt in stone. The rest of the Roman enclosure served as an outer bailey, and this became known as the 'Bail'. It was also the Conqueror's policy to move episcopal sees to centres of population; accordingly a new cathedral was commenced in 1072 under the supervision of the first Norman bishop, Remigius. Land was granted opposite the castle, in the south-east corner of the upper enclosure. The Minster was consecrated twenty years later but building went on for several centuries, some of it occasioned by structural failure and fires.

The political decisions taken by William had important ramifications, social, economic and topographical. New streets were created surrounding the two monuments, while those displaced from their houses had to be rehoused; the suburb of Newport to the north of the city walls may have developed considerably as a result. Further expansion both inside and outside the walls took place, including an area on the north side of Brayford Pool known as 'Newland'. Reclamation is probably implied; it is certainly evidenced from archaeological work.

The first Norman decades also saw the number of parishes climb to almost fifty, and street frontages were built up throughout the town. Markets were held by various trades in different parts of the town. From the late 12th century domestic houses were being built in stone; the two so-called 'Jews Houses' still survive on Steep Hill (Mikelgate), an important commercial street. Other fine town houses are known from illustrations, while a contemporary survival, St Mary's Guildhall in lower High Street (in the suburb of Wigford), served the city's premier socio-religious guild. It may have originated as Henry II's town residence at the time of his crown-wearing at Christmas 1157. Architectural and documentary study has identified and elucidated more medieval residences including several in the area of the Cathedral, while excavations have revealed many good-quality stone houses, particularly in the lower walled city. In due course, the city saw the foundation of a range of monastic establishments, though for some, land was only available in the suburbs or on the urban fringe. The Greyfriars, now the City and County Museum, represents the best surviving fragment. It was probably the Franciscan infirmary.

The medieval city was perhaps at its greatest extent at about 1300, with the friaries in place, and the Close Wall under construction around the Cathedral and the properties which had been acquired by the Dean and Chapter; most of these lay to its east beyond the former Roman wall. Some sort of fortification was at least commenced at the edges of the suburbs of Newport and Wigford, while the former Roman city walls, no doubt with some refurbishment, continued to serve the medieval town. The Roman south wall subsequently went out of use as the east and west walls were extended to the new riverfront, more than twenty-five metres south of the original line. It was probably in the 12th and 13th centuries that vertical wharves were provided for the first time, and a stone bridge was erected (*c*.1140) to carry the High Street across the river. Much of the structure still survives.

The study of pottery and animal bones from excavations seems to indicate the changed requirements of the new Norman elite from the late 11th century. Similarly, detailed archaeological work is throwing new light on matters poorly covered by the literary sources; for instance, several houses excavated in the suburb of Butwerk east of the lower city were of good quality and indicate considerable wealth. In due course, further analysis of artefacts and bones might help us to differentiate socio-economic groups across the city.

The city's wealth was based to some extent on the cloth and wool trades. Fine cloth was widely exported but when its manufacture failed to compete with Flemish products there was a serious economic effect on the city. Moreover, with the introduction of the fulling mill, the wool trade moved into rural areas. A similar fate befell the local pottery industry at a later date. Sites of kilns have been found at three locations in Wigford: that to the east of St Mark's was producing pottery and tile in the mid to late 14th century.

Lincoln also suffered along with other towns from the economic problems of the 14th century and from the Black Death of 1349. Advantages had come from the control of foreign trade; in 1369 the removal to Boston of the Staple, only gained in 1326, was a further serious blow.

Both the historical sources and archaeological evidence suggest a decline in population and in at least some aspects of living standards from this time, a trend not reversed until the end of the 17th century. Churches were demolished and parishes combined. The city was as badly affected as any place of its former importance. Like other towns, it petitioned the King for some remission in taxation, but these cries for assistance took some time to be heard and met with limited success. Urban life contributed, but more as a county town than a regional or provincial capital. In 1066 Lincoln had counted in the top five towns; a subsidy of 1524 suggests that the city had fallen to 19th place in England. Later maps and archaeology indicate that it was the areas beyond the main streets which had become empty.

Notes and further details on page 138.

Medieval Lincoln: *c*.1300

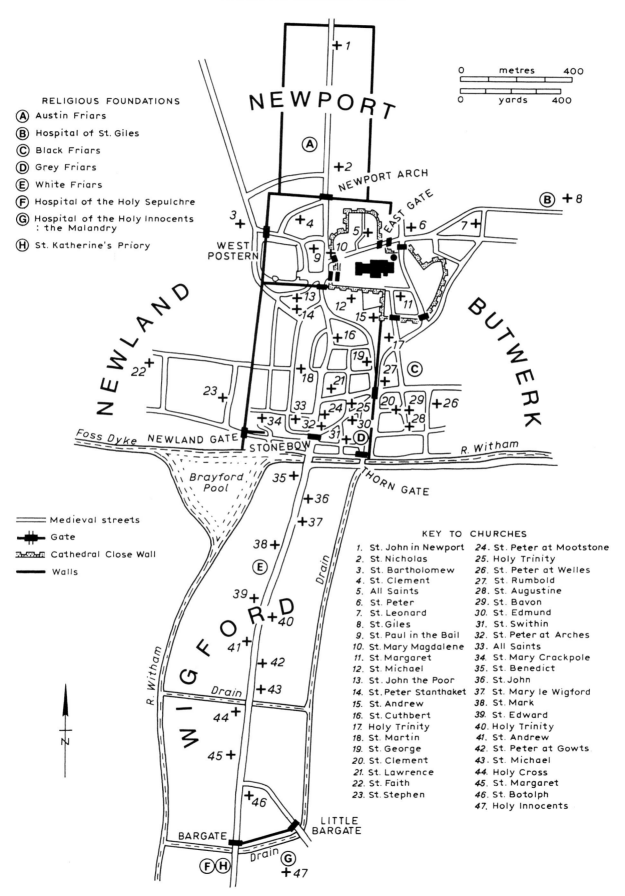

RELIGIOUS FOUNDATIONS
(A) Austin Friars
(B) Hospital of St. Giles
(C) Black Friars
(D) Grey Friars
(E) White Friars
(F) Hospital of the Holy Sepulchre
(G) Hospital of the Holy Innocents : the Malandry
(H) St. Katherine's Priory

=== Medieval streets
+■+ Gate
Cathedral Close Wall
— Walls

NEWPORT

NEWPORT ARCH

EAST GATE

WEST POSTERN

BUTWERK

NEWLAND

Foss Dyke   NEWLAND GATE

STONEBOW

Brayford Pool

THORN GATE

R. Witham

R. Witham

WIGFORD

Drain

Drain

Drain

BARGATE

LITTLE BARGATE

Drain

KEY TO CHURCHES

1. St. John in Newport	24. St. Peter at Mootstone
2. St. Nicholas	25. Holy Trinity
3. St. Bartholomew	26. St. Peter at Welles
4. St. Clement	27. St. Rumbold
5. All Saints	28. St. Augustine
6. St. Peter	29. St. Bavon
7. St. Leonard	30. St. Edmund
8. St. Giles	31. St. Swithin
9. St. Paul in the Bail	32. St. Peter at Arches
10. St. Mary Magdalene	33. All Saints
11. St. Margaret	34. St. Mary Crackpole
12. St. Michael	35. St. Benedict
13. St. John the Poor	36. St. John
14. St. Peter Stanthaket	37. St. Mary le Wigford
15. St. Andrew	38. St. Mark
16. St. Cuthbert	39. St. Edward
17. Holy Trinity	40. Holy Trinity
18. St. Martin	41. St. Andrew
19. St. George	42. St. Peter at Gowts
20. St. Clement	43. St. Michael
21. St. Lawrence	44. Holy Cross
22. St. Faith	45. St. Margaret
23. St. Stephen	46. St. Botolph
	47. Holy Innocents

0   metres   400
0   yards   400

Some 2,300 place-names are found in the folios of the Lincolnshire Domesday and all but a handful can be identified with about 790 settlements which exist today or are known from earlier sources. It would be a mistake, however, to suggest that the survey provides a comprehensive account of 11th-century settlement, for its principal concern was with estates rather than villages. The Domesday Inquest was initiated by William the Conqueror at Gloucester in 1085. Since the Conquest, almost all the major landholdings in England had changed hands and, with the threat of invasion from Scandinavia, the king urgently needed to reassess the resources of his realm in order to prepare for the coming onslaught. The first priority was to take stock of his own income, the regular provision of the crown in terms of geld (that is taxation) and royal estates. However, the king was hardly less concerned with the estates of the tenants-in-chief, for he regularly received several types of due from them, notably military service, and, more exceptionally, the profits of wardship, forfeitures and the like.

Domesday Book was compiled as an account of these estates and their value to their lord. It is arranged by county, but within each a chapter is devoted to each tenant-in-chief and the basic unit of textual organisation is the manor through which seigneurial wealth was accumulated (*see* 18 Domesday Estate Structure.) Various sources went into its making. Pre-existing geld-lists, arranged geographically by twelve-carucate hundred, provided a comprehensive account of landholders and their tax liability, and these were checked and updated by reference to the verdicts of hundred and wapentake juries (*see* 19 Medieval Administration). The jurors' knowledge, however, was limited to little more than the identity of the tenant, the location of his land, its value to him and his legal right; most of the detail of manorial structure and stocking was supplied by the lords themselves or their agents in oral or written returns arranged by manor. The Domesday text was compiled from these returns in the light of the jurors' evidence.

The identifying names of Domesday entries were variously drawn from both of these sources. The nomenclature of geld lists was widely employed in the south of the county. Hundred names alone are given in twenty or so entries, but the fact is usually not explicit. Thus, three estates are identified as Tydd St Mary, but only the king's manor was situated in that settlement; those of Ivo Taillebois and Guy de Craon were actually located in Long Sutton which was a member of the hundred and is otherwise only incidentally noticed in the text. Estate names, however, are not unknown. Robert of Vescy's manor identified as Caythorpe encompassed the settlements of Frieston, Normanton, West Willoughby and part of Ancaster and extended into four hundreds. But hundred names are probably more common in this area. In Lindsey, by contrast, estate names are the norm since the hundreds were much larger than in the south, and their names therefore did not identify land so precisely. Throughout the county, however, the constituent elements of manors are given when estates were dispersed. Count Alan's manor of Waltham, for example, extended into at least fourteen settlements outside the estate centre, although it did not hold all the land in each.

Place-names, then, usually identify organisations rather than villages, and there are therefore few clues to the nature and distribution of habitation. The Domesday scribe does occasionally differentiate settlements of the same name. Market, Middle and West Rasen, for example, are explicitly noted in the text. Generally, however, such divisions are not noted. Thus, the entries relating to Elkington are undifferentiated, but the notice of two churches suggests that North Elkington was already distinct from South Elkington. In such cases the existence of settlements can only be suggested by the location of the fees in the later Middle Ages. The form of settlements is as elusive as the number. Occasional references sugggest nucleated settlements with a penumbra of farms or hamlets–the account of land 'in Drayton itself' implies a central village with outlying elements, and a number of references to sokemen who held tofts may imply a degree of dispersed settlement in some areas– but generally Domesday Book is a poor guide.

Despite its deficiencies, it nevertheless provides a remarkable insight into the society and economy of the county in the 11th century. The 790 or so places named represent no less than 75 per cent of the total number of place-names recorded in the early 14th century when settlement reached its furthest extent. The number of places must have been higher, for where a place-name does not appear in the Domesday text the presumption must often be that the settlement it refers to was a subsidiary element in a larger whole, in the absence of evidence for a later origin. Although many villages may have been loose collections of farms with a common identifying name rather than the nucleated communities of much of the county in the post-medieval period, the distribution of settlement largely conforms to later pattern. The woodland of southern Kesteven was already exploited and settled as was the more thinly populated cliff to the north. Likewise, the Wolds and coastal marsh were also peopled. It was only on the silts and peat fens in the south-east that settlement was more circumscribed than in the later Middle Ages. Various references to marsh held by individual lords suggest that reclamation was already under way. Nevertheless, it is clear that most of the fenland settlements only came into existence in the following centuries. With this exception, by and large the settlement geography of medieval Lincolnshire had already been established by 1086.

Notes and further details on page 138.

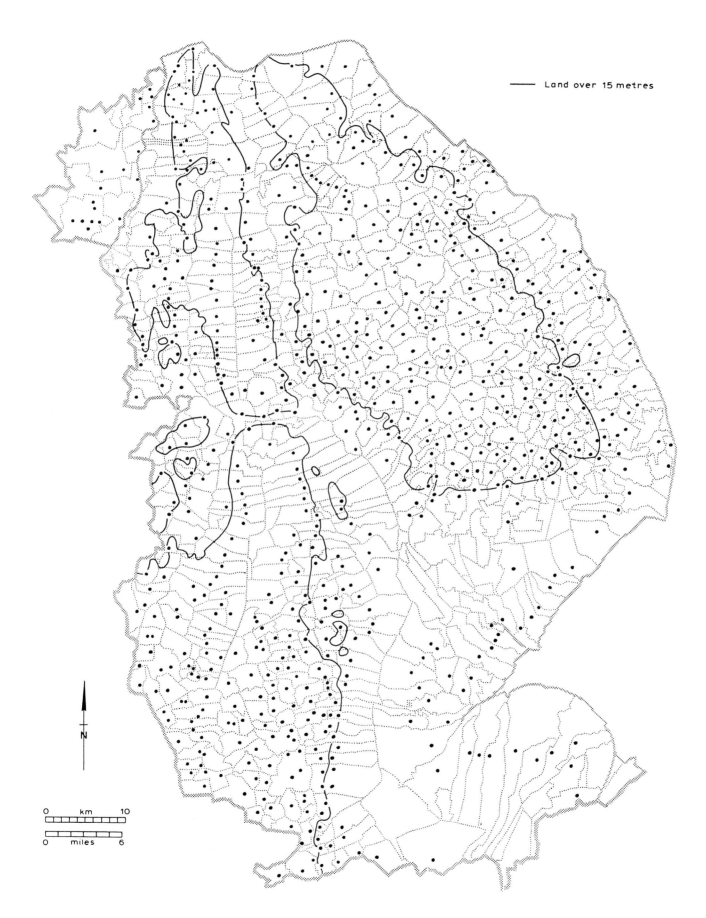

Land over 15 metres

0   km   10

0   miles   6

David Roffe

Estates were of central interest to the Domesday commissioners and in consequence the account of estate structure in the survey is comprehensive. The basic social and economic unit in the late 11th century was the manor. The word, equivalent to the English 'hall', was a Norman importation with the root meaning of 'lord's residence', but in Domesday Book it was used to refer to the whole estate. In many areas of Midland and Southern England manor, parish and vill were coterminous. Estates of this kind were not unknown in Lincolnshire; they are relatively common in northern Kesteven, for example. But most manors were dispersed. They typically consisted of a small demesne (that is, home farm) close to the lord's hall, and a number of often widely-flung satellites which are identified as berewicks (that is, detached demesne) or, more usually, sokelands.

The map depicts Domesday estates in the wapentake of Elloe in the south-east corner of Lincolnshire. The complex of inter-related interests in this area is relatively simple when compared with manors on the fen-edge and in the Wolds, but the structure and characteristics of tenure are generally representative of the county as a whole. Beyond the hall and demesne, which functioned as the estate centre, none of the lords owned the soil of the manor, in the modern sense, in either 1066 or 1086; they were merely entitled to services and dues such as the profits of justice, day labour in the form of ploughing, sowing, reaping and the like, a food or monetary rent, and ecclesiastical tithes from freeholding peasants. The burden of service was considerable for villeins and probably the landless bordars. Most land, however, was held by sokemen who apparently enjoyed a high degree of freedom from seigneurial control, and the dues they rendered were exceptionally light.

The prevalence of this class of free man has led some to characterise the Lincolnshire manor and soke as a loose association of equals which, having its origins in the settlement of a free Danish army in the late ninth and early tenth centuries, was held together by voluntary subjection to the jurisdiction (*soca*) of the lord. However, it is clear that the soke was not an *ad hoc* collection of lands. Although sokemen often had freedom of person and could sell their lands, the soke dues from them could not be unilaterally withdrawn. Patterns of tenure frequently indicate that they were formerly organised in large compact estates. In Elloe, for example, the structure of Guy de Craon's land, all held by Aethelstan in 1066, echoes that of Ivo Taillebois' which had belonged to Earl Aelgar, and it would seem that the fee had its origin in a grant of a portion, here apparently a sixth, of each element of the larger estate. Crowland's lands had likewise been granted by Earl Aelgar or his predecessors, and thus it is likely that Elloe had once consisted of a single estate held by one lord.

The same process of estate formation can be observed throughout the county. Some manors may well have come into being by the more or less untrammelled activity of entrepreneurial freemen, but most appear to have been created by overlords out of extended estates. This mechanism is found in all parts of England. From the early Anglo-Saxon period, if not before, food-rent and labour services of groups of hamlets and villages had been assigned to local centres for the support of a leader, whether a tribal chief or king. From the eighth century such shires or sokes, as they were known, began to fragment as land and services were granted to individuals. In Lincolnshire the process was accelerated by the Danish colonisation of the county, and by 1086 it was only the larger sokes which bore witness to a system of land tenure which had become outmoded. Most sokemen no longer rendered their services to the king; they had become the men of lords who had taken his place as the recipient of tribute, if not of specifically royal service *(see* 19 Medieval Administration).

The Norman Conquest saw little immediate change in the nature of tenurial relationships or the constitution of estates. Almost all Anglo-Saxon lords, the king's thegns who were directly responsible to the Crown, had forfeited their lands by 1086, but their Norman successors, in Lincolnshire at least, derived legal title to their honours from them. Continuity was therefore a precondition of the Norman settlement, and indeed where sokemen formed the bulk of the population, 11th-century manorial structures often survived into the 15th century. However, the introduction of feudal ideas gradually produced new and more burdensome tenurial relationships. By 1086 there were already sokelands in Elloe which were held by villeins and it would seem that some free men had suffered a depression in status at the hands of their new lords. The change was fostered by the grant of manors to vassals in return for military service. At first many of these tenants only held for life, like their pre-Conquest counterparts, the median thegns who were tenants of the king's thegns. In the course of time, however, manors were conveyed in hereditary fee or granted in perpetuity to religious houses, and peasants became subject to closer control and exploitation. The manor of Spalding, for example, became one of the main demesne estates of the priory which was established there by Ivo Taillebois. By the mid-12th century many lords and their men had assumed near-proprietorial rights over much of their estates. Throughout much of Lincolnshire the manor had become all but private property and the peasants who worked it had no other recourse than to the manorial court of their lord.

Notes and further details on page 138.

Domesday Estate Structure in the Wapentake of Elloe

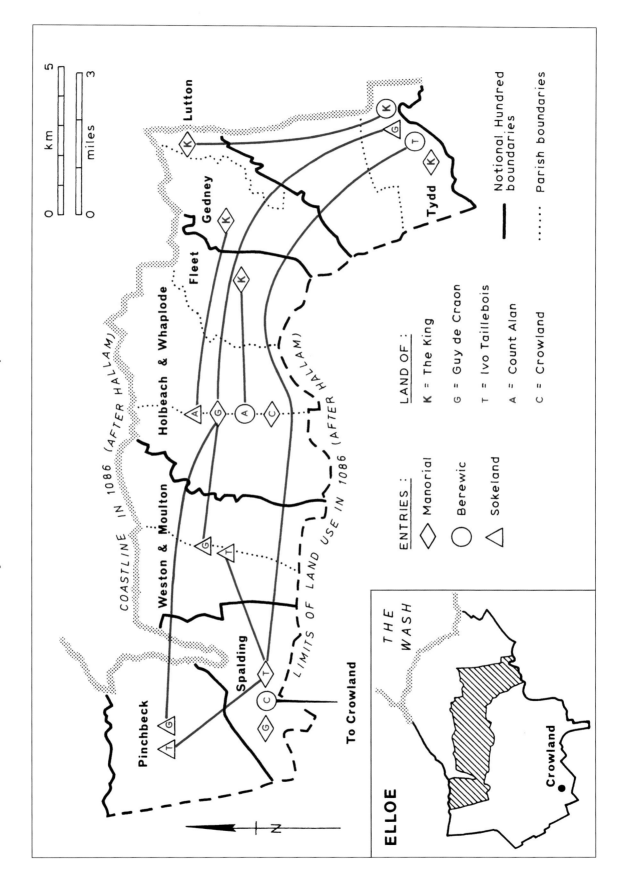

In the medieval period, Lincolnshire was composed of the three parts of Lindsey, Kesteven and Holland. Lindsey had a long history as an area of administration; divided into north, south and west ridings, it originated as a sub-Roman or early Anglo-Saxon kingdom. By contrast, Kesteven and Holland may not have come into existence as discrete units until the eighth or ninth century, for until then they were occupied by a group of small tribes. By 700 the whole area had come under the hegemony of Mercia; Lincoln remained a political nexus in the north, while the south may have looked to Leicester if not to a more local centre. Throughout the area, however, local government was the immediate responsibility of royal vills. Many of these survived, directly or institutionally, as soke centres into the post-Conquest period. Nevertheless, it is clear that by the ninth century the structure was beginning to disintegrate with the grant of dues and rights to individuals, a process which was accelerated by the Scandinavian colonisation of the area in the following century. Lincoln and Stamford became Danish boroughs, with the territories of Lindsey, and Kesteven and Holland, respectively, assigned to them, but no new administrative structure was introduced; the relationship between military stronghold and its territory was essentially one of lordship between Danish jarl and client.

A formal administration was only introduced after the English reconquest. The campaigns of Edward the Elder, king of Wessex, and Aethelflaeda, lady of the Mercians, between 910 and 921 saw the assimilation of Kesteven and Holland into a united English kingdom, and a burghal system, an organisation for the defence of the borough of Stamford and the maintenance of the peace in its territory, was apparently introduced. Lincoln and Lindsey, however, remained part of a still independent Danish Northumbria until at least 927 and may not have been finally conquered until 942. With the submission of York in 954, an integrated system of local government was introduced. The whole area was divided up into wapentakes, the Danelaw equivalent of the hundred elsewhere. Some perpetuated the territories of earlier sokes, but the wapentake was essentially independent of estate structures. New royal courts were set up in each and charged with the collection of taxes, maintenance of the king's peace, and the enforcement of military service through a network of twelve-carucate hundreds, a novel system of frankpledge in which groups of villages were mutually responsible for the behaviour of their members. Under king's reeves, some nineteen wapentakes in Lindsey were assigned to Lincoln and fourteen in Kesteven and Holland to Stamford. However, neither borough was autonomous, for both were joined to Leicester, Nottingham and Derby to form the confederacy of the Five Boroughs under the control of an ealdorman.

The whole apparatus appears to have been designed to divorce the Danes of the East Midlands from their kinsmen in a still unstable North by fostering a sense of separate interest and identity. In the event the organisation failed in its central purpose when King Swein of Denmark invaded in 1013. The East Midlands sided with the invaders and with the North, and the confederacy collapsed. In the aftermath the shire of Lincoln emerged when the territories of Lincoln and Stamford were combined under a single earl who was directly accountable to the king. By 1086 the shire and the oversight of its wapentakes and hundreds was the responsibility of the king's shire-reeve or sheriff, and the efficiency of the system was such that it had become a formidable instrument of royal power. On the one hand it facilitated the collection of taxation and the muster of an army for the king's use only. On the other it curtailed seigneurial power in local government. The wapentake court coordinated policing and provided a forum for the settlement of minor trespasses and crimes which were beyond the competence of manorial courts, while the riding and division courts along with the county courts held at Lincoln and probably Stamford dealt with more serious matters such as felonies.

This structure formed the framework of local government throughout the Middle Ages. In the course of time, however, its effectiveness was eroded and it was supplemented by new institutions. From the 12th century the shire began to lose its judicial autonomy as the more important criminal and civil cases were brought for resolution before itinerant royal justices. At the same time shrieval administration was increasingly subject to feudal pressures. The grant or assumption of view of frankpledge by manorial lords created leet jurisdiction, and as a result by 1250 the hundred had largely given way to a system of vills which more closely approximated to manorial structure. More seriously, wapentakes were granted to local lords, and estates were taken out of the jurisdiction of the sheriff by the grant or assumption of return or estreat of writs, that is the liberty of executing the king's orders through a private court. It was in this way that the great sokes of Grantham, Kirton and Horncastle acquired discrete administrations.

Theoretically, such courts were always deemed to be royal. In reality, however, the effectiveness of shrieval government was seriously compromised. In consequence, from the 14th century omnicompetent commissions were appointed by the Crown for each of the three Parts to keep the peace. It was from this practice that justices of the peace emerged, and from the mid-15th century, within the quarter sessions, they assumed all the judicial functions of the sheriff in the localities. In the following century the manorially-dominated vill was superseded by the parish as the basic unit of local government and the wapentake only remained as a system of policing under the supervision of the high constable and the justices of the peace. It was a structure which was to survive into the 19th century.

Notes and further details on 139.

NORTH

YARBOROUGH

West Halton

MANLEY *1

WEST

AXHOLME *1

● Barnetby le Wold

*2 BRADLEY

Caistor

RIDING

● Waltham

Kirton in Lindsey

CORRINGHAM

HAVERSTOE *2

LUDBOROUGH

RIDING

WALSHCROFT

ASLACOE

LOUTHESK

WELL

● Gayton le Wold

Stow

WRAGGOE

SOUTH

LAWRESS

● Wragby

GARTREE *3

CALCEWATH

Nettleham

● Belchford

HILL

Lincoln

Bardney

● Greetham

GRAFFOE

● Branston

Horncastle

RIDING

LANGOE

● Bolingbroke

CANDLESHOE

BOOTHBY

HORNCASTLE *4

FLAXWELL

*3 BOLINGBROKE

Caythorpe

Ruskington

LOVEDEN

Sleaford

SKIRBECK

KESTEVEN

ASWARDHURN

Ancaster

● Drayton

THREO

Grantham

KIRTON

WINNIBRIGGS

Folkingham

AVELAND

HOLLAND

● Spalding

ELLOE

BELTISLOE

● Edenham

N

NESS

0 km 10

0 miles 6

Stamford

The castle emerged in 10th-century France at a time when central government was breaking down and royal rights and duties increasingly accrued to local lords. The context was nascent feudalism, and the castle embodied the identity of the public with the private which characterised that society. Thus, it not only functioned as a fortification at which military service was rendered and as a centre of local government and law, but also as a lord's residence and estate office. These developments were foreign, in both senses, to Anglo-Saxon society. In the 10th and 11th centuries private lordship in England was subordinated to a strong monarchy which governed the country through a network of royal courts. Military service was always reserved to the crown, and the identity of the common good with the king's peace was well-developed. The concept of the castle was essentially antipathetic to good government. Indeed, when a castle was built by Norman retainers of Earl Ralph in Herefordshire in (*sic*) 1051, it was seen as an outrage and affront to the king's authority, since such activities could only be a challenge to a well-ordered society. By temperament, experience, and necessity, the Normans did not share these sensibilities. The castle was at once the means of their conquest of England and the symbol of the new regime they initiated.

However, the introduction of the castle was not accompanied by untrammelled feudalism. The Norman kings maintained and extended the system of royal government and attempted to control the construction of fortifications. Castles become difficult to define. Size of defences was an early criterion as castle blended into *maison forte* and *maison forte* into moated homestead, but this soon gave way to crenellation as the definitive feature. Nevertheless, sites could be called castles in one context and manor houses in another, and it would seem that circumstances, if not whim, determined categorisation. Both contemporary perception and later tradition compound the problem. Many sites, especially impressive earthworks, and later tower houses which drew on the symbolism of the keep but adopted little else of the castle, have been elevated in status by local enthusiasm and popular antiquarianism. Medieval usage has been the primary criterion of selection employed here, along with tenurial context and size of defences where early references are wanting. In consequence, earthworks like that at Corby Glen and Wybert's Castle in Wyberton have been excluded on grounds of function, while often slight remains, such as Moulton, have been included since they were known as castles in the medieval period.

The major castles in Lincolnshire were almost all established within a hundred years of the Conquest. The earliest are Lincoln and Stamford which were built for the king in 1068 as regional strongholds. Both were situated on major routes and commanded access to and from Lindsey and Kesteven respectively and, like other castles in county towns, were vital instruments of the Norman settlement. Subsequently, strategic castles such as Gainsborough and Owston on the Trent were established by tenants-in-chief to control other lines of communication. Considerations of this kind were always important. In the anarchy of Stephen's reign, many adulterine, that is unlicensed, castles like Barton on Humber were built to protect estates and exert influence over their neighbourhoods. Similarly, in the civil war of the late years of the reign of King John, other castles were built and manor houses, like that of Thomas de Moulton in Moulton, were transformed into castles to counter local disorder and protect interests.

From early on, however, castles were also established at honourial centres where the knights of the barony attended their lord and discharged their various obligations. The motte and bailey at Castle Bytham, for example, may already have been in existence by 1086 to function as the *caput* of the estates of Drew de Beurere, the lord of Holderness, in Lincolnshire. Honourial barons, such as Robert or Albert de Gresley in Swineshead who held from the Lancaster fee, soon followed suit in building suitable residences for themselves at which they in turn received the services of their own men. The siting of such castles is largely determined by estate structure. Bolingbroke is not without its strategic importance, but the fact that the settlement was a soke centre before the Conquest must have been a major consideration, while excavation has shown that Goltho, probably the Kyme family's principal residence, was built on the site of a defended pre-Conquest manor house. Distributions therefore largely reflect the geography of the pre-Conquest interest from which tenants-in-chief derived their honours on the one hand, and the pattern of enfeoffment in the aftermath of the Norman settlement on the other.

Few castles were established after *c.*1220; Somerton was licensed in 1281, but this was the exception. Furthermore, not all castles developed beyond the primitive earthwork and timber structures of the 11th and 12th centuries to survive into the later Middle Ages. Following the anarchy and the reign of John some were razed and others were merely superseded by more commodious accommodation. The royal castle of Lincoln was kept in general repair and the more important honourial centres were maintained. Tattershall was even rebuilt on a grand scale in the 15th century. But with the amalgamation of honours, the decay of feudal relations and income, and the emergence of bastard feudalism, many lapsed into dereliction. Stamford was ruinous by the mid-14th century and Bourne and Welbourn did not survive for much longer. Castles were outmoded. Both lords and gentry now aspired to more comfortable residences which, like the tower house, often drew on the symbolism of the castle but were not seriously defensible. By the later Middle Ages the castle had given way to the country house.

Notes and further details on page 139.

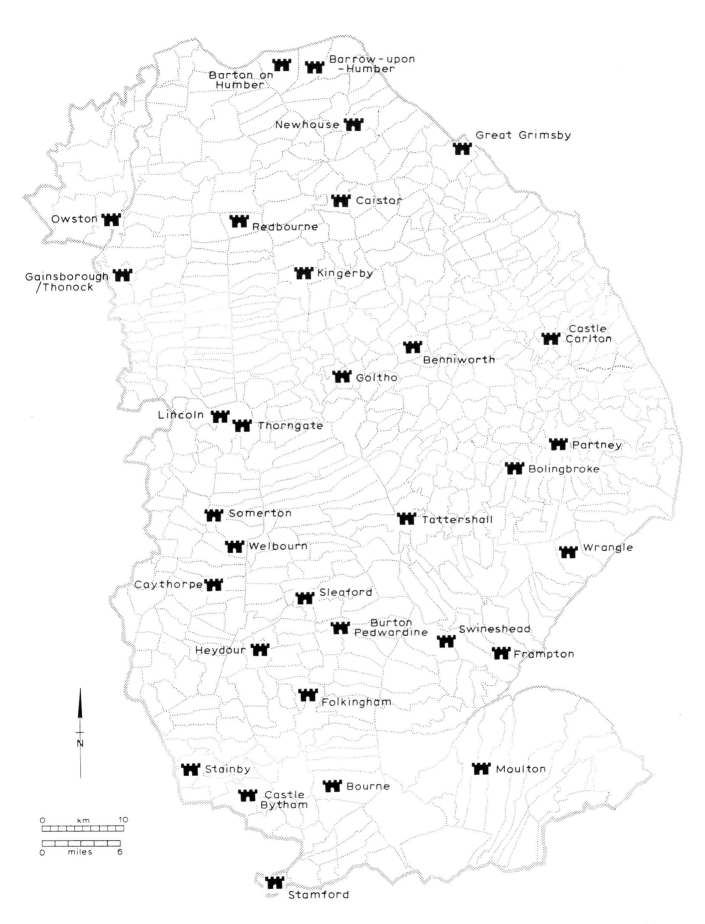

Barrow-upon
-Humber

Barton on
Humber

Newhouse

Great Grimsby

Caistor

Owston

Redbourne

Gainsborough
/Thonock

Kingerby

Castle
Carlton

Benniworth

Goltho

Lincoln

Thorngate

Partney

Bolingbroke

Somerton

Tattershall

Welbourn

Wrangle

Caythorpe

Sleaford

Burton
Pedwardine

Swineshead

Heydour

Frampton

Folkingham

N

Stainby

Moulton

Bourne

Castle
Bytham

0   km   10

0   miles   6

Stamford

41

After the breakdown of Roman administration in the fifth century, urban life all but died out. There are indications that Lincoln remained an administrative centre, and by the seventh or eighth century there was probably a *wic* or trading post there by the River Witham. Throughout the rest of the area, however, there was little else that could be called a town. Most commercial activity took place in rural contexts. In a society which lacked independent forces of law and order, the appointment of sureties was a vital component of any transaction, and many markets and fairs were therefore established at churches and royal estate centres where valid oaths could be made before law-worthy witnesses. Markets at Stow St Mary, Bardney and Partney, and the fair at Stow Green, may have been associated with the early monasteries in the same places, while those at Caistor, Horncastle and Grantham probably owed their existence to the administrative functions of the settlements.

It was the Danish invasions and colonisation of the ninth and 10th centuries that newly stimulated urban growth. Situated in key strategic positions, Lincoln, with its 'suburb' of Torksey, and Stamford were quickly taken and soon became major military and political centres in the wider Viking world of the North. Trade rapidly ensued and manufacturing industries developed on a scale which was unprecedented in England since the Roman period. With the reconquest of the Danelaw by Wessex, city and borough became royal administrative centres and their inhabitants were accorded special status and protection. Not every citizen or burgess held his tenements directly from the king; many were tenants of thegns of the countryside. But their services were generally light, and the townsmen were free from the constraints of manorial administration to pursue trade and industry. The king's courts of Lincoln and Stamford were the focus of the communities and they already articulated some degree of communal identity and action in the late 11th century.

By this time Lincoln was one of the major towns in the country; Stamford was only of slightly lesser importance. With an international trade in wool and cloth and a regional market in manufactured goods such as pottery, metalwork and leather, they dominated the economy of Lincolnshire. However, the growth that they engendered fostered developments elsewhere in the county. As an entrepôt at the mouth of the River Witham, Boston grew within a century from a rural fair into one of the greatest medieval towns in England. No other settlement grew so spectacularly, but others achieved moderate development. Ports situated on the east coast generally flourished, and markets in administrative centres like Kirton in Lindsey assumed a regional role which mirrored their local government functions.

Such developments were largely spontaneous; others were the result of policy. From the 11th century the profits to be made from trade were manifest and lords took conscious steps to foster it. By 1086 the king and the bishop of Lincoln had introduced burgage tenure into Grantham and Louth which, as central places, had probably long had markets. In the next three centuries they were emulated by other lords who sought licences from the crown to establish markets and fairs on their estates and granted liberties to encourage immigration and economic development. Sleaford, for example, was already an important estate centre in the 11th century, but a market was set up and burgage tenure introduced in the early 12th century when Bishop Alexander of Lincoln built a castle there to administer his barony of Sleaford.

Urbanisation of this kind entailed considerable investment. Settlements were often remodelled as burgage tenements were laid out. Thus, part of the manor of Gainsborough was converted into a borough by its lord in the early 13th century and peasant tofts and crofts were divided into the long narrow house plots which are characteristic of towns. Such enterprises were often entirely or partly speculative, and as such did not always have the desired outcome. New Eagle, the only new town built on a virgin site in Lincolnshire, never developed at all, for, badly sited, it lacked a local market and was ill-equipped to exploit the wider economy of the county. Other grants of markets, by contrast, were probably never intended to foster commercial development on a large scale. Bourne was provided with a market in the 12th century when the castle was constructed and streets were apparently realigned to communicate with it. However, it appears that it was only set up for the convenience of the lord of Bourne and the abbey, for no attempt seems to have been made to settle merchants. Supplementing the traditional prescriptive markets where new demand required, such creations existed primarily to service local communities and institutions like honourial courts and monasteries.

By the 13th century, there were few places in Lincolnshire which were further than five miles from a market. Most markets were local and had a hinterland which was protected by custom and law. But they nevertheless contributed to the larger economy, for goods, such as wool on the one hand and manufactured commodities on the other, were exchanged between the localities and the major centres of commerce in the county through the regional towns. In the following century this pattern of trade and commerce began to change. As elsewhere, the county was gravely affected by deterioration of the climate and the plague. But it was the drastic decline of Lincoln, Stamford and Boston, following the migration of new technologies and industries from the restrictive control of urban guilds and the severing of diplomatic relations with the Low Countries, that precipitated a new order. By the 16th century it was the regional markets which were the main centres of exchange. Lincolnshire had become a county of market towns.

Notes and further details on page 139.

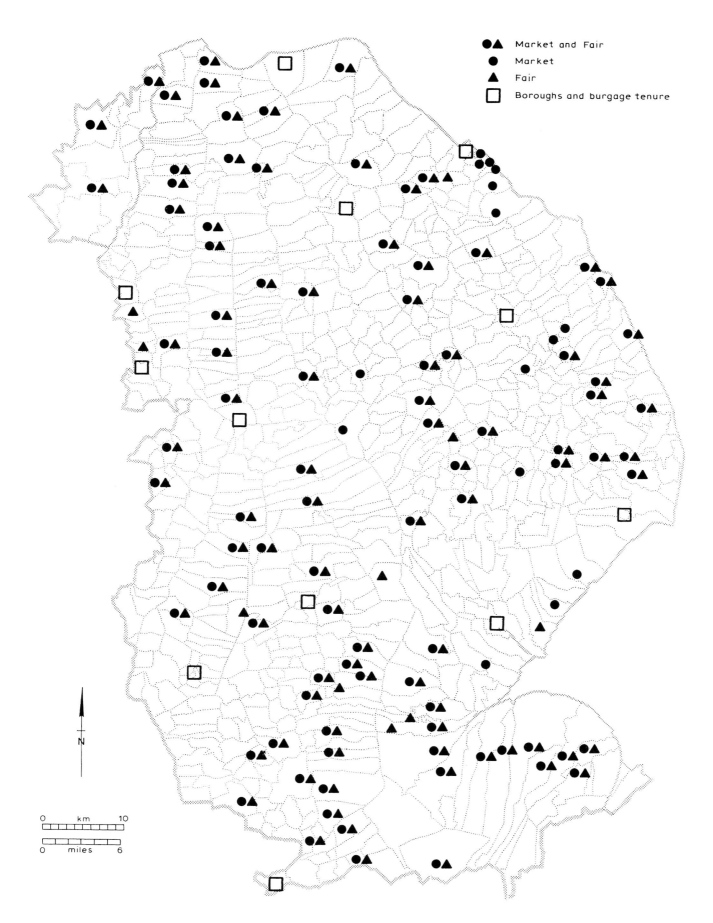

Market and Fair
Market
Fair
Boroughs and burgage tenure

0 km 10

0 miles 6

N

43

Watermills were reintroduced into England (after disappearing with the departure of the Romans) at some time in the middle Saxon period, perhaps around the year AD 700. Although the theory that they originated in the eastern counties and spread westwards in ensuing centuries is now thought to be over-simplistic, their ubiquity in Lincolnshire by the 11th century still reflects at least two or three hundred years of development and evolution.

Domesday Book gives our first picture of the number, distribution and value of watermills in Lincolnshire. As always with this survey, the evidence was recorded in the form of manors rather than settlements and it can be read in various different ways. The process of reconstructing the number and location of the mills on a map is therefore far from straightforward.[1] The completeness of the record is also open to doubt. For instance, was the mill recorded at Skirbeck (near Boston) in 1091 really not in existence in 1086?[2] Nevertheless, the main elements of the picture presented by the map must be broadly accurate.

The survey lists not only whole mills but fractions, shared between different manors and settlements. Sometimes, these can be added together meaningfully. At either Fulbeck or Leadenham, for example, there was half a mill worth 10s. 0d. and in neighbouring Caythorpe was a matching half mill of the same value. At Linwood, one manor had one-third of the mill and another the remaining two-thirds. Often, however, such fractions cannot be neatly reassembled into whole mills, a further indication that the record is not necessarily complete. There were also a number of 'mill sites' (separately marked on the map) where, for whatever reason, no mill was currently operating.

Each mill or fraction was normally assigned an annual rental value, expressed in cash. This should be understood as over and above the value of the manor as stated in Domesday Book. They were probably customary or 'notional' figures and (like the mills themselves) often of some antiquity by 1086. Many are multiples of the Danish *ora* or silver penny (16d.). In one case (at Ulceby) an eel render is part of this valuation because fisheries were frequently attached to mills, the mill pond being a convenient place to erect and maintain a weir. Despite the dearth of eel renders in Lincolnshire compared with some other counties, there remains the suspicion that in some places (such as Bourne) the fishery was more profitable than the attached mill and was the main reason why it was shared between a number of manors.

In Lindsey, watermills were widely scattered in clusters of between one and three mills, with concentrations in areas like the southern Wolds (densely populated in the 11th century), the region around Louth, and the foot of the cliff north of Lincoln. Places such as Tealby, Thorganby and Nettleton had large clusters of mills, shared among a number of different manors. At Nettleton there were nine mills shared among five different manors and at Tealby seven manors shared 14 mills. Yet the overall value of such mills was low; in Nettleton, for example, about 2s. 0d. a year. These settlements made use of relatively small but fast rivers flowing off the Wolds, where positioning the mill on a steep gradient produced sufficient power for a small mill and the number of mills made up for the very limited capacity of the individual sites. Manors in neighbouring villages often had rights in these places (sometimes amounting only to a share of one of the mills) because suitable sites were so rare.

In Kesteven, the distribution of the mills recorded by Domesday Book was very different. There were fewer settlements with mills, but where concentrations occurred they were in clusters of much higher value. A good mill stream needed to maintain a strong but predictable flow of water throughout the year, without either drying up in the summer or freezing over in the winter. In Kesteven, there were several such rivers which were the focus of large-scale milling activity, their mills probably grinding corn brought from some considerable distance away.

The upper reaches of the Witham in the area around Grantham were intensively exploited, but the most important cluster of mills in 11th-century Lincolnshire was on the Slea. Besides the eight high-value mills on the bishop of Lincoln's manor at New Sleaford, there were seven others at Quarrington, Old Sleaford and Evedon. The three mills at neighbouring Ruskington were worth £4 12s. 8d., easily the most valuable small cluster anywhere in Lincolnshire. Yet there were no other mills (except one low-value one at Burton Pedwardine) anywhere else in the surrounding wapentakes of Flaxwell or Aswardhurn. Such patterns of mill distribution not only demonstrate the extent to which physical geography affected where mills were located, but give rise to some interesting speculations about the role earlier Anglo-Saxon administrative units may have played in their development.

All the mills listed in 1086 were watermills: there were no windmills in England until the late 12th century. The higher-value mills were undoubtedly the modern vertical-wheeled type. Some of those with low values may have been examples of the smaller horizontal (or 'paddle') wheeled mills, which were probably still common in the 11th century.

One other striking feature of the distribution map is the scarcity of mills in Holland or on the Isle of Axholme. In such areas, whilst there was no shortage of water, there were very few watercourses with sufficient flow to power a mill. For this reason, the absence of mills in the fens extended into neighbouring Cambridgeshire as well. The one exception noted in Domesday Book was the mill at Fishtoft near Boston, which could have been a tide mill.

Notes and further details on page 139.

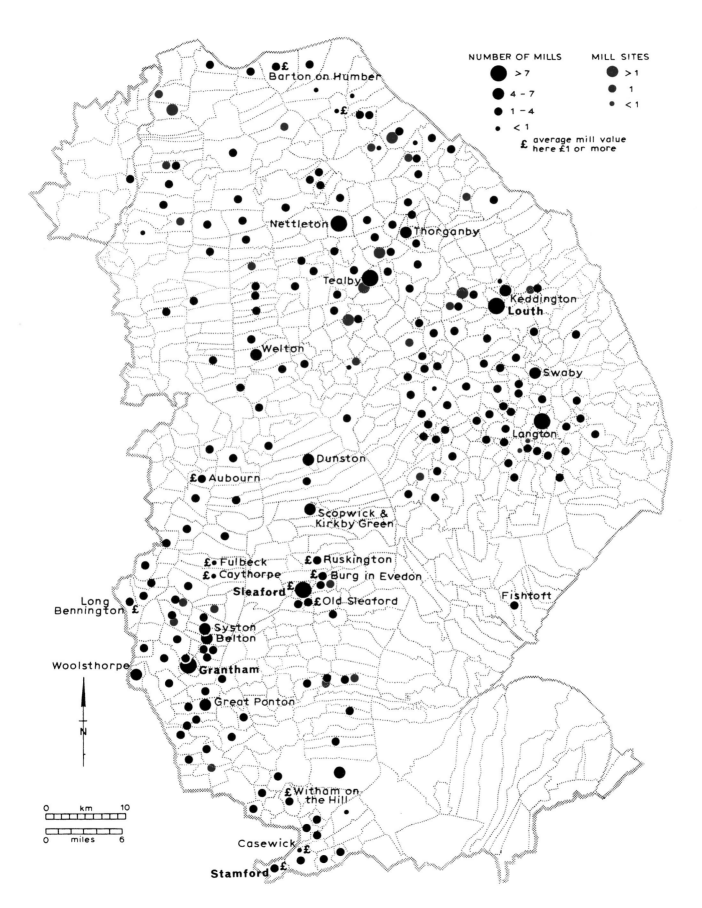

NUMBER OF MILLS
● >7
● 4 - 7
• 1 - 4
· < 1

MILL SITES
● >1
• 1
· < 1

£ average mill value here £1 or more

Barton on Humber £

Nettleton

Thorganby

Tealby

Keddington
Louth

Welton

Swaby

Langton

Dunston

£ Aubourn

Scopwick &
Kirkby Green

£ Fulbeck
£ Caythorpe
£ Ruskington
£ Burg in Evedon
Sleaford £
£ Old Sleaford
Fishtoft

Long
Bennington £

Syston
Belton

Woolsthorpe

Grantham

Great Ponton

£ Witham on
the Hill

Casewick £

Stamford £

km
0   10

0   miles   6

N

45

The parish churches of England developed from two principal sources. The earlier of these was the minster church, or *monasterium*. Such churches were frequently founded on royal estates. They would be staffed by a body of clergy, serving a wide area, or *parochia,* of the surrounding country. In this area, there might grow up a network of chapels, each dependent on the minster church. The existence of such dependencies is one means of identifying a former minster church; examples can probably be seen at Horncastle and at Grantham, and possibly also at Caistor.

During the 10th and 11th centuries, the great landed estates, royal, aristocratic and ecclesiastical, became fragmented. At the same time, village settlements were evolving into coherent communities. These two processes were mirrored in the developing pattern of religious foundations. The large *parochiae* of the minster churches began to be broken up by the creation of local churches. Some of these were offshoots of the great minsters themselves, gaining parochial rights and revenues of their own. Some were proprietary churches, or *Eigenkirche,* built by landowners on their estates to serve their families and their tenants. Others may well have been established as a result of corporate action taken by parishioners. The creation of such local churches, whatever their origins, had the effect of diverting some ecclesiastical revenues away from the ancient minsters, leading to their decay, to a point at which they became virtually indistinguishable from the local churches.

The areas of jurisdiction of the new churches were threatened in their turn by the creation of chapels in outlying settlements. Some of these chapels might themselves be substantial church buildings. Dry Doddington, in the parish of Westborough, and Marshchapel, in the parish of Fulstow, survive as church buildings to the present day but neither became a parish church during the Middle Ages. Other chapels, such as Dembleby, in the parish of Scott Willoughby, and Stain, in the parish of Withern, did by the 14th century achieve independent parochial status. But there were many others which remained as parochial chapels, dependent on the mother church of the parish. They were prevented from developing into fully-fledged parish churches because, from the early 12th century, the boundaries of the existing parishes were becoming more firmly established and in consequence their incumbents were able with increasing success to resist any encroachments on their territory and revenues.

By the early 14th century, the English parochial system had reached the peak of its medieval development. At this point, in about 1320, there were in Lincolnshire some 700 parochial benefices. After this date, few parochial chapels achieved independent status as new parish churches, while on the other hand losses of churches, both in deserted villages and in declining urban areas, began to take place.

By the mid-19th century, a few additions had been made to the parochial map. The draining of the fens produced a number of new parishes, first in the southern fenland at places such as Cowbit and Gedney Hill, and subsequently further north at Carrington, Midville and elsewhere. Some dependent chapels eventually gained parish status. Gonerby and Londonthorpe were separated from Grantham, West Ashby and High

Toynton from Horncastle, and the various chapelries, such as Sutton St James and Sutton St Nicholas, from Long Sutton. In the mid-19th century came the creation of the first new urban parishes in the county, in the churches of Holy Trinity at Louth and Gainsborough.

Losses of parish churches began to be significant in the later Middle Ages, when parishes which had been settled on marginal land were deserted, and their churches in many cases fell into disuse and eventually disappeared altogether. Many of these churches were in the Wolds: North and South Cadeby, Fordington and Maidenwell. The last vicar of West Wykeham was instituted in 1382; by 1397 the church was in ruins and the parish united to Ludford Magna. Dunsthorpe, on the southern edge of the Wolds, was united to Hameringham in 1438. In a different category was the church of St Peter, Mablethorpe, which was said in 1603 to have been swallowed up by the sea more than fifty years before. The highest concentration of lost medieval churches was in the city of Lincoln where 44 parishes had by the Reformation been reduced to fourteen.

Losses continued at a slower rate between the 17th and the mid-19th centuries. The churches of Stain, in the marsh, Calceby and Hallington, on the edge of the Wolds, and Skinnand, in the Witham vale, all disappeared during this period, as did three churches which became redundant through their close proximity to another parish church: Ludford Parva, Middle Rasen Tupholme, and St Gabriel, Binbrook.

The period from 1850 to 1950 saw the disappearance of only a handful of Lincolnshire churches, such as Castle Carlton and Cawkwell. Since 1950, however, the rate of destruction has quickened dramatically. The wolds and the marsh have again been badly affected, with churches demolished at Asgarby, Miningsby, Muckton and elsewhere. Many other churches have been declared redundant. The Withern group of parishes illustrates the decline vividly. Where there were 13 parish churches in the Middle Ages, and 11 at the end of the 19th century, there are now only five.

Notes and further details on page 139.

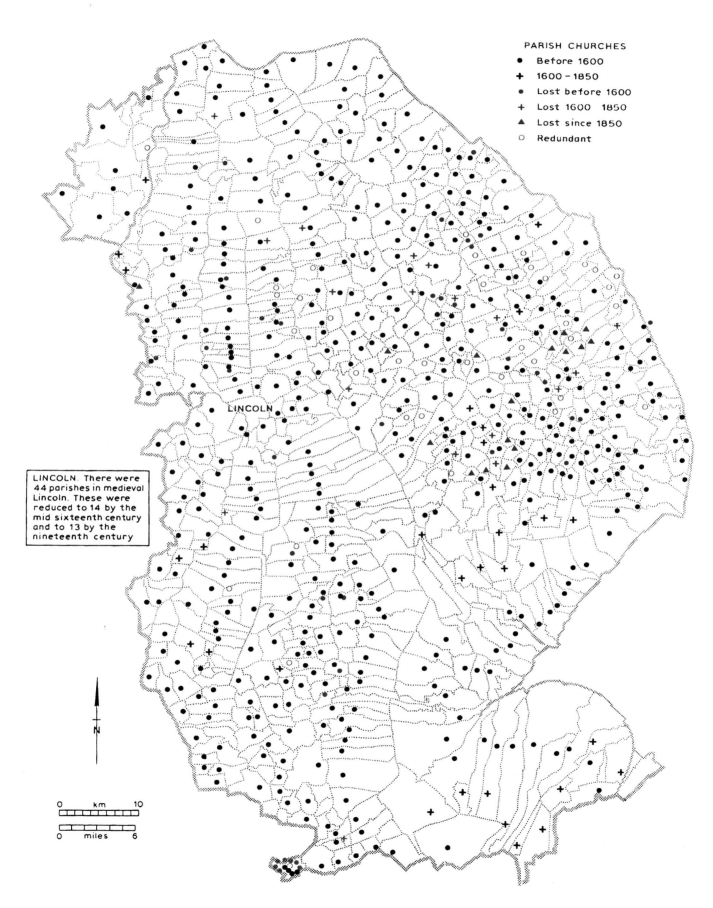

PARISH CHURCHES
● Before 1600
+ 1600 – 1850
● Lost before 1600
+ Lost 1600 1850
▲ Lost since 1850
○ Redundant

LINCOLN

LINCOLN. There were
44 parishes in medieval
Lincoln. These were
reduced to 14 by the
mid sixteenth century
and to 13 by the
nineteenth century

N

0   km   10

0   miles   6

47

The monastic life arrived in England from opposite directions: one strain brought from Italy by Augustine in 597 and the other introduced from the north by Aidan shortly afterwards. By the end of the seventh century, a third variety based on Gallic influences had made its appearance in the Midlands, notably in Lincolnshire where houses were founded at Bardney, Partney and Barrow on Humber. Around the same time, St Guthlac settled in the remote fens at Crowland where, after his death in 714, another monastery was established. Little is known about these four houses, all of which suffered destruction in the Danish invasions around 870.

The 10th-century monastic revival, centred around the houses founded at Glastonbury, Abingdon and Ramsey, had little impact in the county, although Crowland may have been re-founded towards the end of the century. Further impetus was provided by the arrival of the Normans. By the time of Domesday Book in 1086, there were already established in the county three small cells of Norman priories at Covenham, Haugham and Winghale. On a larger scale were Bardney, re-founded by Gilbert of Gant in 1087, and other foundations at Belvoir (colonised from St Albans) and Stamford St Leonard (colonised from Durham).

All these houses followed the Benedictine order. From the beginning of the 12th century, communities of regular canons, following the so-called rule of St Augustine, began to be established in England, a house being founded at Colchester around 1100. The earliest Augustinian house in Lincolnshire was probably Wellow by Grimsby (perhaps in 1132); by the beginning of the reign of Henry II, others had followed at Bourne, Thornton, Nocton, Thornholme and Kyme.

The growing wealth and success of the older houses prompted a reaction among those who sought a return to an earlier, simpler and more austere form of monasticism. This spirit of reform found expression in the Cistercian order which first arrived in England at Waverley in 1128. Cistercian houses were founded in Lincolnshire at Louth Park, Kirkstead and Revesby. They were preceded by the abbey at Swineshead, which initially belonged to the similar order of Savigny; along with the other Savigniac houses, it was merged with the Cistercian order in 1147. Even more austere than the Cistercians were the Carthusian monks, whose first English house, founded at Witham in Somerset, was notable for producing Lincoln's saintly Bishop Hugh. The only Carthusian house in the county was a late foundation, near Epworth in the Isle of Axholme (1397-8).

The early 12th century also saw the establishment of a new order of canons. These were the Premonstratensians, founded by St Norbert in 1120 and modelled on the Cistercian ideal. The first English house of the order was established in 1147 at Newhouse in north Lincolnshire; this in turn established daughter houses at Barlings, Newbo and Tupholme. Another new order of canons grew from humble origins at Sempringham where St Gilbert founded a small nunnery around 1131. At first, Gilbert wanted his nuns to be affiliated to the Cistercian order, but in 1147 Pope Eugenius III entrusted the care of the new order to Gilbert himself. The order spread, with houses at Haverholme, Alvingham, Bullington, Sixhills and elsewhere. Most were double houses, for canons as well as for nuns, although a few were for canons only, notably St Katherine by Lincoln and Newstead on Ancholme.

The military orders–the Knights Templar and the Knights Hospitaller–were created to protect pilgrims travelling to and from Jerusalem. For their support, they were endowed with rich estates, and houses, known as 'preceptories', were established to supervise these properties. The Templars had houses at Willoughton, Eagle, Aslackby and Temple Bruer. After the suppression of the order in 1308-12, many of their possessions passed to the Hospitallers, who already had preceptories of their own at Maltby and Skirbeck.

Most of the houses of nuns in Lincolnshire were attached, at least nominally, to the Cistercian order. There was one Benedictine house at Stainfield, and a house of Augustinian canonesses at St Leonard, Grimsby. The nunneries at Fosse, Gokewell, Greenfield, Heynings, Legbourne, Nun Cotham and Stixwould, may well have begun as Benedictine, but later claimed to be Cistercian to gain the privileges enjoyed by that order. There was also in the county a rare instance of a house of Premonstratensian canonesses (at Orford in the parish of Binbrook), one of only three such houses in the country.

All of the major orders of mendicant friars had houses in the county. The first to arrive were the Franciscans, who were established at Stamford and Lincoln by 1230, and later at Grimsby and Boston as well. The Dominicans were at Lincoln by 1238, at Stamford by 1241 and at Boston by 1288. There were houses of Carmelites at Lincoln, Stamford and Boston, and of Augustinian friars at Lincoln, Grimsby, Boston and Stamford. Houses of the Friars of the Sack had a brief existence at Lincoln and Stamford; both of these were extinct by the early 14th century. Another short-lived creation of the 13th century was a house of the non-mendicant Crutched Friars at Whaplode, abandoned in 1260.

The houses of the Friars of the Sack and of the Crutched Friars were among the few religious houses in Lincolnshire to disappear before the 16th century. The alien priories also suffered losses after their seizure by the Crown in the 14th century as a result of the war with France. The larger houses, such as Spalding, succeeded in adopting English status but the smaller cells, such as Burwell, were dissolved. The great majority of houses in the county, however, survived until the Reformation.

Notes and further details on page 139.

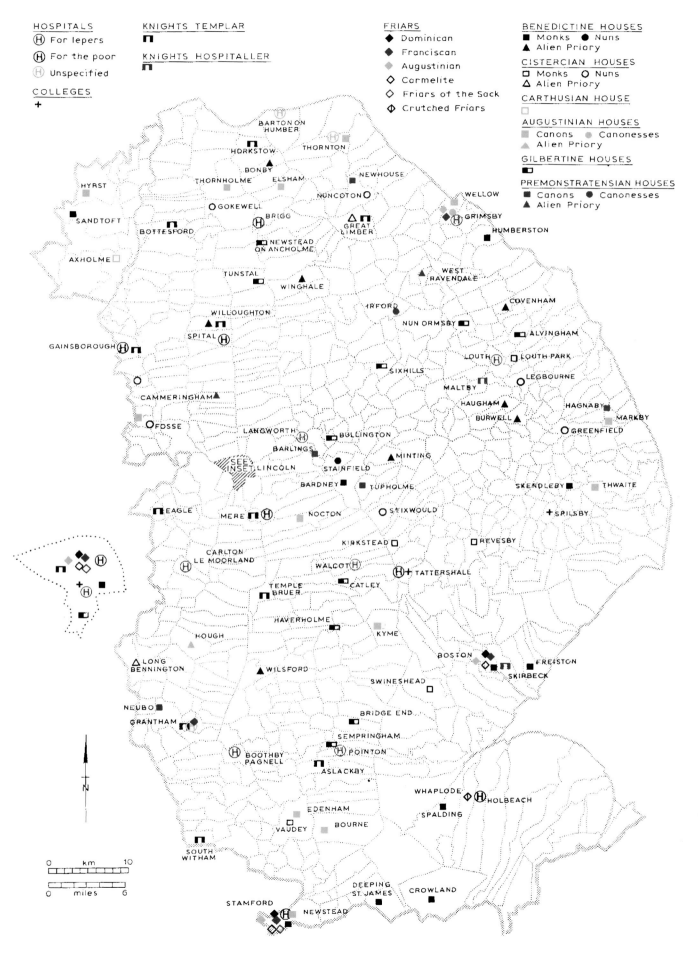

HOSPITALS
- Ⓗ For lepers
- Ⓗ For the poor
- Ⓗ Unspecified

COLLEGES
+

KNIGHTS TEMPLAR

KNIGHTS HOSPITALLER

FRIARS
- ◆ Dominican
- ◆ Franciscan
- ◆ Augustinian
- ◇ Carmelite
- ◇ Friars of the Sack
- ◈ Crutched Friars

BENEDICTINE HOUSES
- ■ Monks ▲ Nuns
- ## CISTERCIAN HOUSES
- □ Monks ○ Nuns
- △ Alien Priory
- ## CARTHUSIAN HOUSE
- ## AUGUSTINIAN HOUSES
- ■ Canons ● Canonesses
- ▲ Alien Priory
- ## GILBERTINE HOUSES
- ## PREMONSTRATENSIAN HOUSES
- ■ Canons ● Canonesses
- ▲ Alien Priory

BARTON ON HUMBER
HORKSTOW
THORNTON
BONBY
THORNHOLME ELSHAM
HYRST
GOKEWELL NEWHOUSE
NUNCOTON
WELLOW
SANDTOFT BRIGG
GRIMSBY
BOTTESFORD GREAT
LIMBER HUMBERSTON
NEWSTEAD
ON ANCHOLME
AXHOLME
TUNSTAL WEST
RAVENDALE
WINGHALE
COVENHAM
WILLOUGHTON IRFORD
NUN ORMSBY
GAINSBOROUGH SPITAL LOUTH LOUTH PARK
SIXHILLS ALVINGHAM
CAMMERINGHAM MALTBY LEGBOURNE
HAUGHAM HAGNABY
BURWELL MARKBY
FOSSE GREENFIELD
LANGWORTH BULLINGTON
BARLINGS MINTING
SEE
INSET LINCOLN STAINFIELD
BARDNEY TUPHOLME SKENDLEBY THWAITE
EAGLE MERE NOCTON STIXWOULD
KIRKSTEAD REVESBY SPILSBY
CARLTON
LE MOORLAND WALCOT TATTERSHALL
TEMPLE
BRUER CATLEY
HAVERHOLME KYME
HOUGH
BOSTON FREISTON
LONG
BENNINGTON WILSFORD SKIRBECK
SWINESHEAD
NEUBO BRIDGE END
GRANTHAM SEMPRINGHAM
BOOTHBY POINTON
PAGNELL ASLACKBY
WHAPLODE HOLBEACH
EDENHAM SPALDING
VAUDEY BOURNE
SOUTH
WITHAM
DEEPING
ST JAMES CROWLAND
STAMFORD NEWSTEAD

0   km   10
0   miles   6

N

49

The medieval diocese of Lincoln extended from the Humber estuary in the north to the meadows of the Thames in the south. In the west it reached to the edge of the Cotswolds and eastwards it stretched as far as the borders of East Anglia. This large area was the result of a union of three ancient dioceses–those of Lindsey, Leicester and Dorchester–following the Viking invasions of the late ninth century.

Measured in terms of parochial benefices, the diocese of Lincoln was by far the largest in England with nearly 2,000 livings within its borders. To cope with the administrative burden which this implied, the first bishop of the diocese, Remigius, established seven archdeaconries whose areas were based largely on the boundaries of the counties which made up the diocese. Thus the archdeaconries of Bedford, Buckingham, Leicester, Lincoln and Oxford corresponded with the counties of those names; the archdeaconry of Northampton included the counties of Northampton and Rutland, and the archdeaconry of Huntingdon comprised Huntingdonshire, Cambridgeshire and a large part of Hertfordshire. In each of these areas an archdeacon was established, the *oculus episcopi*, who was to keep an eye on the state of the diocese and to whom the bishop could delegate much of its routine work.

During the 12th century, two important changes were made to the pattern of archdeaconries in the diocese. In 1109, Cambridgeshire was removed to create the new diocese of Ely; the archdeaconry of Huntingdon was thus reduced to its residual areas in Huntingdonshire and Hertfordshire. Meanwhile, an eighth archdeaconry was gradually emerging in the northern part of Lincolnshire. The first specific reference to the territory of this archdeacon, dated *c*.1145, is to the West Riding of Lindsey. By the early 13th century, the position had become known as archdeacon of Stow. The archdeacon of Lincoln would no doubt have viewed the new creation with a certain degree of hostility, representing as it did the loss of a portion of his archidiaconal revenues, and it is perhaps a testimony to the power and influence of successive archdeacons of Lincoln that the new archdeaconry was ultimately so small in extent.

The archdeaconries of the diocese were further subdivided into rural deaneries, each under the supervision of a *decanus* or dean, a priest enjoying a degree of pre-eminence over his fellow clergy. The boundaries of rural deaneries in England can first be traced in the Valuation of Norwich, drawn up in connection with the levying of a papal tax in 1254, and again in the taxation of Pope Nicholas IV of 1291. In the archdeaconry of Lincoln, 23 rural deaneries are listed, with a further four in the archdeaconry of Stow. In the Valuation of Norwich the deaneries of Ludborough and Louthesk, and those of Horncastle and Hill, were combined; these four deaneries were all returned separately in 1291.

In Lincolnshire, the boundaries of the deaneries bore a close relationship with the boundaries of the equivalent civil divisions, known as wapentakes. It has already been seen that the boundary of the original archdeaconry of Lincoln matched that of the whole county and that the later archdeaconry of Stow comprised the West Riding of Lindsey. This riding contained five wapentakes: Aslackhoe, Corringham, Lawres, Manley and Well. The smallest of these wapentakes, Well, was combined with Lawres to form the rural deanery of that name, and each of the other wapentakes formed a rural deanery of its own, the wapentake names being again used for the deaneries.

This correspondence between wapentake and deanery can be seen over the whole county. There were a few exceptions to this pattern. At Grantham and Horncastle, a local soke was combined with part of the surrounding wapentake to form a rural deanery. The small wapentake of Flaxwell was combined with that of Aswardhurn to form the deanery of Aswardhurn or Lafford, The wapentake of Boothby Graffoe was another exception to the normal pattern. Its lower division formed the rural deanery of Graffoe and the upper division, including the parish of Boothby Graffoe itself, was combined with the neighbouring wapentake of Langoe to create a deanery with the compound name of Longoboby. Another variation in terminology occurred in the city of Lincoln itself, where the deanery was known as that of Christianity, to distinguish the rural dean from the quite distinct office of dean of Lincoln, the principal dignitary of Lincoln cathedral.

The rural deaneries thus created persisted throughout the Middle Ages. At the Reformation, the office of rural dean fell into disuse, its powers and duties being absorbed by the archdeacons, but the deanery boundaries survived unchanged. In the 19th century there was a movement to revive the office and in Lincolnshire some of the larger deaneries, such as Yarborough and Louthesk, were split into smaller units for easier administration. Following the Archdeaconries and Rural Deaneries Act, 1874, a thorough revision of boundaries was carried out, embodied in two Orders in Council of 24 March 1876 and 23 October 1877. By this measure, the archdeaconry of Stow was greatly increased in size to include the area covered by the old deaneries of Yarborough, Grimsby, Louthesk and Ludborough, Walshcroft, Wraggoe, Gartree, Horncastle and Hill. A further change was made in 1934 when Bishop Nugent Hicks announced the creation of an entirely new archdeaconry, that of Lindsey, covering the eastern area of Lindsey. Rural deanery boundaries were amended once more in the 1960s, and at the time of writing change is again in the air with the proposal to reduce the archdeaconries back to two.

Notes and further details on page 139.

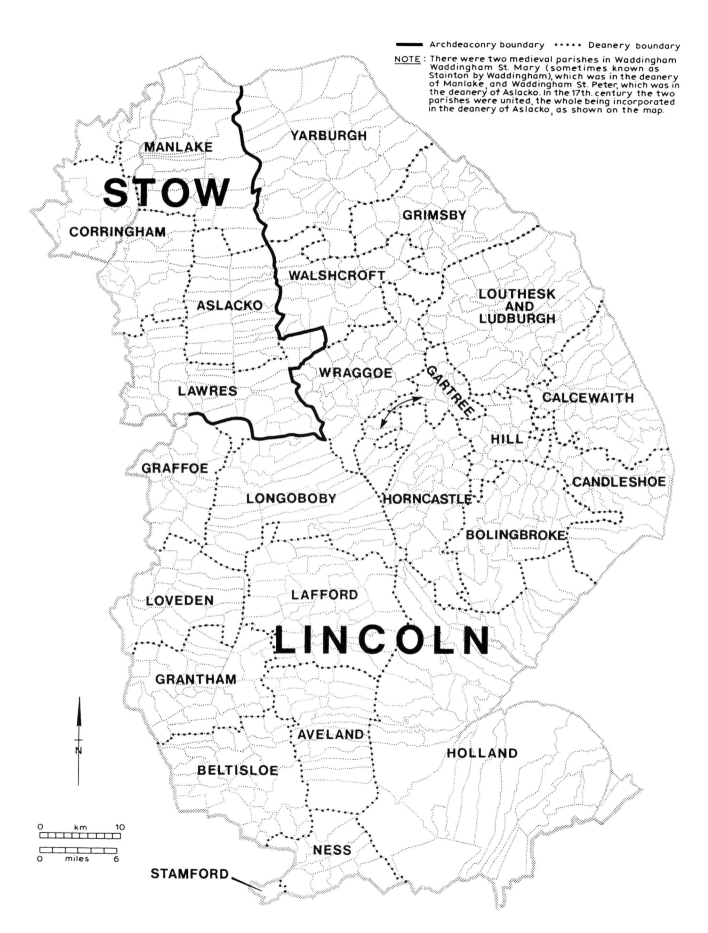

Archdeaconry boundary ━━━ Deanery boundary ••••

NOTE : There were two medieval parishes in Waddingham
Waddingham St. Mary (sometimes known as
Stainton by Waddingham), which was in the deanery
of Manlake, and Waddingham St. Peter, which was in
the deanery of Aslacko. In the 17th. century the two
parishes were united, the whole being incorporated
in the deanery of Aslacko, as shown on the map.

MANLAKE
STOW
YARBURGH
CORRINGHAM
GRIMSBY
WALSHCROFT
ASLACKO
LOUTHESK
AND
LUDBURGH
WRAGGOE
GARTREE
CALCEWAITH
LAWRES
HILL
GRAFFOE
CANDLESHOE
LONGOBOBY
HORNCASTLE
BOLINGBROKE
LOVEDEN
LAFFORD
LINCOLN
GRANTHAM
AVELAND
HOLLAND
BELTISLOE

N

0 km 10
0 miles 6

NESS
STAMFORD

Scattered across the Lincolnshire landscape are over 235 deserted village sites. The distribution of these lost villages is shown on the map opposite and the figures are almost certainly an underestimate of the true total for the county. Lincolnshire, in common with Norfolk, the north-east, and the midland counties, underwent a decline in rural settlement from the 14th to the 18th centuries which has continued, after a brief respite, through to the present day.

Depopulation of the villages began around 1300 as soil exhaustion and disease began to check village growth. The Black Death (1349-51) has often been blamed for much population reduction, although it is unlikely that it wiped out whole communities. More deadly than the Black Death, as far as the demise of villages was concerned, were the changes of land use beginning in the 14th century and leading to the depopulation of many Lincolnshire villages during the 15th and 16th centuries. Economic forces tempted landowners to enclose their land for sheep farming to the detriment of their tenants who relied on their holdings for their living. Deprived of their fields, and sometimes their homes also, the villagers had little option but to seek a living elsewhere and many would have made for the towns. The remains of the 'ridge and furrow' arable strip fields are still visible across much of the Lincolnshire landscape today, and bear testimony to the villages that once lay at their centre. The problem of depopulation of the countryside was so great that conversion of tillage to pasture was made an offence by Act of Parliament in 1489. Nevertheless, landowners continued to risk the penalties and they enclosed land and demolished settlements well into the late 16th century.

Even when the pressure to enclose land for sheep farming diminished, whole villages were moved or destroyed by landowners wishing to landscape their estates and create country parks. This practice reached its peak in the 18th century. In the 20th century, depopulation has accelerated to an alarming rate and village desertion is a continuing process.

The pattern of distribution of Lincolnshire's deserted medieval villages is fairly predictable, the sites favouring the higher ground and slopes in the north-east (on the Wolds) and south-west of the county (around Grantham). There is only one deserted village site known in the fens and only a handful in the Boston area.

In any discussion of this nature, there is always a fundamental problem in deciding what constitutes a village. For the present purpose, 'village' has been taken to mean a group of families living in a collection of houses and having a sense of community, irrespective of actual size. Many Lincolnshire villages have shrunk since medieval times, but not disappeared (Shrunken Medieval Villages) and these are not considered here. The accepted definition of a Deserted Medieval Village is a village where there are now fewer than three inhabited houses.

Deserted villages vary enormously in terms of physical appearance. Some are truly lost, their position only guessed at from vague references in the documentary records. Others are deduced from the scatters of pottery and building material found on the ploughed fields—but no trace of the streets or houses survives above ground. Finally, there are those village sites where the ground plan of the village remains to this day, marked out by the bumps and hollows in the field. Deserted village sites are often occupied by one surviving farm or manor house which has carried the village name through to modern times. In some cases the church (or its ruin) is still standing. Many village names survive as parish names although the village itself may have ceased to exist centuries ago.

Lincolnshire can rightly claim to have been in the forefront of research into Deserted Medieval Villages. The first ever aerial photograph of a lost village site to be published was that of the village of Gainsthorpe, published in the *Antiquaries Journal* of 1925. The previous year, the vicar of Welton had reported the existence of these ancient earthworks close to Ermine Street to Dr. O.G.S. Crawford who flew over the site and photographed it from 4,000 feet. He realised this was not a Roman camp as had been thought previously and, researching the history, found an account of a traveller to the place in 1697.[1]

At the same time as Gainsthorpe was being discovered, Canon C.W. Foster was busy compiling his list of 'Extinct Villages—other forgotten places'.[2] Canon Foster traced his lost villages both through documents and in the field. Of the 141 sites he mentions, 80 are lost or deserted villages.

Following this flying start, the study of Lincolnshire's lost villages went into decline. The Deserted Medieval Village Research Group, formed in 1952, has produced excellent surveys and gazetteers for many English counties, and maintains the list of Deserted Medieval Villages for Lincolnshire but, as yet, no definitive study of Lincolnshire's lost villages has been published.

Deserted Medieval Villages must rank amongst the most evocative settlement sites to visit but they vary enormously in their state of preservation and ease of access. Lincolnshire can boast some of the clearest sites in the country with streets, houses and gardens showing as well-defined earthworks, but it is four hundred years since these green fields saw ready access and most are on private land. The best of the Lincolnshire sites fall into this category and include West Wykeham, North Cadeby, Brackenborough, Maidenwell and Walmsgate, although some of these may be appreciated from adjacent roads and footpaths. Both Biscathorpe (TF228849) and Brauncewell (TF048526) are good sites and have public footpaths running across them. A great many drivers pass Dunsby (TF039515) on the Lincoln to Sleaford road daily without realising what is represented by that one bumpy pasture field in a sea of intensive arable farming.

Notes and further details on page 139.

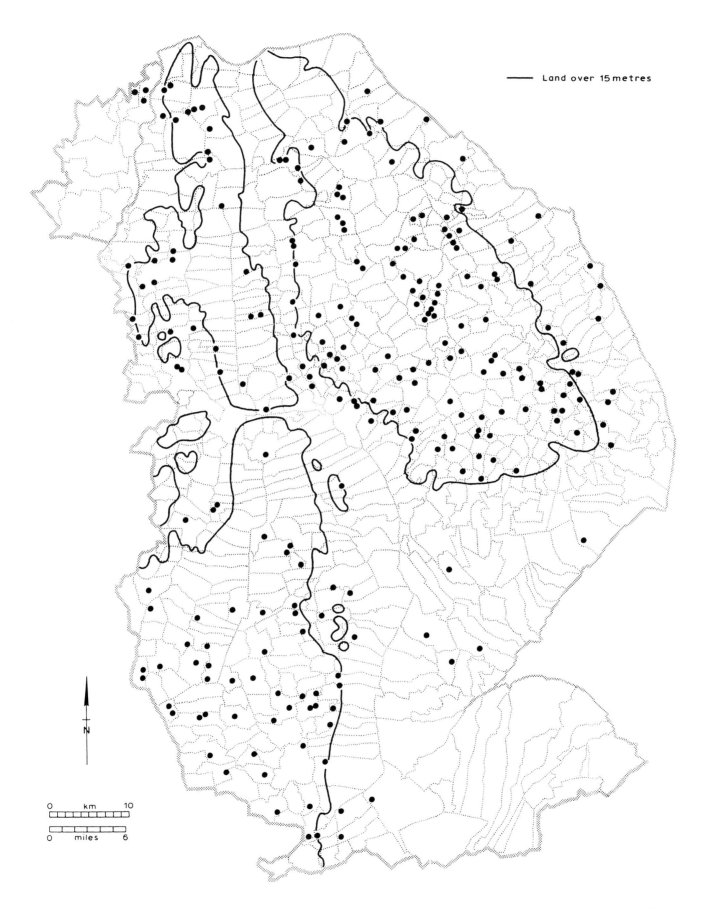

Land over 15 metres

0   km   10
0   miles   6

N

Seven Lincolnshire markets were mentioned in Domesday Book in 1086: these were at Burton upon Stather and Thealby, Barton upon Humber, Bolingbroke (which was said to be 'new'), Louth, Partney, Spalding and Threckingham. There is little indication, however, of the extent to which they reflected either the pattern or the level of trade and commerce in the period.[1]

The regular enrolment of royal grants of markets and fairs from the 13th century provides a measure of their existence. There is no way of knowing the extent to which these grants involved the creation of a new market or merely licensed ones which were already there, but there were a number of cases where markets which had developed by prescription were ratified in this way.[2] For example, wine was being traded at Brigg in the 1180s and a market was already established there by the early 13th century, but the town's lord did not get a charter for a market and a fair until 1235.[3] The charter for Market Rasen's weekly market which was granted in 1219 moved an existing Sunday market to Tuesday, an example of a process which had begun earlier in the century, stimulated by the Church's opposition to Sabbath desecration.[4]

Markets and fairs were licensed at 131 places from the 12th to the 15th centuries. The largest number of grants made in the five 50-year periods between 1200 and 1449 was the 55 made from 1250 to 1299. Thereafter the number was insignificant.[5] While these grants reflect the increasing effectiveness of royal licensing procedures, they are also indicative of increasing trade. The market charters which the lords of such places as Appleby and Bonby obtained in 1267 and 1318 respectively may represent an over-optimistic assessment of their commercial potential, but at other places grants of markets and fairs were associated with larger villages.[6] The diversification of the agricultural economy of the fens of south Lincolnshire led to the establishment of markets and fairs in almost every town or village in that part of the Holland division of the county as well as in the settlements which skirted the fens.[7]

Most market grants were associated with the right to hold a fair, usually annually, but in some cases more frequently. While markets served a local hinterland, fairs dealt in goods from a wider region. Those at Boston and Stamford attracted merchants from overseas as well as from the major English towns and cities.[8] Traders dealing on a large scale attended Burton upon Stather's two 15-day fairs which were a major outlet for the produce of the area. Their situation on the River Trent meant that, in common with Lincolnshire's other major medieval fairs, they benefited from their proximity to navigable water. The majority of the county's fairs were, however, smaller, lasting for three days, usually in May, June and July, while there was a second group in September and October.[9] The number of markets in Lincolnshire had shrunk to between thirty and forty by the 16th century. By 1792 there were 28 weekly markets, while those at Boston, Louth and Stamford were held twice weekly.[10] Among the markets which came to an end were those at Appleby, Broughton, Winteringham and Winterton in the north-west of the county. They were said to be 'decay'd' in 1695, while all that remained of the former trade at Burton on Stather was 'a little inconsiderable market'.[11] However, towns such as Brigg continued to flourish as market centres, in its case as part of a wider network of trade which extended across the Humber.[12]

Annual fairs often continued where weekly markets had declined, and indeed the number that was held increased in several places. Some fairs for which there is no earlier evidence had come into existence by 1792. This meant that there was a total of 51 places with fairs in 1792. Along the River Trent and in the Isle of Axholme they continued without associated markets in villages such as Messingham and Scotter, while new ones had been established at Belton and Haxey. On the other hand, there was a drop in the number of places which had markets and fairs in the fens of south-east Lincolnshire, but the number of fairs increased at Boston, Donington, Holbeach and Spalding.

The goods which were traded at these fairs in the 18th century were the produce of the local agricultural economy—cattle, horses and sheep, with flax and hemp in the Isle of Axholme and the fens, although not all produce passed through them. Wool, for example, was bought and sold by private contract.[13] However, the fairs were the means whereby the products of the region found wider markets and, like the markets, their development reflected the economic life of the county.

Notes and further details on page 140.

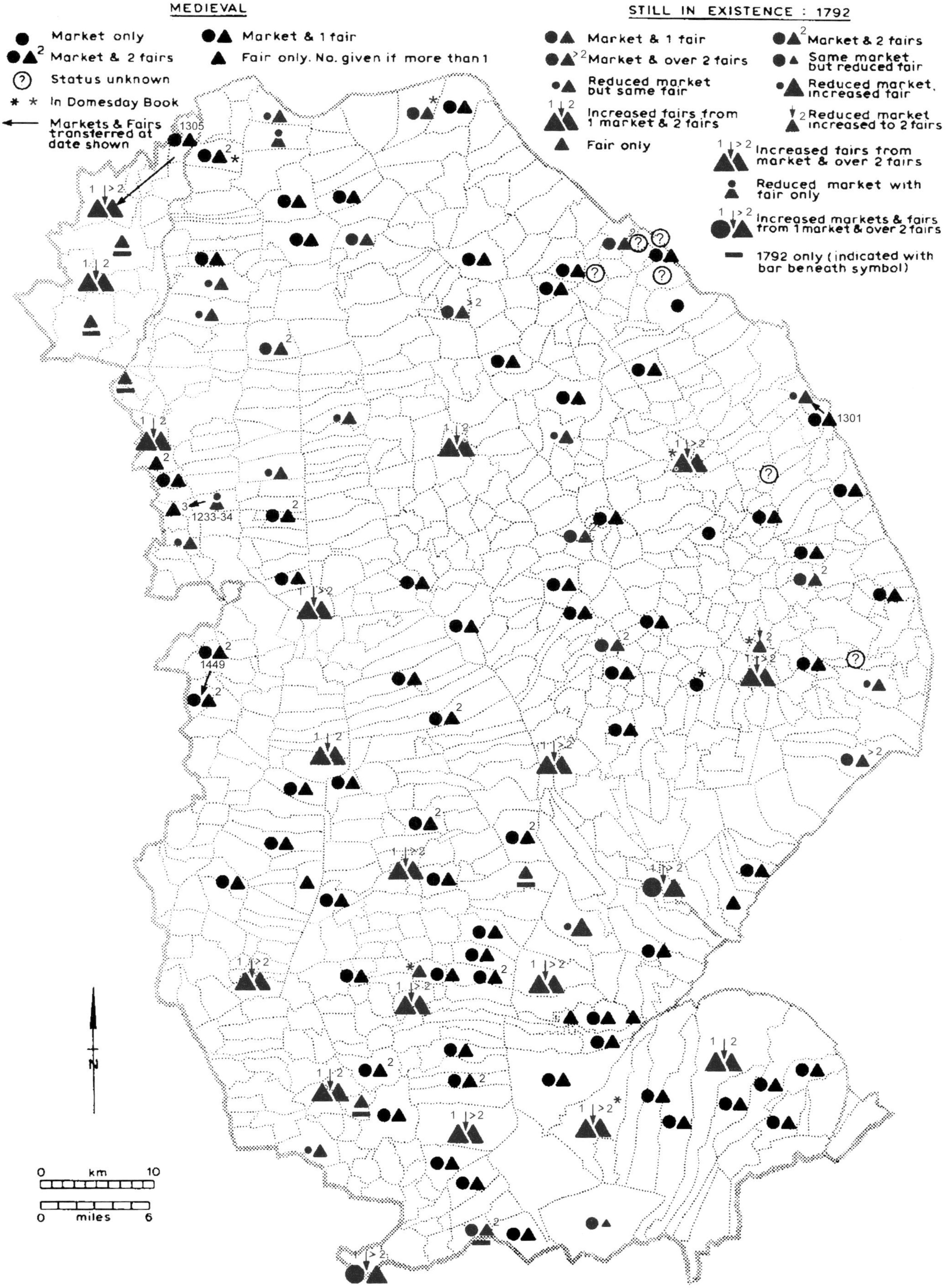
MEDIEVAL
Market only
Market & 2 fairs
Status unknown
In Domesday Book
Markets & Fairs transferred at date shown
Market & 1 fair
Fair only. No. given if more than 1
STILL IN EXISTENCE : 1792
Market & 1 fair
Market & over 2 fairs
Reduced market but same fair
Increased fairs from 1 market & 2 fairs
Fair only
Market & 2 fairs
Same market, but reduced fair
Reduced market, increased fair
Reduced market increased to 2 fairs
Increased fairs from market & over 2 fairs
Reduced market with fair only
Increased markets & fairs from 1 market & over 2 fairs
1792 only (indicated with bar beneath symbol)
1305
1301
1233-34
1449
N
0 km 10
0 miles 6

28 MARITIME TRADE AND FISHING IN THE MIDDLE AGES *Simon Pawley*

In the 13th and 14th centuries, Lincolnshire's coastline was dotted with small ports and havens, many of which are now so far from the sea that it is difficult to imagine the extent of their medieval involvement in maritime trade and fishing. The shape of the coastline has changed beyond recognition since that time. So too has the navigability of many rivers which, in the Middle Ages, provided a natural extension of this commerce. The medieval ship was small and adaptable, and seagoing vessels could once be found as far inland as Lincoln, Horncastle and Gainsborough. They could also pass along the Humber into the Yorkshire Ouse river system and so up to York and beyond.

Many of the places marked on the map were required to contribute ships and mariners to the impressed fleets mustered by Edward III for his various campaigns in France during the Hundred Years' War. Such fleets (used to transport men and supplies across the Channel) were mustered by arresting ships in all recognised ports and havens, and sometimes along the river network as well. The officials who performed these impressments were notoriously corrupt and would frequently demand bribes before exempting smaller vessels. Not surprisingly, any 'staying of ships' was unwelcome to mariners and fishermen, who relied on their vessels for a livelihood. In 1338, for example, the wrongful detention of the Saltfleet fishing fleet in Great Yarmouth was said to have cost the fishermen £40 in lost catches.[1]

The foundation of the widespread maritime trade of the Lincolnshire ports in the Middle Ages was the 'staple port' of Boston, through which all shipments of wool were supposed to pass en route for Calais. Until the end of the 13th century, Boston exported more wool than any other port in England. From that time onwards, it experienced a slow but steady decline. Nevertheless, throughout the medieval period it remained a focus which drew in overseas trade to the numerous small creeks and havens along the county's coastline and so helped to promote a thriving maritime economy there.

Foreign merchants would have been a common sight in a number of Lincolnshire havens in the 14th century. Scandinavian, Flemish and Hanseatic vessels traded through Grimsby, Saltfleet, Skegness and Wainfleet, importing timber, cloth, stockfish and wine and exporting locally produced grain, cloth and wool. The role of Lincolnshire's great medieval religious houses in this trade was central, because they owned many of the large wool-producing flocks. Louth Park Abbey, for example, used Saltfleethaven as a natural focus for its commercial interests. As late as the early 16th century, wool was still being sent from such places in local vessels to join the one or two large fleets which went from Boston to Calais each year. Much wool and other produce also found its way out of the smaller havens, illegally and without payment of customs, throughout the medieval period.

The religious houses also played a vital part in another major element of the county's medieval maritime economy, the trade in salt and fish. Salt was a commodity in heavy demand during the Middle Ages because of its preservative qualities, and salt production was an important industry in the Wash area and in the Lindsey marsh. Peat dug from turbaries in the Isle of Axholme—many of them also owned by the religious houses—was shipped along the Trent and the Humber and imported for use in the manufacturing process in Lindsey.

Some of the Scandinavian merchants who could be found at Lincolnshire ports were buying salt for use in the Baltic herring fisheries; but there were other seasonal fisheries closer to hand. The map shows a number of Lincolnshire ports such as Wrangle which did a thriving trade in salt with the great-annual herring 'fares' or fisheries off the Yorkshire and East Anglian coasts.

Many Lincolnshire ports also had their own seasonal fishing fleets. In the 13th century, Spalding is said to have been an important centre, with the vessels owned (significantly) by the local Prior. Skegness, Wainfleet and 'Skottermuth' (Halton Skitter) are also recorded. By the 14th century, however, Saltfleet was sending easily the largest Lincolnshire fleet to the herring 'fares' off Scarborough and Yarmouth. In 1343, for example, 14 Saltfleet fishing boats went to Yarmouth. They left laden with local salt for sale on arrival and would have returned with cargoes of salted herrings, which were marketed not only at Saltfleethaven itself but at Grimsby and other fish markets in the area.

Until the end of the Middle Ages, fishermen did not normally venture into distant waters in search of catches, but in the 15th century a fishing ground for cod was opened up off Iceland. It was always dominated by the East Anglian fishermen who had first begun it, but in some years there were also small fleets of vessels from Boston and Grimsby (the latter financed largely from the nearby fishing village of Clee). This was a comparatively high-risk venture, involving a long and dangerous voyage and a round trip lasting six months, with uncertain profits at the end of it. Not surprisingly, the smaller havens took no part in it.

By this period, in any case, the heyday of the county's medieval maritime activity was long over. Wool exports from Boston had dwindled, salt production was in decline as the salt marshes grew and the sea retreated, foreign salt of greater purity was beginning to dominate the markets, and havens such as Boston, Saltfleet and Wainfleet were warping up. By the time the underpinning wealth of the religious houses was removed from the equation in the early 16th century, the county's involvement in seasonal fishing and maritime trade was already only a fraction of what it had been in the era before the Black Death.

Notes and further details on page 140.

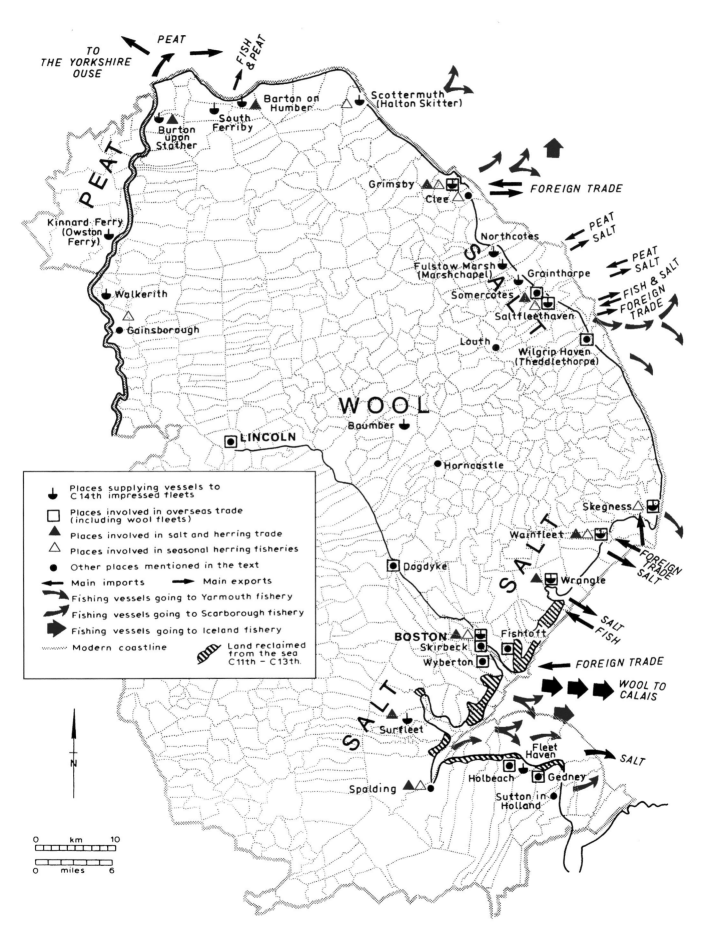

To the Yorkshire Ouse

PEAT

FISH & PEAT

Scottermuth (Halton Skitter)

Barton on Humber

South Ferriby

Burton upon Stather

PEAT

Kinnard Ferry (Owston Ferry)

Grimsby

Clee

FOREIGN TRADE

Northcotes

PEAT SALT

PEAT SALT

FISH & SALT

Walkerith

Fulstow Marsh (Marshchapel)

Grainthorpe

Somercotes

Saltfleethaven

FOREIGN TRADE

Gainsborough

SALT

Louth

Wilgrip Haven (Theddlethorpe)

WOOL

Baumber

LINCOLN

Horncastle

Skegness

Wainfleet

FOREIGN TRADE SALT

Dogdyke

SALT

Wrangle

SALT FISH

Places supplying vessels to C14th impressed fleets

Places involved in overseas trade (including wool fleets)

Places involved in salt and herring trade

Places involved in seasonal herring fisheries

Other places mentioned in the text

Main imports   Main exports

Fishing vessels going to Yarmouth fishery

Fishing vessels going to Scarborough fishery

Fishing vessels going to Iceland fishery

Modern coastline   Land reclaimed from the sea C11th – C13th.

BOSTON

Skirbeck

Fishtoft

Wyberton

FOREIGN TRADE

WOOL TO CALAIS

N

Surfleet

Fleet Haven

SALT

Holbeach

Gedney

Spalding

Sutton in Holland

0   km   10

0   miles   6

57

There can be no doubting the extent of the decline in maritime activity which had taken place in Lincolnshire by the middle of the 16th century. The records of the period are more abundant and specific than anything which preceded them. Growing financial pressures on the Tudor administration had led to a concerted attempt to maximise the yield from customs revenue. In place of the malpractices and slack control of the Middle Ages, a strict hierarchy of head ports, 'members' and creeks was established, with a complex paraphernalia of officials who (at least in theory) checked and recorded every transaction, coastal or foreign, at every possible landing place.[1]

There was also a growing belief, the most notable exponent of which was William Cecil, Lord Burghley, that maritime skills (and especially fishing) needed to be cultivated so that England would have a ready supply of trained mariners: men who, as one later writer put it, would be 'fellows for the nonce and shew themselves right English' when confronted with the enemy at sea.[2] This concern led to frequent investigations into the state of the creeks and havens along the east coast. There was a general belief that fishing, in particular, was in decline. The London fishmongers blamed everything from the abolition of 'fish days' to a general decline in moral standards.

No matter how exaggerated such claims may have been, Cecil can have had little pleasure in the results of several surveys of havens and shipping in Lincolnshire carried out in 1560, 1565 and 1582. Grimsby had a couple of ships in the 80–100-ton bracket but these now looked towards Hull for their trade. At Boston and nearby Dogdyke there were no vessels above 40 tons in size and the majority of the trade was purely short-range coastal traffic, running between the port and the Great Ouse river network leading south to Cambridge and the great annual fair at Stourbridge.

The smaller havens were in a state of total decay. Major repairs had been undertaken at Wainfleet to straighten and widen the serpentine bends of the haven but it was still 'a pore beggarlie markett towne and wherein doethe inhabit no merchaunt or other person that useth any trafique of merchaundise'. Saltfleet and Wilgrip had been totally warped up for twenty years before the 1565 survey. The haven at Saltfleet seems to have been put in order by the 1570s, only to be out of use again by about 1600. This time it was probably inaccessible until extensive new work was carried out in 1648, with Theddlethorpe replacing it as the normal landing place for goods. Many other havens (some not in existence in the medieval period) were now one or two miles from any houses and as far again from the sea, as the saltmarsh had crept outwards and the head of the haven had silted up. Such places offered little or no commercial opportunities.

Trade had not totally ceased, but it had narrowed dramatically both in its volume and in its horizons. The trade in miscellaneous goods at Boston continued on a small scale for most of the 16th and 17th centuries. Small keels from Lincoln, Dogdyke, Spalding and Boston used the Witham and the Wash to gain access to the Great Ouse. Some Humber havens were still trading in peat (mainly with Hull and York) and a little salt was still being manufactured around Marshchapel.

However, the overwhelming bulk of the commerce was a one-way traffic by coasting vessels bringing coal from Newcastle and (at a slightly later date) Sunderland to the rural areas of Lincolnshire which lacked supplies of fuel. The coastal port books of Boston, Wainfleet and Saltfleet contain almost no other entries. This trade had the advantage of not requiring a harbour: a collier could lie offshore and be unloaded at low tide. Such vessels did not normally come from the haven in question but either from Newcastle itself or from Keadby (on the Trent) or Selby. There are records of coasters belonging to Saltfleet in some periods during the later 16th century, but once again the nature of the trade seldom varies: coal brought from the north-east and offloaded for local consumption.

This limited commercial horizon is mirrored by what we know of fishing on the Lincolnshire coastline in the same period. What had been a significant industry in the 13th and 14th centuries had now become a small-scale offshore concern, using boats of only a few tons burden and crewed by men for whom it was a by-employment rather than a full-time occupation. In 1565, there were 34 small boats operating out of landing places like Cleethorpes and Goxhill in the Humber area, sometimes doubling as ferry-boats across the estuary. In the villages around Boston and Wainfleet there were 15 boats of similar size, often owned in partnership between two or more men from the same village, to spread the risk. All of this demonstrates the lack of importance fishing had by this period. Lincolnshire fishermen who left wills in the 16th century made bequests of their land-based assets first, and their probate inventories confirm that such capital as they possessed was normally invested in sheep and cattle rather than boats and gear. It was advice not confined only to the less well-heeled. In 1601, the young Robert, Lord Willoughby, was advised to sell up all the ships he owned as 'a charge intollerable' on his estate.

The map also shows the number of fishermen recorded in various places on or near to the coast in a muster of sea-fishermen which took place in Lincolnshire in 1628. The returns may not be complete, but they again indicate very small-scale operations (mainly in the north of the county) and an occupation usually pursued as a by-employment, rather than as a first means of obtaining a livelihood.

Notes and further details on page 140.

Maritime trade and fishing in the 16th and 17th centuries

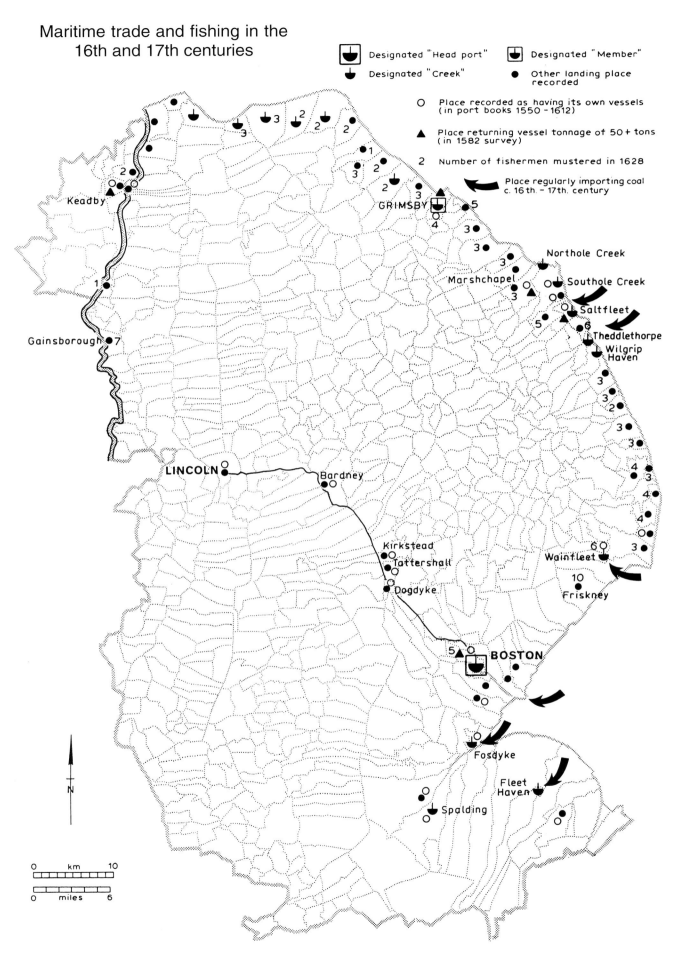

Designated "Head port"

Designated "Member"

Designated "Creek"

Other landing place recorded

○ Place recorded as having its own vessels (in port books 1550 – 1612)

▲ Place returning vessel tonnage of 50 + tons (in 1582 survey)

2 Number of fishermen mustered in 1628

Place regularly importing coal c. 16th. – 17th. century

Keadby

2

GRIMSBY

1

3

2

2

3

2

3

5

4

3

3

3

Northole Creek

Marshchapel

3

3

Southole Creek

5

Saltfleet

6

Theddlethorpe

Wilgrip Haven

3

3

3

2

3

3

4

3

4

4

3

6

3

Wainfleet

10

Friskney

Gainsborough 7

1

LINCOLN

Bardney

Kirkstead

Tattershall

Dogdyke

5 BOSTON

Fosdyke

Fleet Haven

Spalding

0 km 10

0 miles 6

N

THE LINCOLNSHIRE RISING

Ian Beckwith

The Lincolnshire Rising broke out on Sunday, 1 October 1536.[1] By 8 October it was effectively over, although government forces did not arrive on the scene until six days later. Thus the Rising lasted barely a week. It was provoked by a combination of events: the dissolution of the lesser religious houses in the area, a visitation of the clergy, and news that the remainder of a subsidy was due to be collected. Meanwhile rumours were circulating that the King intended to despoil the parish churches and to put a tax on cattle and sheep.[2]

The Rising broke out in Louth on the Sunday and Monday (1-2 October). On Tuesday, the commons of Louth marched to Caistor where they compelled some of the gentry, who were there as commissioners for the collection of the subsidy, to return with them to Louth. In the meantime the commons of Horncastle, Spilsby and Alford rose. On Wednesday the commons of Rasen and Alford came into Louth where at a muster it was announced that each wapentake was to be ready to march under its captain on the following day. Accordingly the commons and gentry gathered at Great Towse and proceeded towards Lincoln. The host lay overnight at Market Rasen, the gentry in the town and the commons on Hamilton Hill where they were joined by a group, said to number 10,000, coming from Yarborough wapentake. Contingents from Horncastle, Spilsby, Wragby and the religious houses in the Witham valley made their way to Langworth Lane, arriving on Friday, 6 October. Meanwhile the marchers from Market Rasen halted at Grange de Lings where they were joined by the commons of the Soke of Kirton.

On Saturday, while the commons mustered on Newport Green, the gentlemen of the two hosts met at Mile Cross to agree on the final form of the demands to be sent to the King. Meanwhile parties were dispatched to Sleaford to escort Lord Hussey and other gentlemen of Kesteven to Lincoln but without success. On Sunday, in the chapter house of the cathedral, the gentlemen read the articles to the commons, and on the following day these demands were sent to the King. On Tuesday a letter arrived from the King which referred, in a famous phrase, to Lincolnshire as 'the most brute and beastly shire in the realm'. The gentry met the commons on Wednesday and argued against advancing further before they received the King's response to their demands. On the same day Lancaster Herald arrived and spoke so persuasively that on Thursday, 11 October the 'rebels' began to disperse to their homes. Meanwhile, the King's forces had reached Stamford. By this time the majority of the commons had drifted away, leaving the gentry to face the royal wrath.

The map demonstrates that this was a rising principally of the men of a limited part of Lindsey, although 'rebels' joined it from Boston and there were signs of unrest around Sleaford. Just over seventy parishes were involved,[3] mainly east and west of Louth, with other clusters around Horncastle, Market Rasen, Alford and Spilsby, and a few scattered along the Humber and the valleys of the Ancholme, Witham and Bain. The larger part of Lindsey, notably the villages and towns on either side of the cliff north of Lincoln and those in the Till basin, the Trent vale and the Isle of Axholme, remained uninvolved.

The parishes in the areas affected by the Rising tended to be more heavily populated. But this could also be said of many parishes which remained aloof, notably in the Isle of Axholme, the marsh and the Witham valley.[4] Many of the districts involved in the Rising were situated near a religious house, for example Louth Park, Bardney and Markby. On the other hand there were many parishes elsewhere in Lincolnshire which had monastic connections but did not become involved. It is not possible to generalise about how far this was either an urban riot or a rural 'jacquerie'. Many urban craftsmen were among the 'rebel' leadership, and market towns were focal points for the Rising, but some towns, such as Gainsborough, Grimsby, and most of those in Kesteven and Holland, took no part.[5] Nor is it possible to say that the prominence in the Rising of the freeholding parishes of the marsh was linked to their 'open' character, since many 'closed' parishes of the wolds and clay vale also actively supported the 'rebels'.[6]

The map also emphasises the significance of the traditional rallying points, in many cases located on hilltops, for the various groups of 'rebels' making their way towards one another from different directions. This suggests that, following the initial chaotic and violent proceedings of the mobs in Louth, Horncastle and elsewhere, the captains of the militia in the wapentakes put in hand an orderly mobilisation, calling up their men to assemble at the recognised mustering places. The orderly quasi-ritual character of the Rising was reflected in the oath of loyalty which the 'rebels' administered to those whom they pressed into joining them as they went along. By this token, the 'rebels' declared their loyalty to the King who they believed was being alienated from his subjects by the evil counsel of wicked ministers, notably Thomas Cromwell. The gentry were obliged by the commons to assume their traditional roles as leaders of the musters.[7] Even the murder of the bishop's chancellor, Dr. Rayne, by the Horncastle mob, urged on as it was by the priests, had a sort of ritual character.[8] In both towns and rural parishes the commons were usually summoned together by the common bell.

The punishment of the 'rebels' was less draconian than had been feared. Many of the ringleaders were still alive to receive the King when he visited Lincolnshire in 1541. The vacillation of the authorities in London and the shires is striking. The slowness of the royal response, with no army in the field until 9 October, is remarkable. The Earl of Shrewsbury at Worksop and Lord Burgh at Misson, both from the safety of the other side of the Trent, uttered brave threats against the rebels but both seem to have allowed discretion rather than valour to play the better part until they were sure that the Duke of Suffolk and the royal forces were in sight of Lincoln.

Notes and further details on page 140.

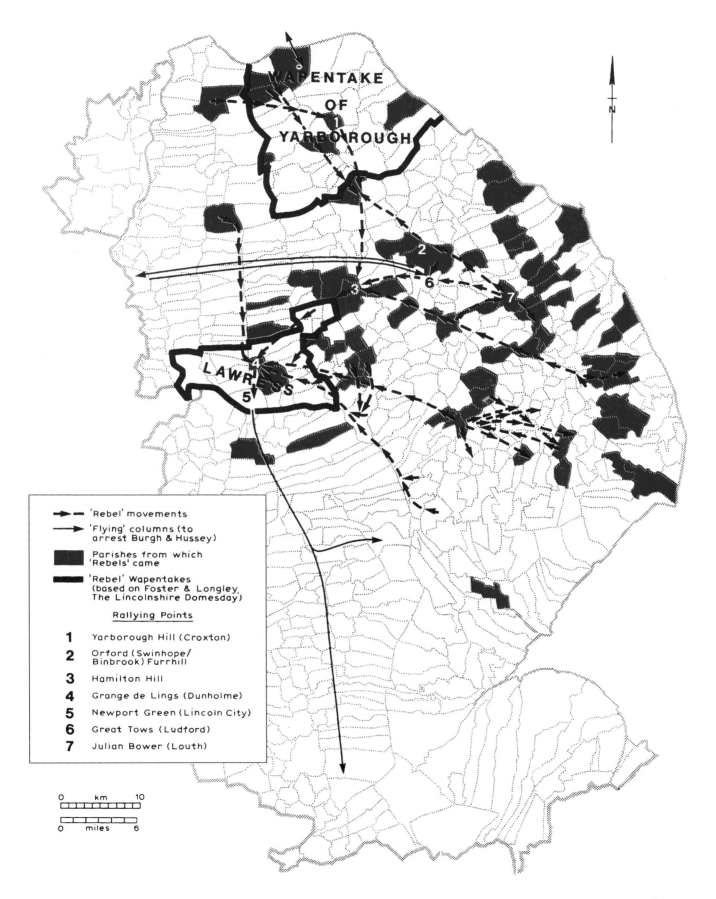

WAPENTAKE
OF
YARBOROUGH

LAWRESS

Legend:

'Rebel' movements

'Flying' columns (to
arrest Burgh & Hussey)

Parishes from which
'Rebels' came

'Rebel' Wapentakes
(based on Foster & Longley,
The Lincolnshire Domesday)

Rallying Points

1   Yarborough Hill (Croxton)
2   Orford (Swinhope/
    Binbrook) Furrhill
3   Hamilton Hill
4   Grange de Lings (Dunholme)
5   Newport Green (Lincoln City)
6   Great Tows (Ludford)
7   Julian Bower (Louth)

0   km   10

0   miles   6

THE EARLS OF YARBOROUGH: INTERESTS AND INFLUENCES

Anne Mitson

In 1564 Sir William Pelham, the founder of the Brocklesby estate, made his first purchase of land in Lincolnshire, the manor of Great Limber, bought for £1,000 from John Hanbye. Sir William's father, from Laughton in Sussex, had died in 1538 leaving a small legacy of £20 per annum to be divided between his three sons. William had to make his own way in life and, like other younger sons at that time, became a soldier. For William, this choice of career proved fruitful. His duties took him overseas and he was able, from the profits of his office as Lieutenant of the Ordnance, to build a considerable estate, amounting to almost 11,000 acres at his death in (upper map) 1587.[1] Although Sir William seems rarely to have lived in Lincolnshire, in some twenty years he had laid the foundations of a landed estate which is still extensive and influential today.

Unlike Sir William, his descendants were content to make their home in Lincolnshire. Although little is known about the early house at Brocklesby, a 'very fine stately building' existed in 1603. The present house is largely a reconstruction of an 18th-century mansion, carried out after 1898 following a serious fire; in 1957-8 this was in turn reduced in size, leaving the present L-shaped house.[2]

Over the next three centuries Sir William's successors enlarged the estate, until, in the 1870s, the 4th Earl of Yarborough inherited some 60,000 acres (lower map). Each Pelham added to the estate, some more extensively than others. The second Charles Pelham, inheriting in 1692, spent over £40,000 in land purchases before his death in 1763. Although Charles was twice married, he left no children and the estate passed to a great-nephew, Charles Anderson. He brought with him land in Broughton and Appleby, including the Manby estate, lying to the west of Brocklesby but close enough to preserve the compact nature of the estate.

Charles Anderson Pelham, created Baron Yarborough in 1794, spent large sums extending his estate, including the purchase in 1804 of 4,675 acres at Thorganby, Croxby and Rothwell, for which he paid £90,000. He enriched his estate in other ways. As a young man he undertook a European tour and met, and later married, Sophia, the only daughter of George Aufrere, a renowned art collector, whose extensive collection eventually went to the Yarboroughs. But the Baron was an art enthusiast himself. On the death of his young wife in 1786, he undertook the building of a mausoleum, employing James Wyatt who created the fine neo-classical building housing Nollekens' figure of Sophia, which is surrounded by Italian monuments to other members of the family.

Despite his achievements, Lord Yarborough left in 1823 an encumbered estate to his eldest son Charles, later created Earl of Yarborough. From the early 1830s, large sums were paid out in interest on a number of mortgages, as much as £20,808 in 1871, but the estate was sufficiently large to support such borrowing.

Between 1823 and 1875, the 1st, 2nd and 3rd earls maintained and added to the estate. Despite some financial worries, each was able to run the houses at Brocklesby and Manby, as well as maintain a prestigious London house in Arlington Street. Each was able to live the lifestyle befitting an earl, whether at Brocklesby, in London, on the continent, or hunting or sailing. At the same time each took a great interest in the estate and its tenants, both the farmers and their labourers. Of particular concern was the provision of schools. Between 1845 and 1895, in addition to regular subscriptions, donations were given for the alteration or rebuilding of 21 schools (lower map). An important consideration was that the schools should provide an education for the children of all tenants, whether members of the Church of England or nonconformists.[3] The family were unusual in allowing nonconformist chapels to be built on their estate.

In 1875 the estate passed to the 4th earl, who was to see enormous changes during his long life. He inherited an estate of some 60,000 acres bringing in a net rental of £68,126 in 1885. By 1896, however, the agricultural depression had reduced the net annual rental to £42,283 and, unlike in the earlier part of the century when there were waiting lists of would-be tenants, farms were now proving difficult to let. The 20th century brought additional problems for the landowner, including vastly increased taxation. The Brocklesby Estate survived largely intact until after the First World War when, along with other large estates, a substantial part of the property came on to the market. Sales took place in 1919, 1925 and 1933. The 5th earl in 1936 inherited a much reduced estate, with tenant farmers once again in financial difficulties, resulting in a number of bankruptcies. Further sales of land in 1944 and 1948 reduced the estate to about half of what it had been at its height.

Nevertheless, the estate today retains much of its importance and influence in north Lincolnshire. Eighteenth- and 19th-century estate buildings survive in almost all the parishes where the Yarboroughs were once landowners, as far south as Claxby, Rothwell and Wold Newton. Substantial farm houses dating from the end of the 18th century survive in Swallow, Melton Ross, Great Limber and elsewhere. Memorial windows in churches, as at Thorganby, Swallow and Great Limber, remain to testify to the importance and influence of Yarborough tenant farmers, such as the Binghams, Farrows and Nelsons.[4]

While the Yarborough influence has been confined in general to the north of the county, it has been wide-ranging. It has made its mark via the rural communities and via urban Grimsby. The Pelhams have provided sporting hospitality for their friends and tenants; they have provided employment on their large estate; they have been involved politically at both local and national levels. Although the role of the aristocracy has radically changed, their influence is still felt. And a new era began as the 8th Earl of Yarborough succeeded to the estate on the death of his father in 1991.

Notes and further details on page 141.

Land purchased by 1st Sir William Pelham 1564-1587

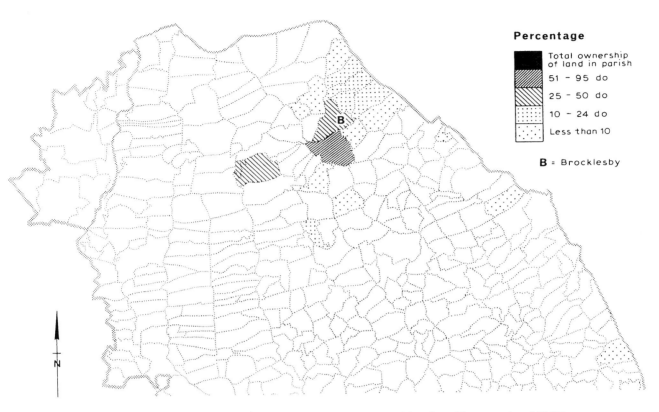

Percentage

Total ownership
of land in parish

51 - 95 do

25 - 50 do

10 - 24 do

Less than 10

B = Brocklesby

N

Distribution of land comprising the Brocklesby Estate in 1875

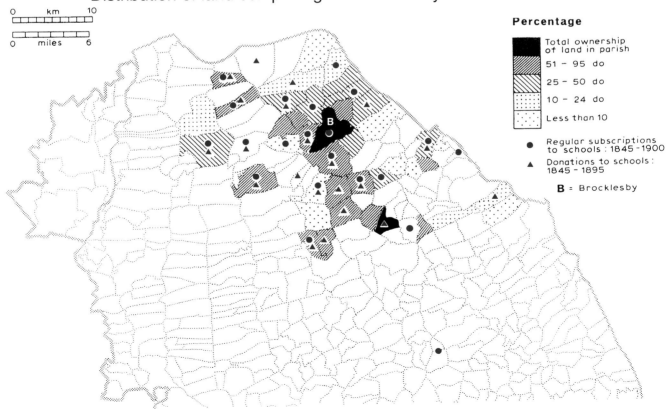

0   km   10

0   miles   6

Percentage

Total ownership
of land in parish

51 - 95 do

25 - 50 do

10 - 24 do

Less than 10

● Regular subscriptions
to schools : 1845-1900

▲ Donations to schools :
1845 - 1895

B = Brocklesby

At the beginning the county wavered. Early in 1642 Parliament appointed, as lords lieutenant, the Earl of Lincoln and Lord Willoughby of Parham, while the King appointed the Earl of Lindsey to be his lieutenant in the shire. In June, Lord Willoughby took the view of arms at Lincoln. On 13 July, the King came in person to Lincoln to meet the Community of Lincolnshire. The following day, the gentlemen of the county presented a petition to Parliament supporting the King and subscribed 172 horses and men. The noticeably thin distribution of those who offered men and horses for the King's cause suggests no particular pattern other than a concentration around Lincoln. The Royal Standard had barely been raised at Nottingham on 25 August than Royalist officers raided Coleby Hall south of Lincoln to arrest the occupants. Gainsborough raised a force to defend its neutrality. Grantham checked its weapons. A Royalist ship attempted unsuccessfully to put a consignment of arms and men ashore at Skegness. Parliament ordered forces to be raised in the county. Cressey Hall, near Surfleet, was garrisoned for the King by the Sheriff of Lincolnshire, Sir Edward Heron, but soon afterwards the Sheriff was taken prisoner in a skirmish. Early in November the Royalist army of the Earl of Newcastle was reported advancing towards Lincolnshire.

Whoever held west Lindsey and Kesteven commanded the Trent up to the Royalist stronghold of Newark and beyond. Equally, whoever held the Lincolnshire shore of the Humber estuary threatened the Parliamentary garrison in Hull. To the south, a Royalist force from bases in Holland might break into the counties of the Eastern Association, or the Association's forces (the Ironsides) could strike through Lincolnshire into Yorkshire. Lincolnshire's long coastline offered both sides the possibility of landing reinforcements in the county.

Early in 1643, as Newcastle's army approached, Parliament ordered more forces to be raised to prevent Lincolnshire falling into Royalist hands. Although the Hull garrison raided Thorganby Hall in February, the Royalist garrisons in Grantham, Belvoir, Stamford, Crowland, Spalding, Wainfleet and Gainsborough ringed Lincolnshire and controlled the river passage. In April Colonel Cavendish's cavalry defeated a Parliament force at Ancaster Heath but Cromwell's Eastern Counties army took Crowland. On 20 July Lord Willoughby of Parham captured Gainsborough for the Parliament and four days later Cromwell took Burghley House. The Royalist ring round Lincolnshire was broken, only for Cavendish to lay siege to Lord Willoughby in Gainsborough. However, after a masterly night-time rendezvous at North Scarle between Cromwell's army and Sir John Meldrum's from Nottingham, the combined Parliament force surprised Cavendish's regiment among the warrens on the parish boundary of Lea and Gainsborough, driving it into the carrs where Cavendish and his cavaliers were slaughtered as they struggled in the mire.

But barely had Cromwell and Meldrum relieved Willoughby in Gainsborough than the Earl of Newcastle's army was observed, crossing the Trent at Morton, compelling Cromwell and Meldrum to abandon Willoughby and to withdraw to Lincoln. Newcastle's artillery now pounded Gainsborough until its inhabitants demanded that Willoughby surrender.

Throughout August 1643 the Parliamentary forces in Lincolnshire pulled back in disarray to Boston and thence into the Eastern Counties, while the Royalists overran Lincolnshire, garrisoning Lincoln, Tattershall, Bolingbroke and Mablethorpe. However, Newcastle was reluctant to advance into the Eastern Association's country while the garrison at Hull remained at his rear. Instead of pressing on to take the demoralised garrison in Boston, Newcastle turned away to besiege Hull. This cost the Royalists Lincolnshire.

Parliament appointed the Earl of Manchester as Commander-in-Chief in the Eastern Counties. With Newcastle engaged before Hull, Manchester made Boston the springboard to gain the initiative in Lincolnshire, taking Wainfleet and investing Bolingbroke. As Manchester's army lay quartered around Horncastle, a Royalist force sought to relieve Bolingbroke. As the sun broke through the autumn mists on the morning of 12 October, Manchester's army broke the enemy line at Winceby, leaving the field covered with the Royalist dead and wounded. The Parliamentary victory at Winceby had a domino effect. In turn Parliament took Lincoln, the coastline was brought under control, Brigg, Burton Stather and Gainsborough fell, and Newark was besieged. Royalist fortunes temporarily revived in the spring of 1644 when Prince Rupert broke the siege of Newark, and Lincoln, Gainsborough and Sleaford were retaken. A month later, however, Manchester was back in Sleaford and Parliament held Stamford and Grimsthorpe Castle. In May Manchester's forces stormed over the upper city in Lincoln. While Manchester made ready for the advance into Yorkshire which was to lead him to Marston Moor on 2 July, the Royalists in Newark recaptured Stamford and garrisoned Irnham House. But on 6 August, following Marston Moor, Manchester was back in Lincoln and Parliamentary detachments were quartered in front of Newark at Claypole, Beckingham and Brant Broughton.

In September Manchester moved into the Thames valley, leaving Royalist raiding parties from Newark once more free to harass Lincolnshire, striking at Sleaford, Caistor, Crowland, Louth, Torksey and Great Gonerby. In June 1645 Royalist forces captured Hougham House near Grantham and defeated a Parliamentary force at Riby Gap near Grimsby in what was probably the last battle ever to be fought on Lincolnshire soil. In August a Royalist unit slighted Torksey House. Nine months later the King gave himself up and the garrison in Newark finally surrendered, having held out since December 1642.

We know the sympathies of only some of the land-owning class. The distribution of those Lincolnshire landowners who were penalised for their support of the King reveals nothing significant in the alignment of the loyalties of the three parts of the county. More noticeable, as four years earlier, are the many parishes in which support for the King was either undeclared or non-existent.

Notes and further details on page 141.

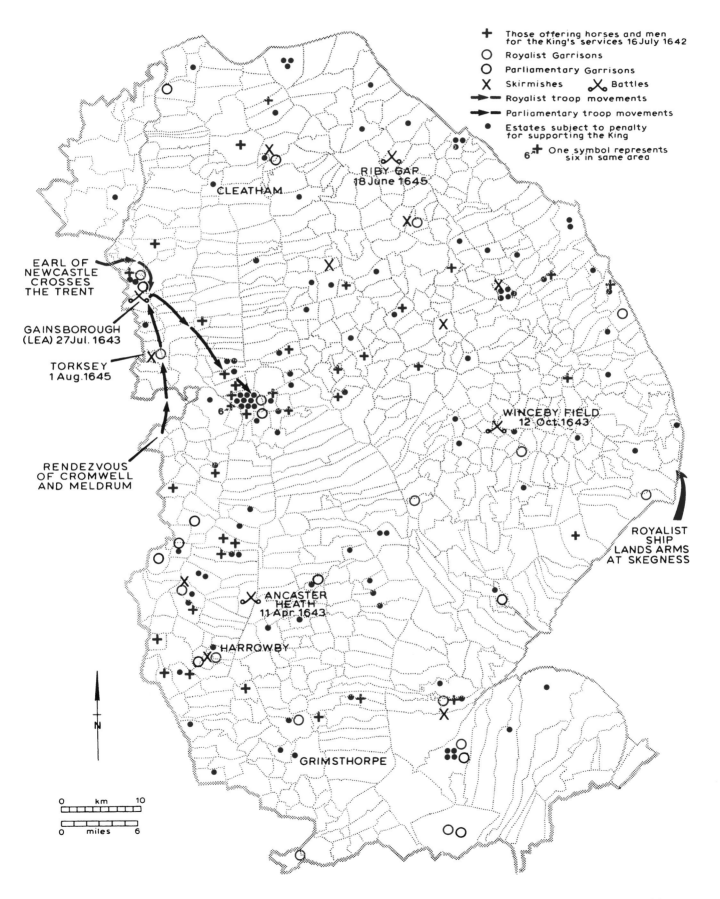

Those offering horses and men
for the King's services 16 July 1642

○ Royalist Garrisons

○ Parliamentary Garrisons

X Skirmishes   Battles

Royalist troop movements

Parliamentary troop movements

• Estates subject to penalty
for supporting the King

6 One symbol represents
six in same area

CLEATHAM

RIBY GAP
18 June 1645

EARL OF
NEWCASTLE
CROSSES
THE TRENT

GAINSBOROUGH
(LEA) 27 Jul. 1643

TORKSEY
1 Aug. 1645

6

WINCEBY FIELD
12 Oct. 1643

RENDEZVOUS
OF CROMWELL
AND MELDRUM

ROYALIST
SHIP
LANDS ARMS
AT SKEGNESS

ANCASTER
HEATH
11 Apr. 1643

HARROWBY

N

GRIMSTHORPE

0   km   10

0   miles   6

I: The Detached Kitchen

The detached kitchen is often regarded as a feature of houses built principally in lowland England. Many reasons have been proposed for its existence, from fire-hazard to unpleasant odour from cooking cabbage. A departure from this functional aspect to that of social distinction is found in clergy housing, mainly of the 17th century, recorded in the terriers or lists submitted to the bishop setting out the buildings as well as the land belonging to a particular parish. It was, at some points in the chronicle of a celibate priesthood, undesirable that women cooks and scullery maids should be housed under the same roof.

By the 17th century such notions were increasingly disregarded, yet quite a high proportion of clergy houses still had kitchens like the one at Bassingthorpe described about 1577 as '... remote from ye house'. It is very marked that the housing described in 16th- and 17th-century terriers is not far removed from that of the laity. If comparisons of parsonages, laymen's cottages and farmhouses are made, several have indications that cooking was done away from the main house. The two-roomed plans of substantial farmhouses sometimes include contemporary bake-ovens and capacious cooking hearths in one downstairs room with the other fitted for a parlour. Others have what appear to be two parlours to which attached kitchens were built later, leaving the impression that their original arrangement included a detached kitchen. None of the parsonages which were recorded by the 17th-century terriers is now known to survive. As though to stress the impression that clergy and lay housing were closely comparable, several detached kitchens still exist but are disused.

Of these the earliest is in Pond Street, Great Gonerby, where a mid-17th-century house of hall and

parlour has its former kitchen built of similar materials, coursed limestone and mullioned windows, several feet away. A slightly later brick house at Firsby has two fine parlours and a similar detached kitchen with oven and set boilers. In the elegant Regency houses of Welland Terrace in Spalding, several appear to have had their kitchens separated across a narrow yard. The accommodation suggests that on the garrets over kitchen and scullery, there was a housekeeper's room and a larger one for the maids.

The demise of the detached kitchen is difficult to determine. It is certain that some outhouses in many Lincolnshire villages were used for cooking well into the 20th century, particularly when the paraffin stove was at the height of its popularity. The kitchen has always been regarded as an inferior room by Lincolnshire people. In the period when pantile had become common, photographs record that the, usually, lower-built part housing the kitchen was still thatched, seemingly to stress that inferiority. At Stixwould, '... one outhouse cal[l]ed the kitchen conteyning two bays' (terrier, 1601), or at Great Steeping (terrier, 1612), '... one kitching ... 2 bayes [built of] earth and covered with strawe', the descriptions serve to underline an attitude which has endured for centuries.

In many villages now the kitchen-and-parlour sort of house has generally been 'gentrified' by the addition of a short wing housing the kitchen to give its tenant the dignity of a separate dining-room and a sitting-room. The gradual progress of housing towards the three-roomed plan of kitchen, hall and parlour, adopted for the better farmhouses from the late 16th century, is virtually complete.

House (parlour and hall)   Detached Kitchen

Farmhouse in Great Conerby, now 1 and 3 Pond Street, as it may have appeared before alteration by the Brownlow Estates in the 19th century.

The detached kitchen

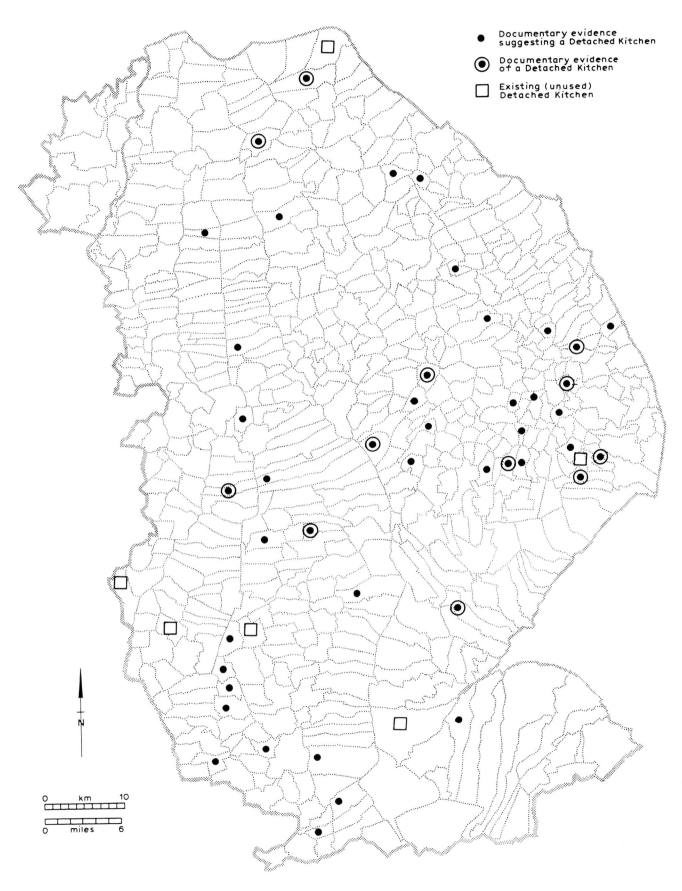

Documentary evidence
suggesting a Detached Kitchen

Documentary evidence
of a Detached Kitchen

Existing (unused)
Detached Kitchen

N

0   km   10

0   miles   6

II: The Distribution of Domestic Crown Post and King Post Roofs

Lincolnshire is known as a county where houses and their barns or outhouses were commonly built in 'mud and stud' during a period begun in antiquity and ended during the middle years of the 19th century. A distribution map of such structures surviving today would be misleading. Where not a single survivor now exists there is often secure documentary evidence for several, inhabited well into the 20th century. This method of building (an oak frame of posts, tie-beams and wall-plates covered by laths of hazel or other coppice-wood supporting a daubed covering of what was, basically, mud) became common throughout the county as well as in surrounding ones. Of more practical use to an historian is an indication of particular techniques or design characteristics. The incidence of a particular roof frame type has much more to tell than a map liberally sprinkled with symbols. Known crown post roofs present a sparse county-wide distribution.

Roof-types in Lincolnshire evolved from a base common to most areas of England, at least that is what the little surviving evidence suggests for those of the 12th and 13th centuries. The common rafter roofs of these early buildings employed timbers of similar scantling, some five to seven inches in section. These timbers were jointed into 'A' frames, of two rafters joined by a collar at about the midpoint. As time went on, various experiments, or perhaps outside influences, suggested improvements aimed at making the roof-frame more rigid, less likely to bow or rack (the toppling of trusses towards one or other end of the building under wind pressure) and to decrease the quantity of timber, usually oak, used in framing. A roof is usually fitted on the wall-head of a building by means of a sort of ring-beam or wall-plate. At regularly spaced intervals a tie-beam spans the building, assisting in making the wall-head stable. The 'bay' is the volume of the building between these tie-beams, including the space enclosed by the roof. In Lincolnshire the bay interval may be as little as six feet in small buildings, about eleven or sixteen feet in most, up to a maximum of twenty-two feet. The most obvious secondary function of a tie-beam is to use it as a main support for flooring roof-space as garrets but for the most part this practice first occurred in the late 16th or early 17th centuries. In medieval building the tie-beam more frequently served, additionally, as a framing member for the bulkhead walls dividing the building below into rooms. In Lincolnshire this use is underscored by the use of 'room' in the sense of 'bay' in many 16th- or 17th-century documents, which can cause some confusion in interpretation.

One of the types of 'stiffening' employed in roof construction is the crown post. It is associated with better quality framing, commonly called half-timbering, masonry or brick structures. Here a vertical post tenoned into the centre top-side of the tie-beam has its head tenoned into a long timber passing below the collars of the 'A' frame. The vertical post, the crown post, is then further supported by braces, two from the top of the tie-beam to mortices in its flanks and two from its other faces reaching up to the underside of the long timber supporting the trusses, the collar purlin. A type of stiffening sometimes regarded as a relative is the king post.[1] Here the supporting post morticed into the top of the tie-beam is carried up past the collars to carry a long timber supporting the rafter apices, called the ridge purlin.

So far, few of either type have been recorded in Lincolnshire, but it is suspected that many more await discovery. Most crown-posts occur in houses of more than average quality, in official building and in churches. A similar pattern occurs in Yorkshire where one of the earliest crown-post roofs is that of the Templars' Foulbridge, Snainton, in the North York Moors, with a dendrochronological date of about 1288.[2] This plain structure is obviously a close relative of the similarly plain Lincolnshire ones.[3] In contrast are the display crown-posts wrought as gothic pillars with cap and base mouldings. It should be noted that plain crown-posts occur in southern England too.[4] Plain crown-post roofs also occur in Nottinghamshire and in York.[5] Lincolnshire is thus surrounded by the national distribution.

The sequence of recorded Lincolnshire crown-post roofs starts in the mid-13th century with that of the medieval lodgings at 18 James Street, Lincoln, the earliest of the group in that city, followed by the roof over the parsonage hall at Coningsby of the mid-14th century.[6] Ralph, Lord Cromwell, began his major brick rebuilding at Tattershall Castle in the 1430s and the gate- or guard-house there (before 1472) has a spindly crown-post roof virtually contemporary with that over the Guildhall and Shodfriars in Boston.[7] The remaining Lincolnshire roofs were constructed after that date and before 1600. Cromwell House in Louth, although drastically altered in its lower storeys, has the run of roof interrupted by a more usual clasped purlin roof where the central stack passes through. The house is jettied, like Shodfriars, which identifies the building as one belonging to the better class of citizen, perhaps a merchant.

The type of distribution might perhaps have been divided into two classes, that over a framed building or that over a masonry structure including those of brick. By so doing the distribution could be demonstrated as variants, one belonging to the brick and crown-post area and the other to that of a framed tradition. This, however, produces a division into socio-chronological strata impossible to comprehend in such a distribution.[8] For that reason it is essential that the distribution is seen to be part of a national one related to others outside Lincolnshire.[9] Survival of buildings in Lincolnshire seems less than the national pattern and the few discussed here seem likely to represent a considerable body of such roofs built during the three centuries before 1600 with the largest group being in the city of Lincoln and the remainder in market towns.[10] Extended fieldwork will undoubtedly identify more examples in the county.

Notes and further details on page 141.

Crown and King Post roofs

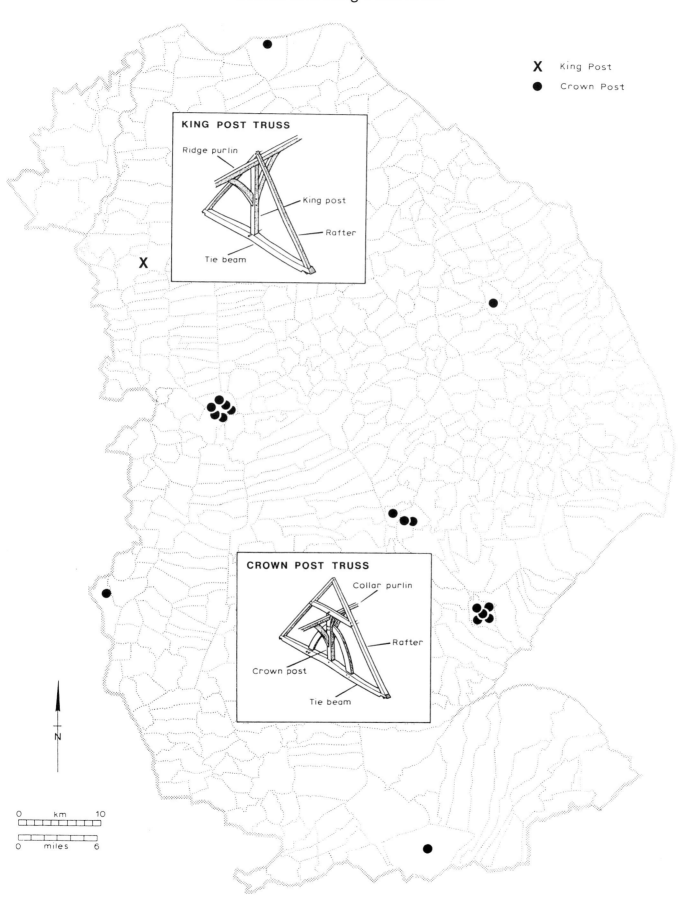

X   King Post
●   Crown Post

KING POST TRUSS

Ridge purlin

King post

Rafter

Tie beam

CROWN POST TRUSS

Collar purlin

Rafter

Crown post

Tie beam

N

0   km   10

0   miles   6

With the introduction of the Poor Law Act in 1601,[1] the government of Elizabeth I addressed for the first time the problem of the deserving poor, as distinct from the vagrant class of 'rogues and vagabonds' who continued to be punished as criminals.

The day of the manor and the monastery as providers for the poor had long gone, and attempts at encouraging charities[2] and authorising collectors for the poor[3] through the church had failed to halt their increasing numbers. The attendant begging, vagrancy and crime became real threats to the maintenance of law and order; new measures were therefore necessary. As the foundations of local administrative machinery were now in place in the parishes, the government devised the means for poor relief by placing the burden of its operation on the parish vestries. The Act of 1601 introduced the compulsory payment of rates and the annual election of overseers of the poor. This financial and administrative system remained in force with supplementary legislation until the Poor Law Amendment Act of 1834.

Any definite conclusions as to the operation of the poor law in Lincolnshire are hampered by the uneven survival rate of parish records and the limited research so far undertaken, but there is enough evidence to gain a general impression. The main discussion revolves around the methods chosen by the parishes for the provision of poor relief and, in particular, the extent to which workhouses were adopted prior to the union workhouse system introduced in 1834.

Setting the poor to work was approved in a vague way in 1601, but Acts of 1722[4] and 1782[5] gave more explicit encouragement for parish workhouses. Many parish vestries, however, continued to use the system of outdoor relief in the form of regular payments in money or in kind with other benefits such as medical aid. Parishes often kept 'poorhouses' but did not provide work; in some cases the poor were farmed out to employers but were not housed institutionally. Spinning schools[6] for children were also tried. Practices varied at different places and at different times. It is known that Sleaford was setting the poor to work as early as 1616, although the institutional workhouse is not evident in the records until 1728. There is early evidence of other Lincolnshire workhouses at Boston in 1730, Bourne in 1735 and the parish of St Swithin, Lincoln, in 1737.

Some workhouses were built specifically for the purpose; references to such building work can be found in overseers' accounts. Other workhouses were merely existing cottages owned by the parishes or by charities. In general the indoor work to which the poor were set involved combing wool, spinning materials such as worsted, flax and wool, and making stockings and other clothes. It is interesting to note that White's 1826 *Lincolnshire Directory* lists George Barker as 'stocking manufacturer and governor of the workhouse' of Winterton. The map illustrates those parishes which were using the workhouse system in 1776 and also those which headed incorporated unions of parishes before 1834. There is documentary evidence to show the existence of workhouses in a large number of other parishes, some of which may have served neighbouring parishes as well on a contractual basis, but charting them on a comparative map would be hazardous when some may have lasted only for short periods.

Out of 701 parish returns recorded in response to the government enquiry in 1776,[7] 47 parishes claimed to use a workhouse. There is evidence, however, that Burgh le Marsh and Kirton in Lindsey also supported workhouses, although they do not appear on the return. In addition, some workhouses which had been established before 1776 had not endured. At Messingham, for example, a workhouse was built in 1747 but by 1757 there were increasing debts and thereafter it disappears from the records.

The results of government enquiries in 1803[8] and 1813-15[9] show which parishes were participating in the workhouse system, but they do not distinguish which parishes operated independent workhouses and which contracted with neighbouring parishes. The observations published in the 1803 report state that 131 Lincolnshire places out of 701 maintained all or some of their poor in workhouses. The observations in the 1813-15 report indicate that 184 places out of 711 in the county maintained the greater part of their poor in workhouses.

A union of several parishes in north Lincolnshire, using a workhouse at Winterton, was formed in 1782. Lincoln city parishes with some rural parishes (including one Nottinghamshire parish) subscribed to a house of industry in Lincoln operated by directors of the poor under a local Act of 1796. A number of these parishes had previously supported a workhouse in Lincoln. Caistor formed a Society of Industry for 19 parishes in 1800, under the guiding influence of William Dixon of Holton le Moor. By 1813 a total of 50 parishes were using the workhouse. A workhouse in Claypole built in 1818 served 14 parishes in Lincolnshire as well as six parishes in Nottinghamshire. The parish of All Saints, Wainfleet, headed a union of six parishes and one hamlet in 1828.[10]

The government reports and documentary evidence show, therefore, that the majority of Lincolnshire parishes were unable to support a workhouse before 1834. One major reason why so many parishes preferred to provide outdoor relief may be that the application for relief by agricultural workers was seasonal—when there was no work on the land. The predominance of rural parishes with populations of less than 300 may also have meant that workhouses were not viable in many individual parishes.[11]

The workhouses which were established were, with some exceptions, in the more populous market towns where there were local manufacturers prepared to set the poor to work or neighbouring parishes willing to participate. The influence of local leaders, as at Caistor, was no doubt also a reason for adopting the workhouse system.

Notes and further details on page 141.

Parish Workhouses: 1776-1834

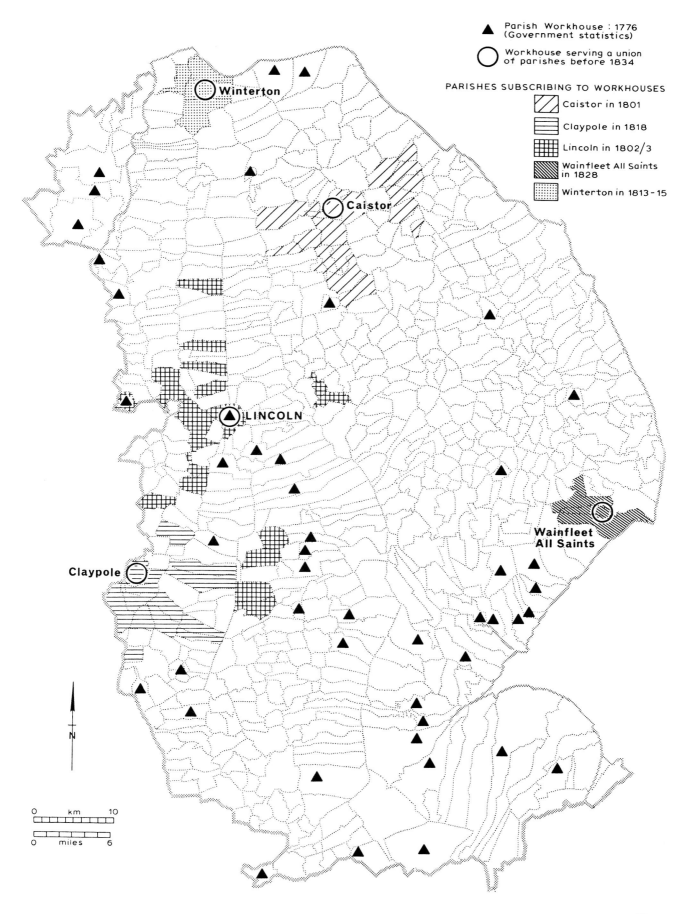

▲	Parish Workhouse : 1776 (Government statistics)
◯	Workhouse serving a union of parishes before 1834

PARISHES SUBSCRIBING TO WORKHOUSES

	Caistor in 1801
	Claypole in 1818
	Lincoln in 1802/3
	Wainfleet All Saints in 1828
	Winterton in 1813-15

Winterton

Caistor

LINCOLN

Wainfleet All Saints

Claypole

0 km 10

0 miles 6

The first attempts to control the waters of Lincolnshire were by the Romans: the Fosse Dyke connecting the Trent and Witham, improvement of the Witham from Lincoln to Chapel Hill, and construction of the Car Dyke as a catchwater drain around the inner edge of what was later to become fenland. Sea-level then was around twenty feet lower than now, and the marshy coast was sheltered by offshore banks and shoals. Sea-level started to rise from the second century and the fenland lagoon quickly silted up, with a bank of coarser material from Wainfleet to Boston and Spalding and round to Long Sutton. By Domesday, settlements were established on this natural bank, and the peatlands of the inner fens and the Isle of Axholme had formed. By 1300 the enlarged 'townlands' of the fens had taken in small areas of saltmarsh and a wider zone of freshwater 'fen', leaving the inner arc from Postland Fen to East Fen as intercommoned grazing. Between Mablethorpe and Skegness, the coastline was at least half a mile further east than now.

The 13th century heralded a period of dramatic change as rising sea-level overwhelmed the offshore banks and combined with tidal surges to reshape the coastline. This led to deterioration of natural drainage through lessening of gradients. Commissions of Sewers struggled to maintain flows and to contain tidal inundations; the medieval patchwork of defensive clay banks are still misnamed 'Roman'. Inland the intercommoned grazing was reduced to summer only, and peatlands became 'foule and flabby quagmires'. Conditions continued to deteriorate but plans to drain large areas in the 16th century were thwarted by the long-established practices of intercommoning.[1] However, some limited coastal reclamation was possible within the shelter of the growing spit of Gibraltar Point (1555 and 1589), and the Maud Foster Drain was cut in 1568.

With the advent of Sir Cornelius Vermuyden in the Isle of Axholme in 1626 there began a remarkable decade of drainage and reclamation activity. By agreement with Charles I, Vermuyden was to make drowned land 'fit for tillage and pasture', for which the participants would receive a third of the land to be drained. Under pressure from the participants for a return on their investment, the main work was carried out within eighteen months. However, the drains, from the wet west across the warplands to the Trent, were inadequate, while opposition from rioters and bank wreckers was considerable, and the work was far from a success.

Vermuyden was disliked and it was Sir Philibert Vernatti who undertook the drainage of Deeping and Croyland Fens in 1631 for the Earl of Bedford. Drains converged on Pode Hole and thence by Vernatt's Drain to the Welland; 'washes', that is natural overflow reservoirs, were created alongside the Welland and Glen. Also in the 1630s, Sir Anthony Thomas started drainage in West Fen (1631-4) with Newham Drain to Anton's Gowt on the Witham, the Earl of Lindsey drained 30,000 acres of common land in Kesteven with the South Forty Foot Drain (1635-8) and Sir John Monson employed Dutch workers to drain the carrlands of the Ancholme with the New Cut from Bishopbridge to a sluice at Horkstow (1637). On the coast Vermuyden embanked 1,120 acres of saltmarsh at Tydd St Mary in the Nene estuary (1632) and Endymion Porter 1,000 acres at North

Somercotes (1632-8); 600 acres were reclaimed at North Cotes and Marshchapel (1638) and 300 acres at Friskney (1641). Coastal reclamation continued after the civil wars and by 1660 a massive 17,374 acres had been embanked from Gedney to Moulton, and the whole of Bicker Haven cut off from the sea.

For the next century the only new works were the draining of the 10,000 acres of Holland Fen with the North Forty Foot Drain by Earl Fitzwilliam in 1720, and reclamations in the Nene estuary in 1720 (1,322 acres) and 1747 (762 acres). The efficiency of gravity drainage continued to decline because of rising sea-level and wind pumps became essential. The meandering Witham downstream of Chapel Hill was a particular problem; reports and plans for straightening the river produced little action until the Witham Act of 1762 and the construction of the Grand Sluice at Boston in 1766.

Other improvements resulted from the Black Sluice Act of 1765, and in 1774 the Vernatt's Drain was extended to join the Welland nearer the sea at Surfleet. Smeaton's reports of 1771 and 1776 on the Isle of Axholme revealed problems of inadequate drains and difficulty of discharge into the tidal Trent. The cutting of the Mother and Folly Drains in 1795 did something to help the situation. Between 1777 and 1797 some 25,000 acres of the Witham Fens were drained and enclosed. During this period of Parliamentary enclosure, the ings and marshes along the Humber bank were secured, saltmarsh was reclaimed at Tetney (1778-9) and Wainfleet/Croft (1789) and the South Holland Embankment was built from Fosdyke to Gedney (1793-1811) to reclaim 4,695 acres.

John Rennie was the engineer who made the most impact in the early 19th century with the drainage of 40,000 acres of the still intercommoned East, West and Wildmore Fens (1801-14). His principles were catchwater drains to collect highland water, arterial drains to conduct lowland water as near as possible to the outfall of the main river, and to control that outfall (although the Witham Cut had to wait until 1884). One third of the land had to be sold to pay for the works.[2] Within half a century steam pumps became necessary on the East Fen (at Lade Bank, 1866), having earlier been installed for Deeping Fen at Pode Hole (1827), in the Isle of Axholme on the Mother Drain (1828) and Bourne Fen (1846). On the Ancholme a new sluice was built at South Ferriby (1825). All drained fenland required continuous improvements and bigger pumps in response to the effects of rising sea-level. Yet on the coast reclamations continued—in 1809 at Wainfleet and Friskney, from the 1840s to the 1860s on the north-east coast, and in the 1860s and 1870s from the Witham to the Nene. In the 20th century, the main work had been on the Wash coast—in 1948 and 1977-8 at Wainfleet and Friskney and also in the 1970s at Butterwick and Freiston, the first reclamation here for over 450 years.

Notes and further details on page 141.

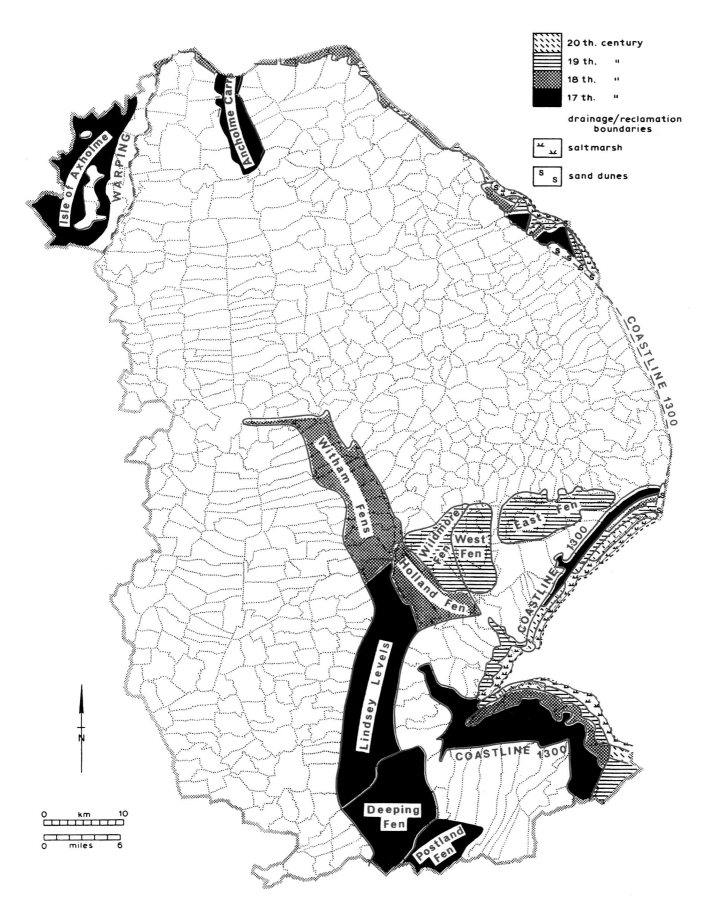

Legend:

20 th. century
19 th. "
18 th. "
17 th. "

drainage/reclamation boundaries

saltmarsh

sand dunes

Isle of Axholme

WARPING

Ancholme Carrs

COASTLINE 1300

Witham Fens

Wildmore Fen

West Fen

East Fen

Holland Fen

COASTLINE 1300

Lindsey Levels

COASTLINE 1300

Deeping Fen

Postland Fen

0 km 10

0 miles 6

N

The Toleration Act of 1689 meant that the places of worship belonging to Protestant dissenters from the Church of England became an officially recognised part of local life. There was a total of 110 dissenting meeting houses in Lincolnshire by the first quarter of the 18th century, of which 57 were Baptist (mostly General Baptist), 28 Quaker, 12 Presbyterian and two described as Presbyterian or Independent. There were also 11 of unspecified denomination.[1] Their geographical distribution reflected the development of the dissenting churches in the 17th century. The Baptists were more closely associated with rural settlements than the Presbyterians or Independents, while seven of the ten Presbyterian congregations which existed between 1715 and 1729, together with one Independent congregation, were situated in towns.[2]

By 1773, the number of Baptist and Presbyterian congregations had declined to 17 and six respectively. While the Baptists had left some rural communities such as Hacconby and Melton Ross, new congregations had been established in at least five places, including Horncastle.[3] The Society of Friends, or Quakers, were relatively strong in north-west Lincolnshire, especially in the Isle of Axholme, in the villages to the south-west of Lincoln and in the fens, although the number of meetings had declined to 17 by 1800.[4] Like those of other dissenters, Quaker meetings included people gathered from parishes which did not have meeting houses.

By the mid-19th century the religious map of the county had been transformed as a result of the evangelical revival which had begun to have an influence on the people of the county from the 1740s. The growth in the number of dissenting places of worship registered with the Bishop of Lincoln from the middle of the 18th to the middle of the 19th centuries—a total of 1961—provides an indication of this, although they are not an exact measure of the permanent strength and distribution of nonconformity in the period.[5]

The 1851 Census of Religious Worship, which included most nonconformist chapels and meeting houses as well as meetings held in hired rooms and private houses, is a measure of the nature and extent of Protestant nonconformity at this date.[6] The impact of Methodism on the county can be seen from the 462 places of worship which were returned as belonging to the Wesleyan Methodists. Nearly all the chapels had been built since 1800 when there were some 25 in Lincolnshire.[7] The next largest nonconformist body, the Primitive Methodists, which had been established in the county since 1817, had 221 chapels and meeting places. The Wesleyan Reform movement had only had a limited impact by 1851.

The evangelical revival also affected some of the older dissenting churches. The development of the New Connexion of the General Baptists from 1770 led to a growth in the number of General Baptist chapels to 34 by 1851. There were also 22 Particular Baptist chapels or meetings. The 38 places of worship described in the census tables as 'Independent' also included Congregational churches. They had little direct connection with the older dissenting congregations, being largely the result of the work of the Countess of Huntingdon's preachers in the later 18th century and the activities of students from Hoxton Academy and Highbury College in the early 19th century.[8] The Latter Day Saints or Mormons had also appeared in the county in the 1840s but only had five scattered congregations in 1851.[9]

The position of the Wesleyan Methodists as the leading nonconformist denomination in the county in 1851 was also reflected in the accommodation they provided in terms of number of seats. Their provision of 78,862 sittings—28 per cent of the total for all the churches of the county—far outstripped that of the next largest provider, the Primitive Methodists. The Primitives, with just under half the number of chapels and meeting places of the Wesleyans, had only 25,164 seats. This reflected the smaller size of their chapels and meetings which had an average capacity of nearly 114 seats compared with nearly 170 for the Wesleyans.[10] The 11,508 sittings belonging to the Independent churches were outnumbered by the total of the Baptist churches (13,620), largely divided between the New Connexion General Baptists (7,948 sittings, giving an average capacity of 256) and the Particular Baptists (4,786 sittings, providing an average of just over 217).

The erection of a nonconformist chapel or the opening of a room for worship depended on the availability of land in a place and the goodwill of its owner. This influenced their distribution so that areas such as south-west Lincolnshire where landlord control was strongest had relatively few nonconformist places of worship. The importance of settlements in divided ownership as centres of nonconformity is apparent from the number of chapels and meetings in areas such as the fens, the Isle of Axholme and the marsh where there were significant numbers of freeholders. Moreover the divisions of Methodism meant that in many places there were two or even three places of worship belonging to its various branches as well as those of other dissenting churches. Where there were larger parishes, as in the fens, the proliferation of nonconformity was also a response to dispersed settlement and local chapels often developed into the social as well as religious centres of isolated communities. Indeed, whatever the local circumstances in which nonconformity developed—in town, village or hamlet—or whether meetings and services were held in chapel, hired room or private house, its distribution in Lincolnshire by the middle of the 19th century is a measure of its importance in the religious and social life of the county.

Notes and further details on page 142.

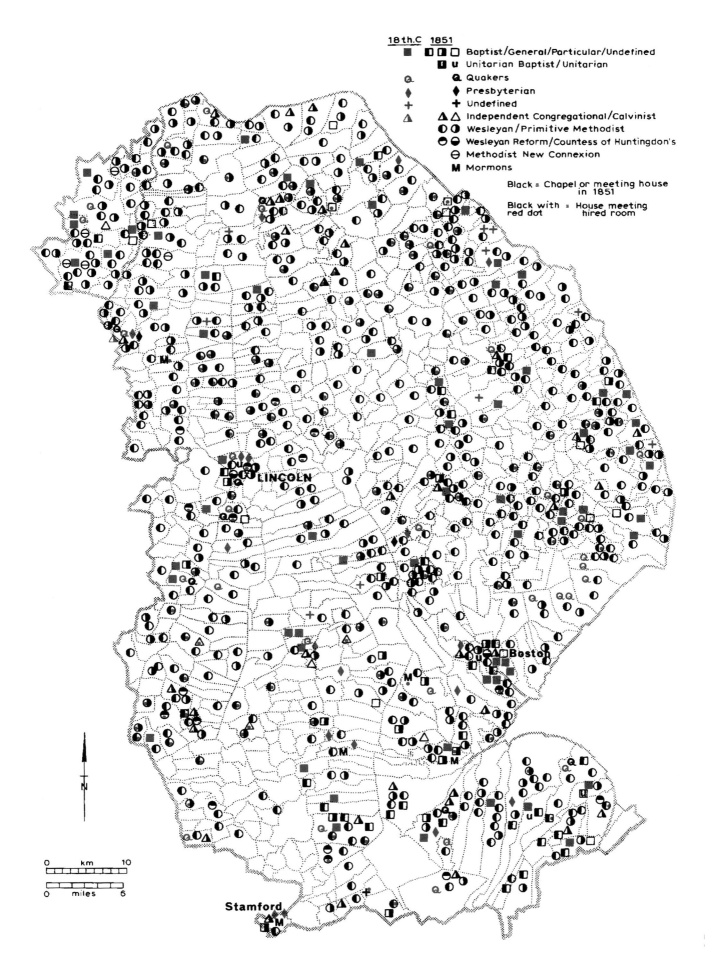

The legend on the map reads:

18th.C 1851

■ ▯▯□ Baptist/General/Particular/Undefined
▯ u Unitarian Baptist/Unitarian
ɑ ɑ Quakers
◆ ◆ Presbyterian
+ + Undefined
△ △ Independent Congregational/Calvinist
◑ ◑ Wesleyan/Primitive Methodist
◒ ◒ Wesleyan Reform/Countess of Huntingdon's
⊖ Methodist New Connexion
M Mormons

Black = Chapel or meeting house in 1851

Black with red dot = House meeting hired room

LINCOLN

Boston

Stamford

0 km 10

0 miles 6

N

The children of the poor and labouring classes gained their education, if at all, either at home, in dame schools or through a local charity. Between 1529 and 1674, 18 free grammar schools were established in the county, many of which still continue today. There were also some forty-five 'petty' or charity/dame schools recorded in the county before the end of the 17th century.[1] Many such charity schools were small, with as few as two children at Goxhill in 1754, four at Dorrington, six at Eagle, yet others such as Cowbit (Free) had 30 children on the register. Usually the grantor bequeathed capital or a cottage and land for a school house, a schoolmaster and occasionally a schoolmistress, maybe the master's wife. At Stickford, the wife was to instruct the girls in knitting and sewing. The charity often specified how many children should receive a free education: at Billingborough, 12 poor children; at Ewerby, 16 boys; at Sedgebrook, 15 poor children of tenants of Sir John Thorold's estate. If the master so wished, he could exceed the specified number by taking fee-paying pupils; at Bolingbroke the register showed 40 pupils, though only 25 were free. Payments were sometimes required for extra provision: at Digby, 1s. per year for fire money, and at Ropsley, pens and ink cost 1d. per week and the children had to find their own books!

Attendance differed considerably between summer and winter: East Kirkby had 60 in winter but only 31 in summer; Fishtoft, 28 compared with ten. This is a clear reflection of the need for children to support the family income by working on the land–sowing, weeding, harvesting, herding. Some schools made provision for the harvest. At Morton cum Hanthorpe, five weeks' holiday were given at harvest and three weeks at Christmas.

The 'three Rs' were usually expected as the curriculum, and, in the dame schools, were frequently specified. Beyond the basics, teaching might have to be paid for: at Ropsley, 2s. 6d. per quarter for land surveying and maths; at Ewerby, reading and spelling were free but writing and arithmetic cost 3d. per week. A few schools prepared pupils for entry to the free grammar schools and Latin, Greek and Hebrew were not uncommon. Most schools reflected the views of the philanthropists who set up the charities, that the pupils should receive moral teaching to fit them for working life. While girls were schooled in spinning, weaving and knitting to enable them to cope with the demands of family life, or of work in the local great houses, the moral teaching was achieved through attention to the fundamentals of Christian education. Ruskington children had to learn the Church catechism by heart, and repeat it every Saturday, go to Church every Sunday and holiday and see that they behaved themselves decently. Sedgebrook demanded the teaching of the catechism, the creed, the Lord's prayer and the ten commandments.

In the free grammar schools the curriculum was rather wider but the classics were essential since these 18 schools prepared pupils for entrance to the universities of Oxford and Cambridge. Their foundation often reflected a university connection; Richard Fox founded both Grantham School (1529) and Corpus Christi College, Oxford; Caistor was founded in 1630 by Francis Rawlinson of Sidney Sussex, Cambridge. Others were established under royal approval: Great Grimsby (1547), Louth (1551), Horncastle (1571) and Gainsborough (1589).

In the case of many early schools the name of the founder is recorded and shows the interest of the lords of the manors and clergy in providing education: Faldingworth (1662) by the Countess of Warwick; Ewerby (1667) by Henry Pell; Grantham Girls Charity School (1671) by the Rev. Thomas Hurst; Brigg (1669) by Sir John Nelthorpe. This early tradition came to fruition with the establishment in 1698 of the Society for the Propagation of Christian Knowledge (SPCK). From then onwards there was a surge of school establishment followed by a period of consolidation. Sixty-three schools were founded in the first quarter of the 18th century, and then only 29 more in the next 75 years.

Of the 63, the greater number were the result of local worthies taking up the challenge that the SPCK had thrown down. The clergy in particular were involved in the spread of education, achieving their aims by raising capital, using glebe land as sites, and by using rents from land to guarantee the salary of the master. The salaries varied widely: Whaplode (1704), £10 4s.; Ewerby (1667), £10; Navenby, £18 for the master but only £13 for the mistress–proceeds from the enclosure award of 1772. Yet the master at Butterwick was endowed with £250 per year while the Hansard school at Caistor had £30 for the master and £15 for an usher. In 1829 Edmund Turnor provided a capital sum of £1,000 for the Colsterworth school to gain £30 per year interest for the master.

The rural nature of the county was reflected in the slow dissemination of ideas in education: the monitorial systems of Bell (1797) and Lancaster (1798) reached Alford in 1819 and Burton Coggles in 1839. The British and Foreign School Society founded in 1801 is mentioned at Theddlethorpe in 1810 and at Welby in 1824. The monitorial system gained its greatest impetus with the establishment of the National Society in 1812. Yet in the following 20 years only 16 new schools were built in the county–five under the auspices of the National Society (probably with grant aid from the Society towards the building costs), nine Church of England and two parochial. This was a very small addition to the total of 140 parishes recorded as having a school. Apart from greater provision, they were all very similar to the earlier schools and continued the tradition of close Church/community relationships with the stress on religion and moral teaching to establish principles for working life. The next phase of school development began when the state decided to take an active interest in education.

Notes and further details on page 142.

Charity Schools: 1500-1830

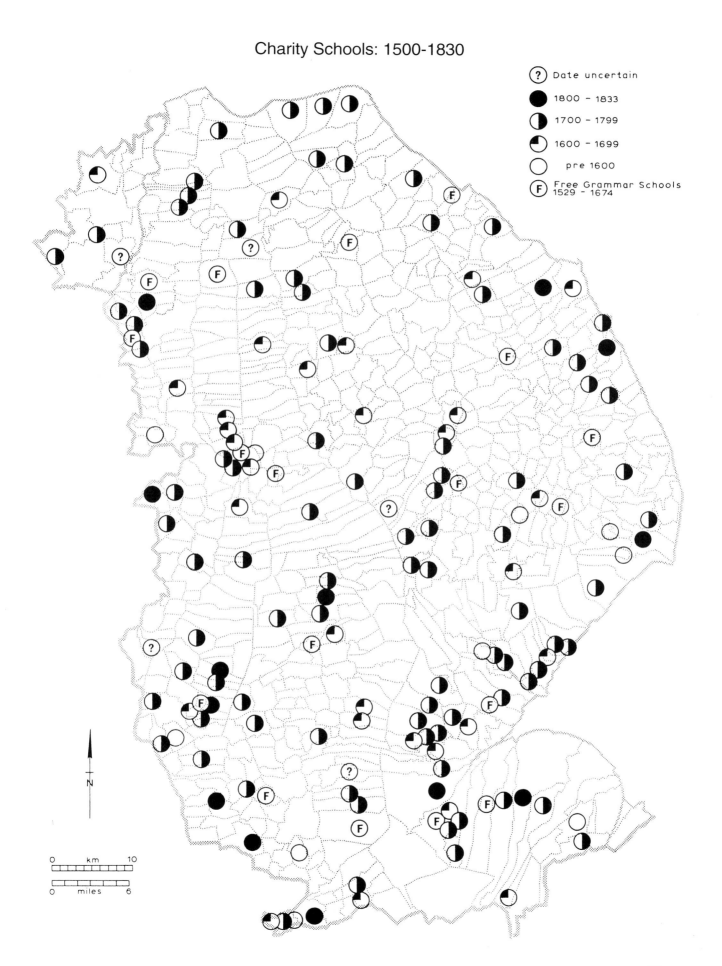

Legend:
- **?** Date uncertain
- ● 1800 – 1833
- ◑ 1700 – 1799
- ◕ 1600 – 1699
- ○ pre 1600
- **F** Free Grammar Schools 1529 – 1674

0 km 10

0 miles 6

N

Responsibility for the maintenance of highways had since 1555 fallen on the parishes through which they passed but, by Georgian times, this system could not cope with the increasing usage and greater maintenance needs of the main roads of the county. The solution was found in the creation of turnpike trusts which would take on responsibility for the repair and improvement of stretches of main road. They would borrow money to pay for the initial works, and, to repay the loan and undertake future maintenance, they would raise funds by levying tolls on the road users. The powers and responsibilities of each trust were contained in individual Acts of Parliament, which were initially for a period of 21 years but were later extended.

The first Lincolnshire roads to be turnpiked were stretches of the Great North Road through the county, from Grantham northwards in 1726 and south to Stamford in 1739. The next Trust, authorised in 1739, was for the road from Lincoln eastwards to the Wolds at Baumber. After 1751 it became easier to obtain Turnpike Acts, and between 1756 and 1765 13 new turnpike trusts were formed for Lincolnshire roads and two others were enlarged. That was the great period of trust creation, and in the following years only a few more roads were turnpiked.

In broad terms the process of creating turnpikes in Lincolnshire started in the south-west of the county, nearest to London, and gradually spread northwards and eastwards through Kesteven and into Holland and Lindsey. Those formed in the 1750s were mainly for roads in Kesteven and across the fens to towns in Holland, and most of the main trusts in Lindsey were formed in 1765. One of the trusts formed in 1756 took over most roads for a distance around Lincoln. The road from Lincoln northwards to the Humber was turnpiked in 1765; this terminated at Barton on Humber from where there was a ferry across the river to Hull. After 1765 almost the only other roads to be turnpiked in Lindsey were four more radiating from Louth which was then the principal town in north-east Lincolnshire.

The passing of a turnpike act did not always mean that the authorised works were carried out and, even if they were, they were not always effective. But on average most turnpikes had more money spent on them than other roads did and they were often notably better. Toll bars where travellers had to pay were usually erected near the ends of a trust's road, on the edges of towns or at major junctions. Side bars were sometimes erected across side roads to prevent people avoiding the main bars. The initial site for a toll bar was not always the best location so the bars, and the adjacent cottages for the collectors, were sometimes moved. In the 1840s one at Boston was moved when the Black Sluice was rebuilt, and another at Alford was moved further out when the railway station opened.

The turnpike trusts in Lincolnshire were set up later, and did not control such a high proportion of the roads, as in counties such as industrialised Derbyshire or Nottinghamshire. By 1837 there were 29 trusts in Lincolnshire controlling 550 miles of roads, with most trusts having between ten and twenty miles of roads. Most main roads were turnpiked for their whole length but that was not always the case. The road between Lincoln and Newark was only turnpiked from Lincoln to the county boundary at Potters Hill, and the road from Newark to Sleaford was subject to a trust only as far as the top of Leadenham Hill.

The isolation of Lincolnshire was made worse by the lack of bridges over some of the major rivers, such as the Trent north of Newark, the Witham between Lincoln and Boston, and the estuaries of the Welland and Nene around the Wash. The improvement of the main roads in Georgian times was accompanied by the construction of new bridges at Gainsborough, Tattershall, Dunham on Trent, Fosdyke and Sutton Bridge. These were also funded by tolls on users in the same way as the turnpike roads, and the one at Dunham is a toll bridge to this day.

The improved roads and bridges made it possible for traffic to travel faster, and in the late 18th-century stage coach services were established through the county. These could cover long distances and at each stage they would stop at a large inn which could provide refreshments and beds for the passengers and coachmen, as well as food and water for the horses. A coach service between Lincoln and London started about 1784 and one to Barton on Humber by 1791. The Barton service was later transferred to New Holland. The growth of passenger traffic led to the reconstruction or extension of old inns and the erection of new ones on the main routes, including the *George* at Stamford, the *George* at Grantham, the *Greyhound* at Folkingham, the *Spital Inn* at Caenby Corner, the *Peacock* at Boston, and many others.

Between 1820 and 1845 the number of coach services increased steadily and road traffic produced a growing income for the turnpike trusts. In the 1830s four of the six toll gates on the Lincolnshire section of the Great North Road were each taking over £1,000 per year. The right to collect the tolls was let out on three-year contracts, awarded on competitive tender. The toll-collectors employed by the contractors were on duty 24 hours a day and their cottages were usually built with a front door right on the street and windows to give a clear view in both directions. No tolls were levied on Royal Mail coaches, the military or people on their way to Sunday worship.

As railways were opened in the 1840s they took over the long-distance passenger traffic. They were cheaper, faster, and could carry far more passengers. Stage coach services disappeared and the income of turnpike trusts and bridge companies plummeted. Most of the turnpike trusts in Lincolnshire came to an end between 1870 and 1872, as Parliament declined to renew their local Acts. The Acts for toll bridges were not time limited, but as their income was not enough to pay off their debts, let alone pay for repairs, they were all, except Dunham, eventually transferred to the local highway authorities, the tolls later being abolished.

Notes and further details on page 142.

78

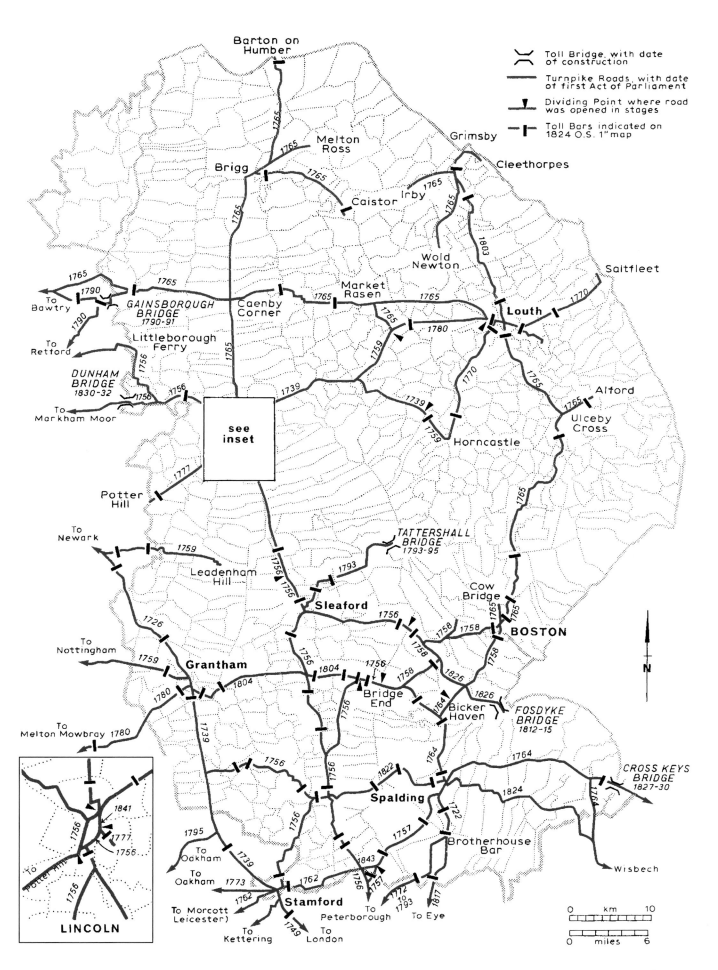

Barton on
Humber

Melton
Ross

Brigg

Grimsby

Cleethorpes

Caistor

Irby

Wold
Newton

Market
Rasen

Saltfleet

To
Bawtry

GAINSBOROUGH
BRIDGE
1790-91

Caenby
Corner

Louth

Littleborough
Ferry

To
Retford

DUNHAM
BRIDGE
1830-32

Alford

Ulceby
Cross

To
Markham Moor

see
inset

Horncastle

Potter
Hill

TATTERSHALL
BRIDGE
1793-95

To
Newark

Leadenham
Hill

Sleaford

Cow
Bridge

BOSTON

To
Nottingham

Grantham

Bridge
End

Bicker
Haven

FOSDYKE
BRIDGE
1812-15

To
Melton Mowbray

CROSS KEYS
BRIDGE
1827-30

Spalding

Brotherhouse
Bar

To
Oakham

Wisbech

To
Oakham

Stamford

To
Morcott
(Leicester)

To
Peterborough

To Eye

To
Kettering

To
London

N

LINCOLN

To
Potter Hill

Toll Bridge, with date
of construction

Turnpike Roads, with date
of first Act of Parliament

Dividing Point where road
was opened in stages

Toll Bars indicated on
1824 O.S. 1"map

0   km   10

0   miles   6

During the Middle Ages major rivers such as the Witham from Lincoln to Boston remained navigable for much of the year, although during dry periods they were likely to become too shallow to be used. The Fossdyke canal between Lincoln and the Trent at Torksey had been first established by the Romans; it was referred to on a number of occasions in the Middle Ages but its condition deteriorated and eventually King James I sold it to Lincoln Corporation.

The first serious effort to revive Lincolnshire's waterways was completed sometime between 1664 and 1673 when a new navigation was created from Stamford alongside the Welland to Deeping St James. From Deeping the river was deep enough for craft to reach Spalding and then lighters took cargoes out into the Wash where they could be transferred to sea-going vessels. In 1671 Lincoln Corporation obtained an Act under which they improved the Fossdyke and erected a sluice at Torksey, but the income from tolls was insufficient to maintain the waterway and it deteriorated again. In 1740 Richard Ellison took a lease of the canal for 999 years at £75 per year and he and his son spent over £3,000 on restoring the waterway. It was reopened in 1744 and the investment soon paid off, for the annual income from tolls rose from £500 in 1750 to £2,367 in 1789.

The major land drains in Lincolnshire were so large that they could easily take lighters carrying grain or other crops, and John Grundy of Spalding was an engineer who was skilled in designing drainage systems that were equally convenient for navigation, and vice versa. The modern age of canals started in the mid-18th century and Lincolnshire might have had one of the first. In 1756, three years before the Act for the Duke of Bridgewater's canal, the citizens of Louth commissioned Grundy to make a preliminary study for a canal from Louth to the sea at Tetney. There were delays in obtaining the Act and construction did not start until 1765. The first section across the marsh was opened in 1767 and the canal finally reached Louth in 1770.

At the same time a scheme was put forward to improve the river Witham for drainage and navigation. The Act for this scheme was obtained in 1762 and the works were virtually complete by 1770. A Grand Sluice was erected at Boston, including a sea-lock, and other locks were built between there and the eastern edge of Lincoln. In 1798 the river and the Brayford Pool in the centre of the city were deepened to make a through navigation from the Witham to the end of the Fossdyke. Subsequently other schemes to improve the Ancholme, the Trent, and the Bourne Eau were carried out.

In the early 1790s Lincolnshire had its share of the canal mania that was sweeping the country. The engineer for many of these schemes was William Jessop, a pupil of John Smeaton. His first job in the county was a survey for an abortive Alford Canal in 1784, and during the 1790s he surveyed routes for the Sleaford Navigation, Horncastle Navigation, Caistor Canal and Grantham Canal. The schemes for the Sleaford and Horncastle navigations, for which Acts were passed in 1792, were closely connected with the improvement of the Witham through Lincoln. The Slea was opened from the Witham to Sleaford in 1794 but the Horncastle project took much longer and was not fully opened until 1802.

Most Lincolnshire waterways followed easy routes down river valleys or across flat fenland and had no need for substantial engineering works but the Grantham Canal, which was authorised by an Act of 1793, was an exception. From Grantham it cut through a ridge separating the Witham valley from the Vale of Belvoir, and then descended down a flight of locks before following the contour round the Vale and eventually entering the Trent opposite Nottingham. This canal was opened in 1797. Two other canals authorised in 1793 were the Caistor Canal, a short line from the Ancholme towards Caistor, and the Stainforth and Keadby which crossed the Isle of Axholme between the Trent and the Don.

Many of the major land drains in the fens were wide and deep enough for navigation, but their primary purpose was for drainage and in dry seasons navigation of the subsidiary drains could be impeded as sluices stayed closed for months. The need for a regular service of boats to transport people, goods and agricultural produce to and from Boston only really arose after land reclamations had led to the building of farms and villages in Holland, East, West and Wildmore Fens. The drains to the west and north of Boston were the ones used most extensively for navigation and many farms and villages in these fens were built on the banks of the drains and used water as their main means of travel. Packet boats ran into Boston every market day until the closing years of the 19th century, and wharves can still be seen at Swineshead Bridge and Hubberts Bridge.

Because so many Lincolnshire waterways connected with the coast or a tidal river, a distinctive feature of the county was the number of tide locks. A normal lock separates two stretches of inland water, one of which is always higher than the other, but a tide lock has tidal water at one end which for part of each day will be higher than the inland water and at other times will be lower. This necessitates two sets of lock gates, to be used according to the state of the tide. There are still such locks at Boston (Grand Sluice), South Ferriby (Ancholme) and Keadby, and there also used to be others at Boston (Black Sluice) and at Tetney (Louth Navigation).

The opening of the railways deprived the canals of some of their traffic but most continued to carry commercial traffic for a number of years. Some like the Caistor Canal closed early but others such as the Trent and the Fossdyke continued into the 20th century. Some of the waterways which ceased to be used for navigation were maintained for land drainage purposes and only lost their locks. In the late 20th century there were schemes to restore the Grantham, Sleaford and Horncastle canals and at least part of the Sleaford navigation has been reopened.

Notes and further details on page 142.

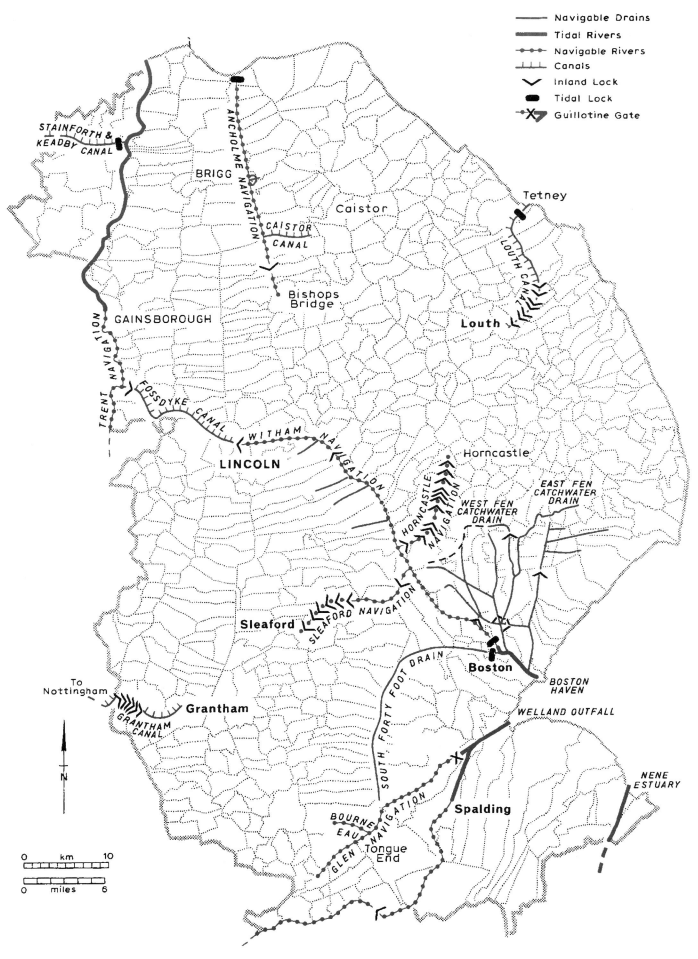

Legend:
- Navigable Drains
- Tidal Rivers
- Navigable Rivers
- Canals
- Inland Lock
- Tidal Lock
- Guillotine Gate

STAINFORTH & KEADBY CANAL

ANCHOLME NAVIGATION

BRIGG

Caistor

CAISTOR CANAL

Tetney

LOUTH CANAL

Louth

Bishops Bridge

GAINSBOROUGH

TRENT NAVIGATION

FOSSDYKE CANAL

WITHAM NAVIGATION

LINCOLN

Horncastle

HORNCASTLE NAVIGATION

WEST FEN CATCHWATER DRAIN

EAST FEN CATCHWATER DRAIN

Sleaford

SLEAFORD NAVIGATION

Boston

BOSTON HAVEN

To Nottingham

Grantham

GRANTHAM CANAL

SOUTH FORTY FOOT DRAIN

WELLAND OUTFALL

NENE ESTUARY

Spalding

BOURNE EAU

GLEN NAVIGATION

Tongue End

N

0 km 10

0 miles 6

41 PARLIAMENTARY AND OLDER ENCLOSURE   *Rex C. Russell and Stewart Bennett*

The map opposite depicts only two aspects of enclosure. The shaded parishes are the older enclosures, those enclosed privately without an Act of Parliament. Those parishes left unshaded were enclosed under the authority of Parliament.[1]

Why did many landowners promote enclosure? Some owners of land may well have thought that the communal nature of open-field farming restricted their initiatives, preventing them getting the maximum return from the strips and the grazing rights which they owned. The change from open-field farming would abolish this communal control.[2] They certainly expected that their rents from post-enclosure holdings would be at least double those from open-field farming. This expectation alone encouraged them to promote enclosure. Their third reason for wanting enclosure was that the Acts could include provisions for the abolition of the unpopular tithes, by awarding land or corn rents in lieu of tithes.[3] The owners of tithes, both clerical and lay, expected to be enriched by the abolition of tithes at enclosure. In this expectation they were not disappointed. The values of church livings improved when land was awarded in lieu of tithes and many major landowners who were also lay rectors added hundreds of acres to their estates.[4] Tithe owners were in a strong position to strike a hard bargain in local negotiations preceding the drafting of the bills to be presented to Parliament. They could delay enclosure if their demands were not acceptable to the other owners of land and common rights. They did so, for example, at Wrawby cum Brig.[5] The tithe owners, who knew very well that owners of land were desperately anxious to get rid of tithes, could and did dictate the terms of such abolition.

Before a parliamentary enclosure, each parish had to obtain its own Act. To begin the process, a meeting was held of the main landowners to discuss the desirability of enclosing the parish. If it was decided that it was, the local sponsors, who were usually the largest landowners, petitioned Parliament for leave to introduce a bill for enclosure. It then underwent the normal passage through Parliament before becoming an Act. The Acts were often substantial documents and contained detailed provisions to be observed in implementing the enclosure. The Act for the enclosure of Middle Rasen runs to 23 foolscap pages, and that for Covenham St Bartholomew and Covenham St Mary is 35 pages in length.

The Act also named Commissioners (usually three) whose role was to effect the enclosure. Their first job was to have a detailed survey undertaken and a plan made of the parish. All people claiming ownership of land or common grazing rights then had to submit their claims, in writing, to the Commissioners who accepted, modified or even rejected claims. All existing land-holdings and common rights were valued. The Commissioners then set about re-planning the entire area to be enclosed, often the whole parish. New roads and water-courses were made; plots of land were allotted to the parish for digging and quarrying road-making materials. Land was awarded in lieu of manorial rights and in lieu of tithes. New plots of land (which had to be hedged and fenced) were awarded to all the owners whose claims were upheld, in direct relationship to the proportion of their former scattered strips or rights of common. The cost of enclosure was borne by all those awarded land, in proportion to the value of each individual award. This did not include the costs of fencing and hedging which were additional and were paid by individual owners. The final act of the Commissioners was to draw up a detailed summary of the results of their work in the form of a written record and, usually, a map record. This Award is the permanent legal record of the local enclosure.

TABLE 1

Lincolnshire Enclosure Acts to 1836

	Lindsey	Kesteven	Holland	Percentage
Before 1760	8	7	0	4.9
1760-1769	30	16	3	15.8
1770-1779	46	22	9	24.9
1780-1789	4	7	3	4.5
1790-1799	28	21	5	17.5
1800-1809	34	19	4	18.5
1810-1819	18	8	9	11.4
1820-1829	4	1	0	1.6
1830- 1836	2	1	0	0.9

The immediate results of parliamentary enclosure, measured by the numbers of people awarded general allotments (that is, excluding those who were awarded land in lieu of manorial rights, glebe and tithes) can be tabulated from a detailed examination of 123 parishes in Lindsey (Table 2).

TABLE 2

Number of people awarded land in 123 Lindsey Parishes

Number of people	Number of parishes	% of total parishes
More than 100	5	4.1
50-100	12	9.7
26-49	26	21.1
15-25	34	27.6
10-15	17	13.8
Fewer than 10	28	22.7

The five parishes where there was most diverse ownership were Crowle (169 people), Barrow on Humber (145), Barton on Humber (126), Kirton in Lindsey (122) and Goxhill (121).

The 309 enclosure Acts over this period affected substantially more parishes, since in some cases more than one parish was included in a single Act. For example, the 1794 Act for New Sleaford also included Holdingham and Quarrington. Enclosure brought about a revolutionary change not only in the appearance of parishes but also in farming methods, agricultural economics and in social relationships.

Notes and further details on page 142.

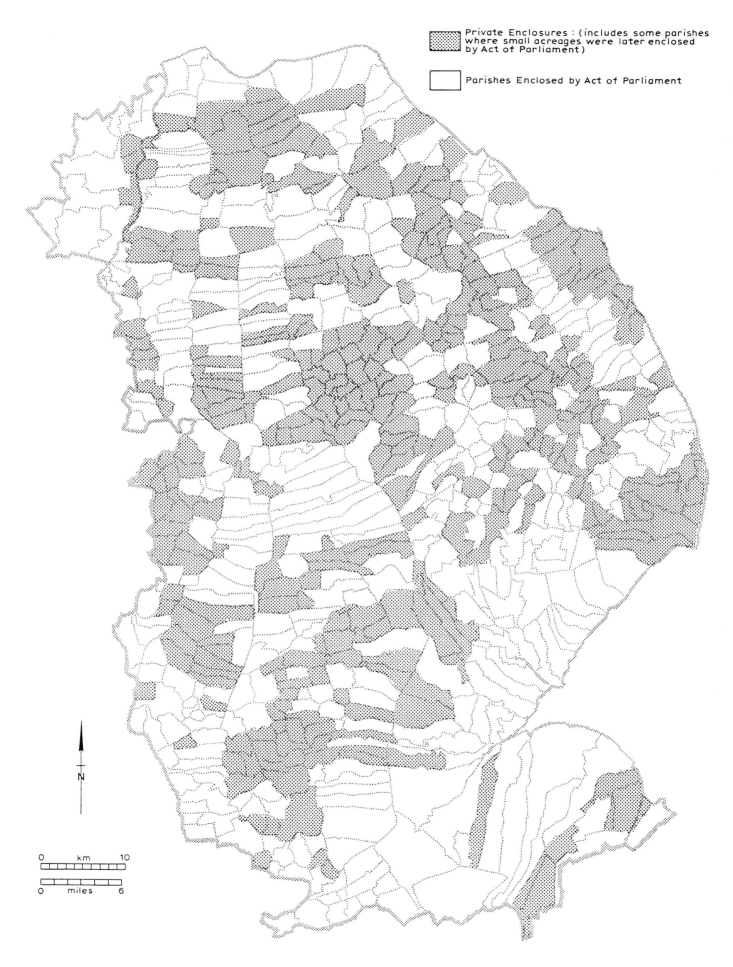

Private Enclosures : (includes some parishes
where small acreages were later enclosed
by Act of Parliament)

Parishes Enclosed by Act of Parliament

0   km   10

0   miles   6

83

Waithe before enclosure: 1807

I

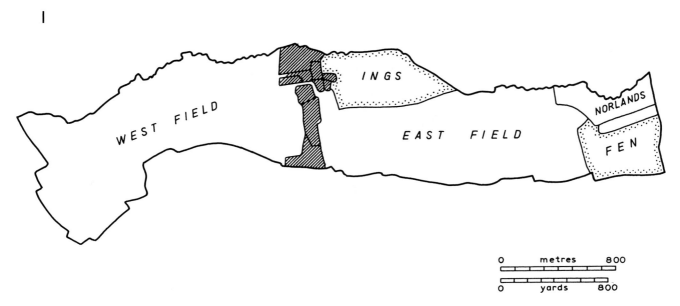

Waithe after enclosure: 1811

II

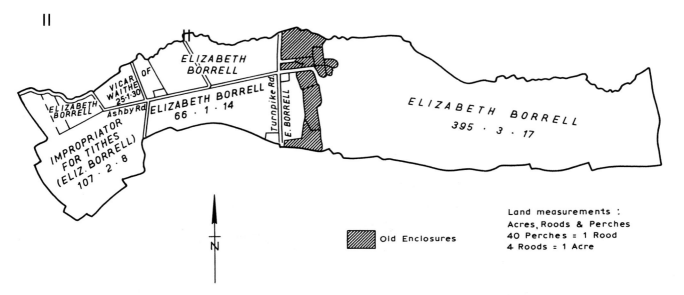

The case studies on these pages show two contrasting enclosures. The Waithe enclosure, begun in 1807 (MAP I), was completed in 1811 (MAP II). Prior to enclosure, the parish consisted of two fields from which only one person, Elizabeth Borrell, received a general allotment. She also received 107 acres in lieu of tithes. Before the enclosure of Heapham (1774-6), there were four fields (MAP III); as a result of the enclosure, 17 persons were awarded land (MAP IV).

The maps of both parishes show the position of old enclosure located around the village and taking the form

of small fields, gardens and allotments, although in Heapham there were a few small parcels of enclosed land in other parts of the parish, The maps also show the loss of the common. This loss was generally a blow to the poor, although some major landowners may have hoped that at enclosure the disappearance of commons would promote greater social stability.

The view of Arthur Young on the ill-effects of commons is well known: 'I know of nothing better calculated to fill a country with barbarians ready for mischief, than extensive commons, and divine service

Heapham before enclosure: 1774

III

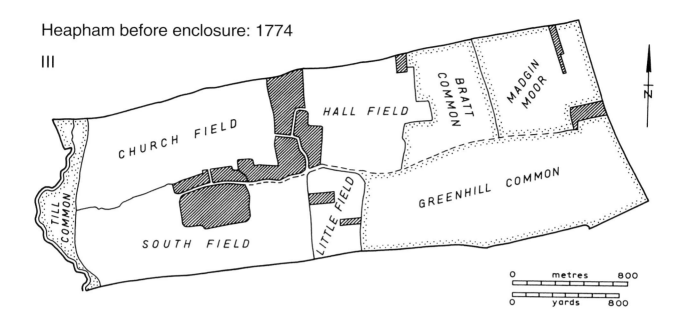

TILL COMMON

CHURCH FIELD

HALL FIELD

BRATT COMMON

MADGIN MOOR

SOUTH FIELD

LITTLE FIELD

GREENHILL COMMON

N

| 0 | metres | 800 |
| 0 | yards | 800 |

Heapham after enclosure: 1776

IV

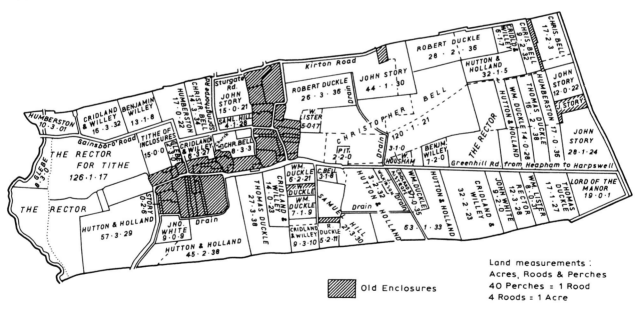

HUMBERSTON 10·3·01

CRIDLAND & WILLEY 16·3·32

BENJAMIN WILLEY 13·1·8

CHRISTR. BELL 14·3·34

HUMBERSTON 11·7·0·22

Dr Meadow Bings

Sturgate Rd.

JOHN STORY 15·0·21

SAML HILL 4·1·28

Kirton Road

ROBERT DUCKLE 26·3·36

JOHN STORY 44·1·30

Drain

ROBERT DUCKLE 28·2·36

CRIDLAND & WILLEY 9·17

CHRIS. BELL 9·2·32

CHRIS. BELL 17·2·3

HUTTON & HOLLAND 32·1·5

HUMBERSTON WM. DUCKLE 16·2·38

THOMAS DUCKLE 14·0·28

CHRIS. BELL 17·0·36

THE RECTOR

HUTTON & HOLLAND

JOHN STORY 12·0·22

J. STORY

JOHN STORY 28·1·24

THE RECTOR FOR TITHE 126·1·17

TITHE OF INCLOSURES 15·0·0

CRIDLAND & WILLEY 6·3·27

CHR. BELL 8·3·3

W. LISTER 15·0·17

CHRISTOPHER BELL

120·1·21

3·1·0

PIT 2·2·0

BENJM. WILLEY 7·2·0

Greenhill Rd. from Heapham to Harpswell

LORD OF THE MANOR 19·0·1

THE RECTOR

Gainsboro' Road

STORY 0·26

JNO. WHITE 9·0·9

Drain

HUTTON & HOLLAND 57·3·29

THOMAS DUCKLE 27·3·38

CRIDLAND & WILLEY 14·0·23

WM. DUCKLE 6·2·21

WM. DUCKLE

WM. DUCKLE 7·1·9

C. BELL 2·1·8

WM. DUCKLE 3·2·32

SAMUEL HILL

HOUSHAM

WM DUCKLE

Drain

0·35

Drain

HUTTON & HOLLAND

W. LISTER 8·0·31

CRIDLAND & WILLEY 32·2·23

JOHN WHITE 9·2·0

WM. DUCKLE 12·3·28

THOMAS DUCKLE 17·1·27

HUTTON & HOLLAND 45·2·38

CRIDLAND & WILLEY 9·3·10

R DUCKLE 5·2·11

SAMUEL HILL 21·3·30

HUTTON & HOLLAND 63·1·33

Old Enclosures

Land measurements :
Acres, Roods & Perches
40 Perches = 1 Rood
4 Roods = 1 Acre

only once a month.'[1] At Heapham, the substantial common went the way of commons in most other parishes and formed part of the general allotment.

Enclosure created new landscapes, parish by parish, at different times with widely differing results, still visible on the ground today. The two common factors were the new straight-edged fields and the long straight roads, both planned on the surveyors' drawing boards with straight-edged tools. Fashions in the width of public roads between the hedges changed. In the 1760s and 1770s, roads 60 feet wide were fashionable; in the 1790s and later, a width of 40 feet became normal. Such changes in width may be seen at many parish boundaries.

Notes and further details on page 143.

43 POPULATION TRENDS, 1801-2000 *Stewart Bennett*

The first national census was in 1801 and consisted of little more than a head count by parish. From this time a census has taken place every 10 years except for 1941. Although later censuses collected substantially more information, the concern here is only with population change at the parish level, represented as a percentage growth or decline. It should be pointed out at this stage that some figures should be treated with caution. First, parishes with very small populations only need a very small change to show a dramatic percentage increase or decrease. Second, the change in parish boundaries must be taken into account. This does not affect the figures for 1801-51. However, during the period 1851-1951 ecclesiastical parishes were replaced by civil parishes for census purposes, many parishes being combined. During the last period 1951-91 some further rationalisation has occurred. Every effort has been made to allow for this.

At the first census the population of Lincolnshire was 208,624. In 1991 the population of the historic county (including South Humberside) was 894,624, an increase of 328 per cent.[1] Over this period, however, the population did not increase at a steady rate decade after decade. During the first half of the 19th century the population nearly doubled (95 per cent) while over the second half it increased by less than a quarter (22.5 per cent).[2] The first half of the 20th century saw the population begin to grow more rapidly (41 per cent). The period from 1951 to 1991 saw only a modest growth (26.7 per cent).

1801-51: The most noticeable feature of this period is the outstanding population growth from 208,624 to 407,222. This was caused not by sudden immigration into the county but mainly by the natural rise in the birth rate over the death rate. Large families were common, and although infant mortality rates were high, a larger proportion of children survived into adulthood. While only a few isolated parishes declined in population over this period, there were substantial regional variations. The highest growth occurred in the low-lying areas, particularly the fens of Holland. Population growth tended to be smaller in the upland parishes of the Wolds. Not only was the population rising at this time, it was also very mobile. It is not unusual to find more than half the heads of household in a particular parish, as listed in the 1851 Census Returns, originating from other parishes. This suggestion of high mobility is reinforced by the number of different birthplaces of children. Market towns were also increasing in size, in most cases exceeding the growth rate of rural areas. For example, Gainsborough had a relatively small increase of only 61 per cent whereas Lincoln grew by 140 per cent, Horncastle by 149 per cent and Grantham (including Manthorpe, Harrowby and Spittlegate) by 153 per cent.

1851-1951: Although the total increase in population over this period was 296,605 many parishes peaked by 1881 and then declined to their pre-1851 level by the end of the century. One reason for this was the depression in agriculture during the last quarter of the 19th century. Given the economic background of an agricultural depression it is not surprising that over the decade 1881 to 1891 the population hardly grew at all (0.69 per cent). Even many fen parishes, which had undergone such an

enormous growth in the earlier period, declined. Between 1851 and 1901, the population of Frampton declined from 801 to 777, and that of Donington from 1,867 to 1,486. It took many parishes until the 1940s and 1950s to return to their 1851 level.

By contrast, population in urban areas such as Lincoln tended to increase during this period. In other parishes there were particular reasons for expansion. The development of the seaside resorts of Skegness, Sutton on Sea and Mablethorpe resulted in tremendous growth. For example in 1851 the population of Skegness was only 366; by 1901 it was 2,140 and by 1951 12,529. Scunthorpe and the surrounding area also grew after the establishment of the steel industry there. In 1851 the total population of Brumby, Crosby, Frodingham and Scunthorpe was 789. By 1901 it had risen to 9,322 and by 1951 to 54,255. Other areas of substantial growth were those parishes which bordered the major towns, such as Skellingthorpe and North Hykeham near Lincoln, Brothertoft, Fishtoft near Boston, and Harrowby and Londonthorpe near Grantham, all of which increased by more than 100 per cent. One other reason for notable increases in population was the location of R.A.F. establishments in the county. For example, between 1931 and 1951, Scampton grew from 212 to 1,805, Waddington from 1,140 to 2,676, and Hemswell from 282 to 1,615. At Cranwell growth was even greater. In 1901 there were just 138 parishioners; by 1931 this had risen to 2,378 and by 1951 to 4,025.

1951-2000: Since the Second World War there have been three dominant factors affecting the county's population. The great mechanisation of agriculture has meant that vast areas of land can be farmed extremely productively with very few workers. Therefore many parishes have remained stable or declined. Conversely, with increased personal mobility, some villages have become 'dormitory' settlements, particularly those close to Lincoln and other towns. The third factor is growth associated with particular industries. The area around the steel industry at Scunthorpe stands out as such an example as does the fishing industry at Grimsby, although the economic fortunes of both have more recently changed. In general terms the area to the south of the Humber has grown faster than the rest of the county. The location of some major industries, good motorway links with the rest of the country, and the construction of the Humber Bridge have all had an effect.

Notes and further details on page 143.

Population change: 1801-1851

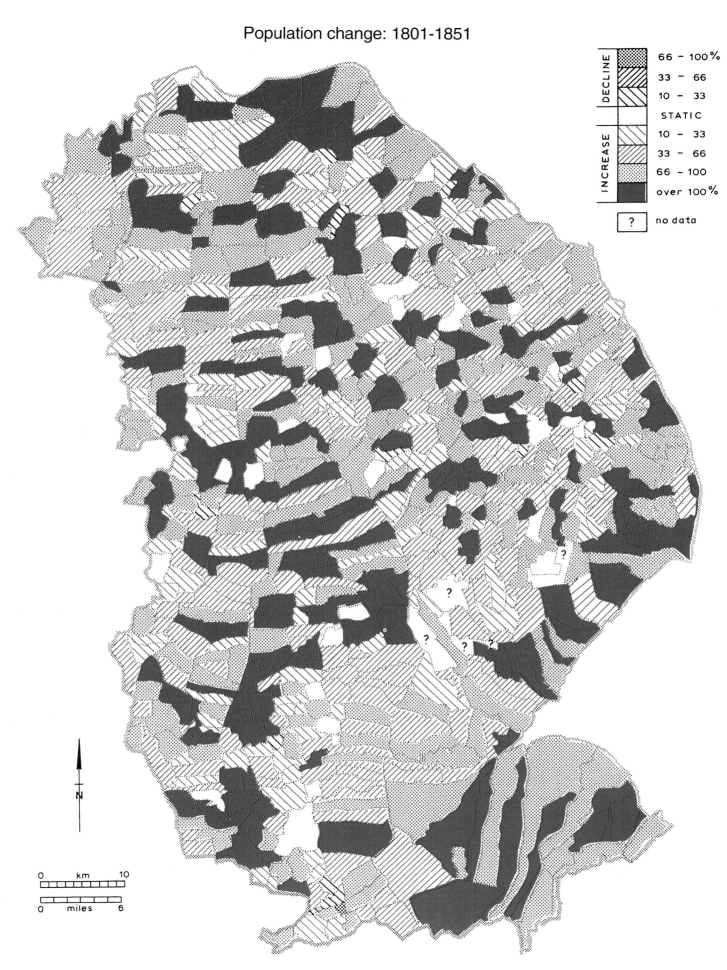

DECLINE	66 – 100%
	33 – 66
	10 – 33
STATIC	
INCREASE	10 – 33
	33 – 66
	66 – 100
	over 100%
?	no data

0 km 10

0 miles 6

Population change: 1851-1851

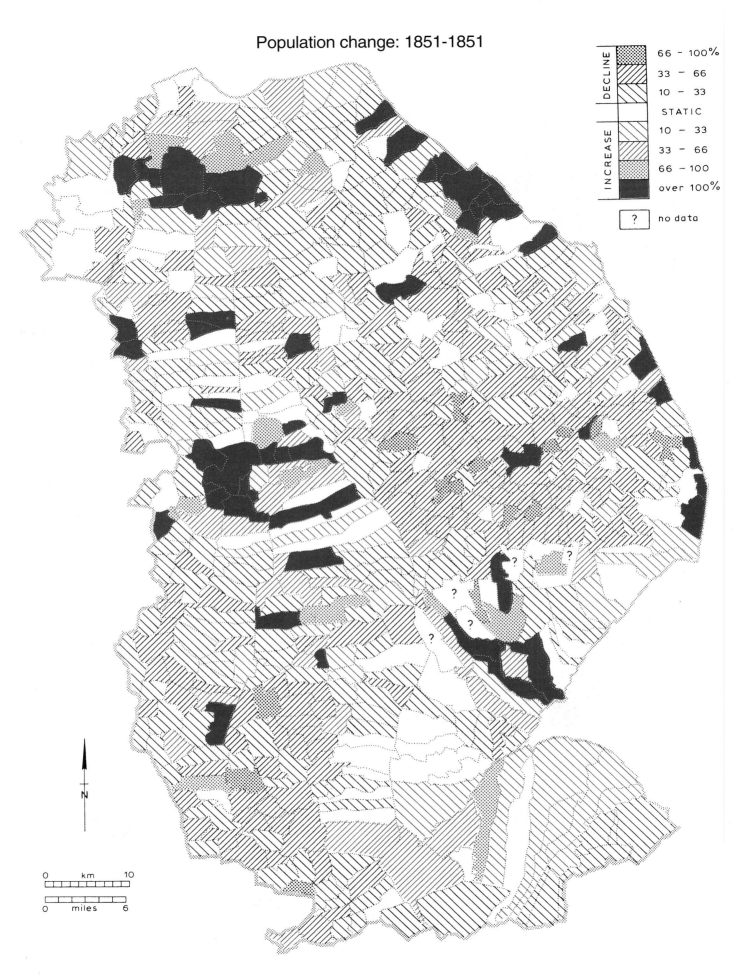

66 – 100%
33 – 66
10 – 33
DECLINE

STATIC

10 – 33
33 – 66
66 – 100
over 100%
INCREASE

? no data

0   km   10

0   miles   6

Population change: 1951-1991

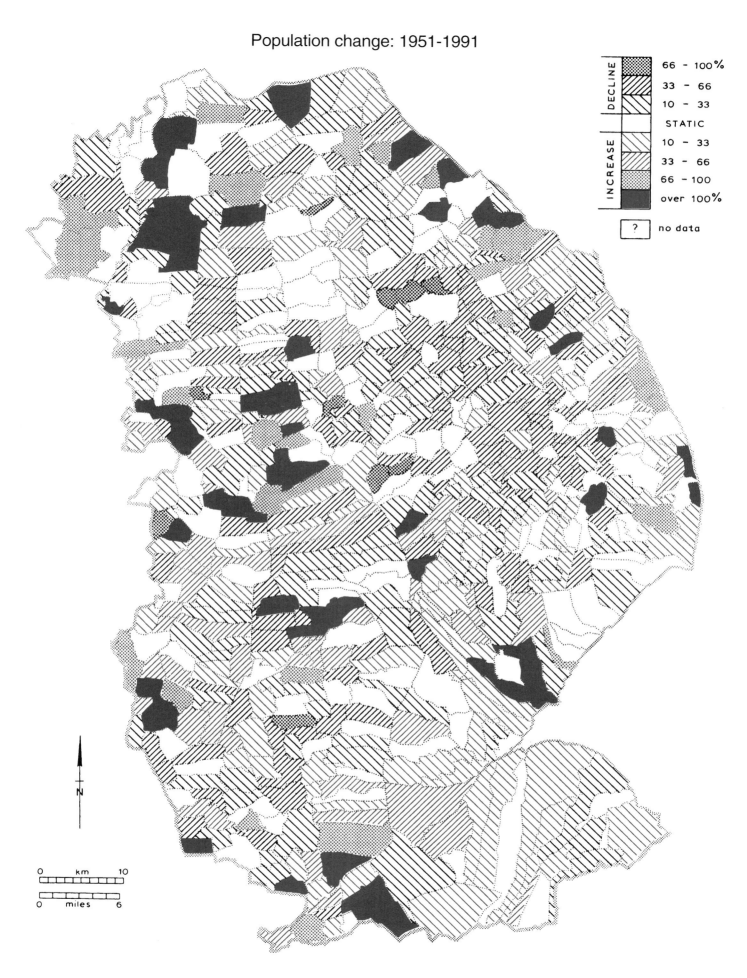

DECLINE
- 66 – 100%
- 33 – 66
- 10 – 33

STATIC

INCREASE
- 10 – 33
- 33 – 66
- 66 – 100
- over 100%

? no data

N

0 km 10

0 miles 6

How did people cope in the past when illness, unemployment or old age prevented them from earning a living? One solution was to seek help from the parish which had a responsibility to care for its poor; another was to turn to a charity. A third solution was to join a mutual assistance society, a 'club'. There were many different kinds of 'clubs' or friendly societies as they were properly called.[1] The most common were sick and burial clubs which normally provided an income during periods of illness and a funeral benefit to ensure a decent burial. Some also provided medical help, unemployment pay and other benefits.

Clubs usually operated on a self-help basis, run by members themselves and financed by members' subscriptions. Friendly societies of this kind expanded nationally in the second half of the 18th century. It is not known how widespread such clubs were in Lincolnshire at this time but the fact that friendly societies were established at Epworth in 1773 and Barton on Humber in 1781[2] suggests that others may also have existed in the county long before such societies were given legal status in 1793. In 1803 overseers of the poor collected details of friendly societies in each parish throughout England and Wales.[3] At that time there were in Lincolnshire 113 societies with 7,530 members, located as shown on the map opposite.

The early societies were usually based at a public house or sometimes at a chapel or church schoolroom. Members met monthly to pay their subscriptions and enact club business. The typical arrangement was for the club to be managed by a master, secretary, treasurer, stewards and a committee all of whom were elected by the members to serve for a six-month or one-year period. The committee considered applications for membership and for benefits and ensured that club funds were properly spent and properly invested. The stewards were responsible for checking claims for sickness benefit and offering appropriate help to members in need. Payments for periods of illness were made and when a member died it was common for all the members to attend the funeral and accompany the coffin in procession to church and then to the burial ground.

Clubs also had a social side which was important, especially in rural areas where 'club night' was one of the main social occasions of the month. Inevitably, drinking was part of this sociability and some landlords found it worthwhile to make available a room on their premises for exclusive club use. Each club held an annual feast day; in Lincolnshire this was usually on Whit Monday or Tuesday. The members would assemble in their club rooms, and march in full regalia and uniform and with banners (if they had such) to the church or chapel for a service. On leaving the church the club would then process round the town or village following a band specially hired for the occasion until it eventually returned to the club room or some suitable hostelry for a grand feast. The considerable amount of drinking associated with club meetings and particularly with club feast days gave clubs a bad reputation in some quarters as it was feared that the poor were being led into debt and bad habits. For this reason many chapels and temperance organisations provided their own clubs as an alternative.

Although the earliest societies were completely independent of each other, from the second quarter of the 19th century the 'affiliated orders' began to establish themselves throughout the country. These orders consisted of locally-based groups linked to a central organisation. Hundreds of different orders developed, each with a name chosen to suggest their reliability, respectability and longevity. The strongest of these orders in Lincolnshire were the Independent Order of Oddfellows (Manchester Unity) and the Ancient Order of Foresters. In the last quarter of the century, further competition came from new national collecting societies, such as the Royal Liver and the Liverpool Victoria Legal. These grew rapidly at the expense of the locally-based branches of orders and independent societies, so that by the early 20th century more people belonged to collecting societies than to any other type of society.[4] By 1905 there were in Lincolnshire 438 registered friendly societies with 69,825 members.[5] Between 1803 and 1905, therefore, there had been a substantial increase, not only in the total number of friendly society members in the county but also in the percentage of the county's population involved.[6]

During the course of the 19th century, the public image of the friendly society movement was transformed; societies had now become an accepted part of a respectable lifestyle. Although club membership expanded considerably in the 19th century, it remained the preserve of a minority of working people. The poorest and women[7] were significantly under-represented. All this changed under the National Health Insurance Act of 1911 which provided for most working men and women. Some friendly societies effectively became agents for the state scheme; 'state' members were added to the existing voluntary members and these societies expanded. Societies which decided not to join the new scheme generally declined and many closed at this time. Friendly society membership reached its peak in the 1940s but the provision in 1946 of free medical care on a universal basis and of a state-run scheme of social insurance established a new order which excluded friendly societies.

The financial benefits of club membership were undoubtedly of vital importance to members. The chance to remain independent of the parish in times of illness, to be 'on the club' rather than 'on the parish', was an important source of pride for working people. Perhaps even more important was the relief of being able to avoid the ultimate shame of ending one's days in a pauper's grave. Friendly societies also provided an opportunity to participate in a self-help organisation; later working men's organisations, such as trade unions and co-operatives, were able to build on the experience of the earlier friendly society movement. Finally, the importance of the social aspects of club life should not be under-estimated, especially in rural areas.

Notes and further details on page 143.

Friendly Societies: 1803 and 1905

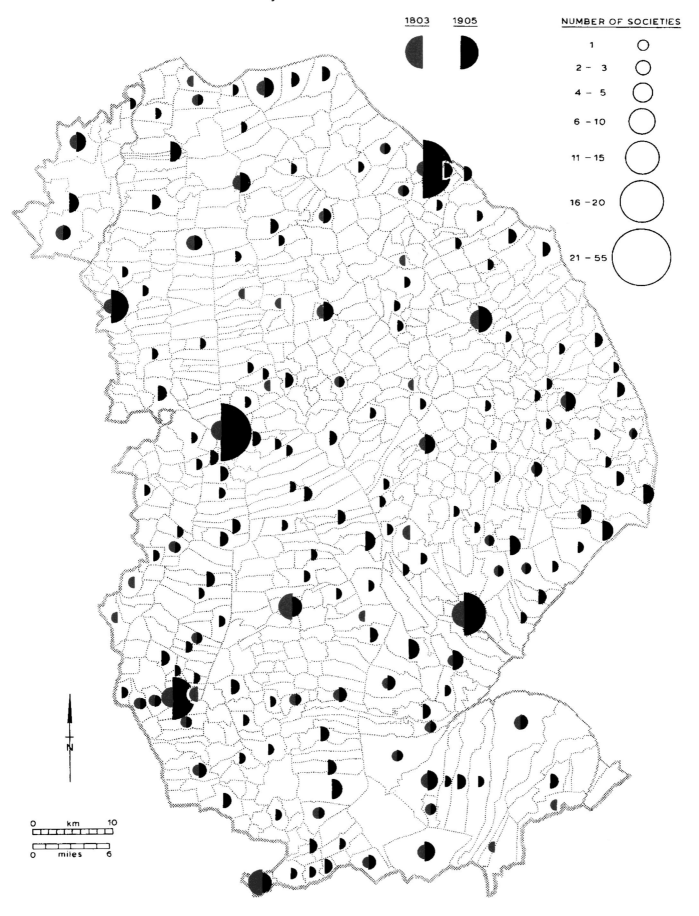

1803   1905

NUMBER OF SOCIETIES

1	○
2 - 3	○
4 - 5	○
6 - 10	○
11 - 15	○
16 - 20	○
21 - 55	○

N

0   km   10

0   miles   6

91

Charles Rawding

The 1801 Crop Returns[1] provide us with the first statistical attempt to measure agricultural land use until the official Ministry of Agriculture returns commenced in 1867.[2] Before looking in detail at the Returns, the limitations of the data provided should be emphasised. First, the Returns were voluntary and a sizeable number of parishes failed to return any figures at all (see Table 1). Secondly, only crop acreage figures were given, no details being provided about any grassland other than rye grass. Thirdly, turnips and rape were often counted together, as were peas and beans, and thus it is often difficult to assess the precise importance of these crops separately. Fourthly, farmers were deeply suspicious of the intentions of the government in collecting such data, the general feeling being that they would be used for taxation purposes as farmers were at this time beginning to reap the profits of high prices during the Napoleonic Wars.

TABLE 1

Number of Parishes Completing Returns

Regions (see map) on page 9.	Parishes completing returns	Parishes not completing returns	% not completing returns
The Marsh	90	27	23.1
The Wolds	111	16	12.5
Ancholme/ Witham Vales	67	12	15.2
Heath and Cliff	131	34	20.6
Isle of Axholme	17	7	29.2
Vale of Trent	48	11	18.6
The Fens	58	30	34.1

At the county level, barley was the most important crop, followed by wheat, oats and turnips. However, if we look at the pattern across the county, there are considerable variations. The Crop Returns have been mapped to show crop patterns by natural region.[3] In the north-west of the county, the Isle of Axholme and the lower Trent vale, wheat was the dominant crop, as it was in the marsh of eastern Lindsey. Wheat liked a soil with a strong body, which was not possible on the heath and Wolds. On the higher northern Wolds, the lighter soils were more suited to turnip cultivation as befitted a region that relied heavily on sheep production. On the lower southern Wolds, barley was the more important crop, with turnip second. Barley was also the most important crop on the heath and cliff south of Lincoln, as it was more successful on less fertile soils, whereas the clays were too stiff to get the best barleys for malting. Oats were most widely grown on the fens at this time because the large areas of newly-reclaimed land were too rich in certain plant nutrients for barley and even wheat. Thus, oats were used as an initial crop for several years to prepare the soils for other crops.[4]

The Returns provided no details concerning grassland acreages. However, by establishing the proportion of total acreage declared as arable, it is possible to make comparative statements about the relative proportions of grassland and arable, although obviously absolute conclusions could not be drawn (see Table 2). The clearest contrasts shown by the table are between the low-lying areas of the marsh and the vales

of Ancholme and Witham, with low percentages of arable land and therefore, one presumes, greater areas of grassland, and the significantly higher returns for the Wolds where grassland was less evident. These figures confirm the farming characteristics described by Arthur Young in his *General View of the Agriculture of the County of Lincoln,* the second edition of which was published in 1813. Young described the grazing land of the fens as 'the glory of Lincolnshire'.[5] Grazing was predominant on the wetter, heavier soils whilst arable expanded rapidly, as a result of the high prices triggered by the Napoleonic Wars, on the former sheep walks of the Wolds. Nevertheless, it would be a mistake to treat the regions purely in isolation. There were, for instance, strong links between coastal parishes and the Wolds, where upland farmers occupied grazing land in the marsh to fatten their flocks.

TABLE 2

Percentage of Arable to Total Acreage

Regions	Total acreage of returning parishes	Arable acreage of returning parishes	% of arable land
The Wolds	205,214	52,595	25.6
Heath and Cliff	333,976	75,109	22.5
Isle of Axholme	54.933	12,322	22.4
The Fens[6]	247,503	53,458	21.6
Vale of Trent	106,642	19,422	18.2
The Marsh	166,379	26,685	16.0
Ancholme/ Witham	142,515	20,806	14.6

Apart from the conventional crops, several aspects of more traditional agriculture were still extant in 1801. On the Wolds and on the heath, especially near Scunthorpe, rabbit warrens were still found, along with extensive areas of gorse and scrub, although both were diminishing in acreage. In the fens, fowling and fishing were important elements in the rural economy, with some areas not drained until the arrival of steam pumps from the 1820s. In places such as East, West and Wildmore Fens, legal complications and disputes slowed down the process of draining as 50 separate parishes had rights of common on these fens.[7] Along with the fens, other low-lying areas of the county such as the vale of Ancholme also based much of their economy on seasonal variations in water levels. The 1801 Returns present a snapshot of agriculture at the mid-point of Lincolnshire's agricultural revolution and provide a valuable insight into variations in agricultural land use.

Notes and further details on page 143.

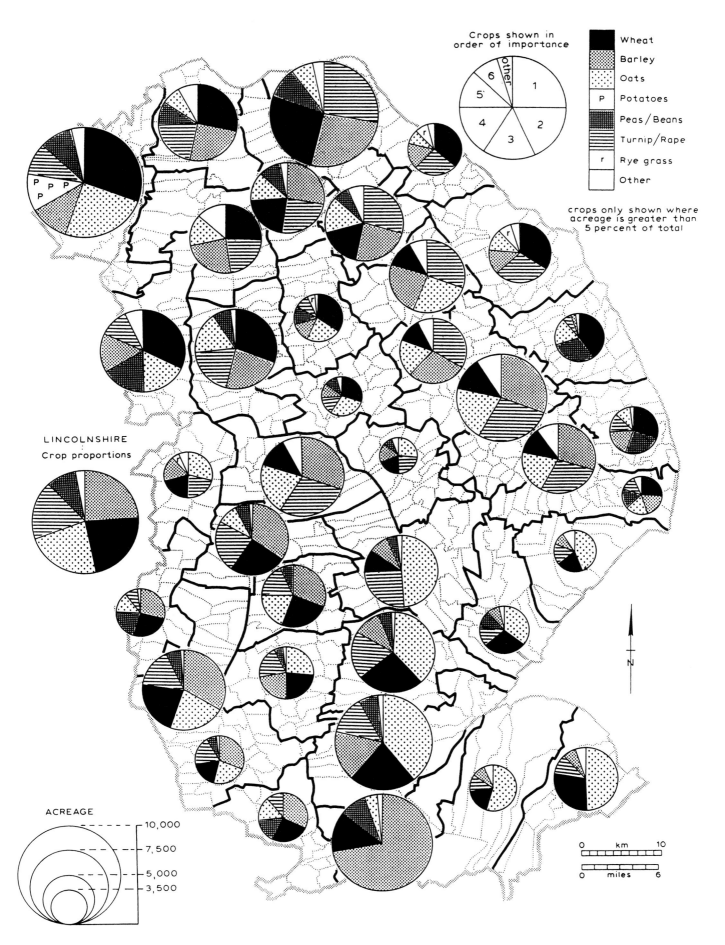

Crops shown in
order of importance

Wheat
Barley
Oats
P | Potatoes
Peas/Beans
Turnip/Rape
r | Rye grass
Other

crops only shown where
acreage is greater than
5 percent of total

LINCOLNSHIRE
Crop proportions

ACREAGE

10,000
7,500
5,000
3,500

N

0   km   10

0   miles   6

The map opposite distinguishes between the landownership characteristics of two types of parish: those parishes in which a few individuals owned most of the land, and multi-owner parishes where there were no dominant owners. This classification is based on the Land Tax returns.[1] The Land Tax, initially levied on land and property, had become by the beginning of the 19th century a tax almost entirely on land. As it was assessed on a parish basis it is possible to estimate the proportion of land owned by individuals from the proportion of the Tax which they paid. This is particularly applicable to large owners.

Parishes with few owners are referred to as 'Close' parishes and are represented by three types. The most extreme were those parishes with a single proprietor, where one person was assessed as paying the entire Tax. The second type comprised those parishes where there were fewer than five proprietors and where the largest paid more than 85 per cent of the Land Tax. The third category was those parishes in which either there were fewer than five landowners or where the largest proprietor paid more than 85 per cent of the total. At the other end of the spectrum were the multi-owner parishes, often referred to as 'Open' parishes. These have been classified into two types. The first category comprised those parishes which had more than 55 landowners and where the largest paid less than 30 per tent of the Tax. The other type of Open parish comprised those in which only one of these criteria applied. For the purpose of this map, the parishes which lay between the extremes have been left unannotated.

The map shows distinct regional variations between parish landownership structures. Open parishes were predominantly found on low-lying, recently-drained land in Holland, the Isle of Axholme, the coastal area north of the Wash and along the Humber estuary. By comparison, Close parishes were more ancient settlements, located on the better-drained uplands, and in particular on the undulating clays south of Grantham, the limestone edge north and south of Lincoln with its associated dip slope, and on the chalk Wolds.

In general these parishes had different social, political and economic characteristics.[2] The population of Open parishes was large, with a higher density and a more rapid growth during the first half of the 19th century. Close parishes tended to be dominated by a 'Gentleman's' residence, large estates and big farms, whereas Open parishes had peasant families and many small proprietors with small farms. There also tended to be differences in non-agricultural occupations, Open parishes having a greater number and variety of industries and crafts, with more shops and public houses.

Open parishes also tended to have a greater degree of religious nonconformity, radicalism and independence in political and social organisations in comparison with those parishes where there tended to be a strong deference to the demands of the dominant owner. Close parishes were often seen by contemporaries as being more orderly and better controlled than Open parishes. Arthur Young, commenting on Lord Carrington's village of Humberstone, described the labourers as 'sober and industrious'.[3] Similarly, labourers living on the estate of the Duke of Ancaster were said to be 'orderly, decent, churchgoing men, who behaved themselves well'.[4] While Close parishes were seen as well-ordered, the opposite was true of Open parishes. The Rev. Samuel Hopkinson described the behaviour of his parishioners at Morton, near Bourne, as lawless and insubordinate, attributing these characteristics to the divided ownership of land.[5]

In Close parishes, landowners had an enormous amount of influence. They provided basic needs in the form of housing and employment. They furnished charities and schools; they could discourage dissenting religious activities by not allowing land to be sold to Methodists and others or by not even allowing their tenants to use their cottages for such purposes. Conversely, they could support the Anglican church in some cases by forcing their tenants and servants to attend. They could influence the voting behaviour of the tenants at elections. They could also allow or disallow feast days and prevent, as in the case of Colonel Sibthorp at Canwick, the building of public houses. Most important, however, they could control settlement even to the extent of demolishing cottages. How widespread this tactic was in Lincolnshire is uncertain but according to Thomas Rawnsley, the Vice-Chairman of the Spilsby Poor Law Union, a policy of 'pulling down cottages or not building them' had been common throughout the period after 1815 to the middle of the century.[6]

The ability of landowners to control settlement was important because the seasonal nature of much agricultural employment meant that it was more economical to employ some labourers on a casual basis. It was important not to have excess labour since the burden of supporting them when unemployed fell on the ratepayer of the parish in which they were resident. It was not unusual to employ agricultural labourers for less than a year because residence in the same parish for a longer period gave the labourer (and his family) the right of settlement and thus the right to be supported at times of unemployment. Subsequently, many labourers were prevented from gaining settlement in the parish in which they worked and resided in a neighbouring Open parish, on which therefore fell the burden of support in times of unemployment. To avoid this expense, it is not surprising that vestries in Open parishes, where settlement could not be so easily controlled, used the Settlement Laws to remove entire families back to their parish of legal settlement.

Notes and further details on page 143.

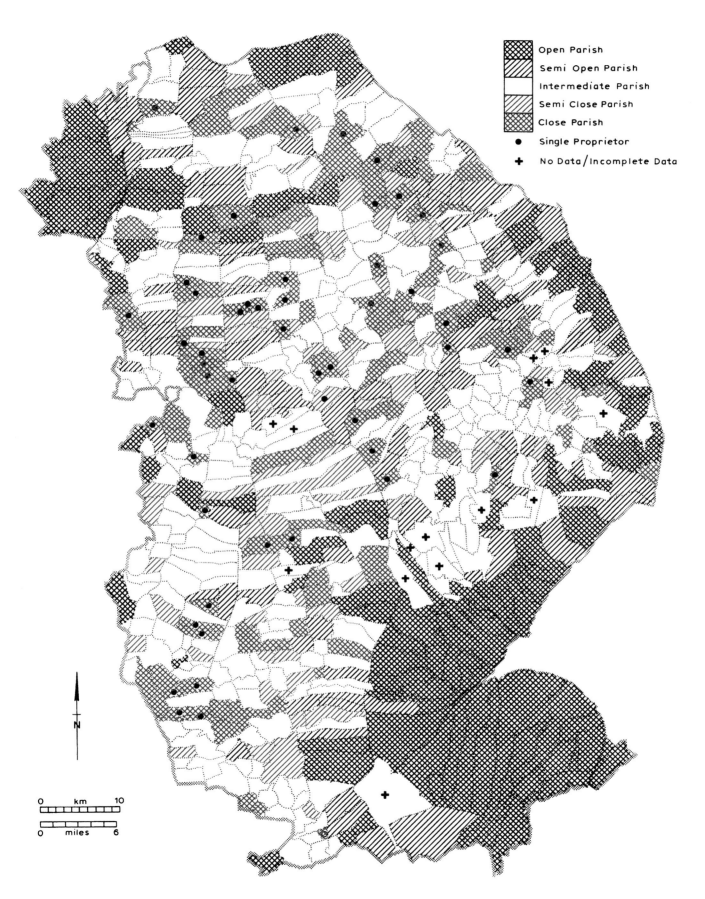

The end of 1830 saw an outbreak of rural discontent in Lincolnshire, which was manifested in arson attacks on the property of farmers. There were 29 attacks on buildings and hay stacks. This was part of a national problem which had begun earlier that year in the south of England as a reaction against the rising price of bread, changing attitudes on the part of rate-payers to the provision for the poor and, most important of all, the introduction of new mechanical methods of threshing corn which was the traditional winter work of many agricultural labourers. At a time of slump, farmers were keen to introduce new methods to reduce labour costs. While labourers could not attack 'changing attitudes' or affect by themselves the economics of farming, they could attack with a vengeance what they saw as the main cause of their plight.

'Swing' was the name given to a fictitious character who rode through the countryside on a white horse, carrying out the various outrages on behalf of the labourers. Fictitious though he may have been, he was real in the minds of both labourers and landowners. At Barton, it was reported that a number of threatening letters had been delivered to farmers, which had been signed 'Swing'.

Lincolnshire saw at least 29 cases of arson, certainly one of the worst records in the country. Few threshing machines were broken (compared with more than ninety in Wiltshire), although threshing machines were being used in increasing numbers.[1] This may have been because of the prompt action of the most important landowners. Sir Gilbert Heathcote, a large landowner in Kesteven, took decisive action to defuse the developing discontent by announcing in the *Stamford Mercury* 'his wish that his tenants shall not any longer use threshing machines'.[2] The outrages might have been worse but for the way the forces of law and order, who had been watching the spread of the troubles from the south, were able to make preparations. Thus when the first case of arson occurred at the beginning of November 1830 they had in place a number of strategies to deal with it. This resulted in more secretive and clandestine activity on the part of the arsonists. Most cases occurred at night and were the work of individuals or small groups. This was in sharp contrast to some other parts of the country where large numbers of labourers went from one farm to another in daylight to argue face to face with farmers.

This does not mean that the threat was less. Threatening letters sent to Lincolnshire farmers tend to support the view that labourers saw their grievance as being against individual farmers rather than as part of a national movement. One such anonymous letter complained about the importation of labour from another parish and the use of new machines, both of which affected the employment of local people:

> mossop you are a damd badun and you may look out we are geten gone on you with out you destroy your mysheen and get out of your farm men and sheperds and take them home to ther one (own) parish with in ten days we will burn you in all parts. weare not speaking on you a lone but all the employs them that dont belong hear so you may look out to your corn and hay. blast and buyer your eyes if you do not imploy your own poor we will burn you in your bed.[3]

The cases at Boston related to the employment of Irish labourers instead of local parishioners, an issue which had been the cause of trouble for some time. At the same time Benjamin Green, a farmer at Great Hale Fen, was sent the following letter:

> Mr green as sure as you are a Bad man you may expete a visit some night before Christmas if you dont let the poor have the Coaille (Coal) ... You will dance without a fiddle Before long. I heard Willian dawsons men give him a good word. But mr edward dawsons men give him a Bad Word so he must mind and sleep with one eye open. Bread or Blood my Boys or Fire and Smoke.[4]

By the time the first case of arson took place at Moulton near Holbeach on 16 November 1830, magistrates, particularly in the south of the county, were organised in an attempt either to prevent outbreaks altogether or at least to contain them. At a time before the introduction of a County Police Force, they had sworn in special constables who were given extensive powers to apprehend 'without warrant' any person who did not have 'visible means of subsistence' or could not give a 'good account of himself'. There was a general belief among landowners and farmers that the troubles were caused by outside influences. Robert Sheffield of Normanby Hall wrote to Lord Brownlow at Belton: 'The Fires are doubtless the work of Vagabonds prowling about the county of which there is now a great influx, and several attempts have been made to inflame the minds of the Peasentary.'[5]

One hundred and eighty two special constables were sworn in from 38 parishes, mainly from the wapentakes of Flaxwell and Aswardhurn where the magistrates were particularly active. Numbers ranged from 129 at Heckington to only two at Dorrington. At Leadenham it was reported 'the whole estate seems to have been sworn in'.[6] One reason for the high numbers of volunteers may have been the three shillings a night and the further three shillings a day payments. Every four or five parishes were to form a Section with up to twenty mounted constables under the operational control of a Superintendent who was to appoint a Commander in each parish. At the moment the Commander knew of a 'Riot or Tumultuous Assemblage' he was to notify the Superintendent, who then informed the magistrate in the adjoining sectors so that in a short time a large number of constables armed with staves could be brought together. This was perhaps the main reason why most Lincolnshire arsons were committed at night.

Notes and further details on page 144.

November to December, 1830

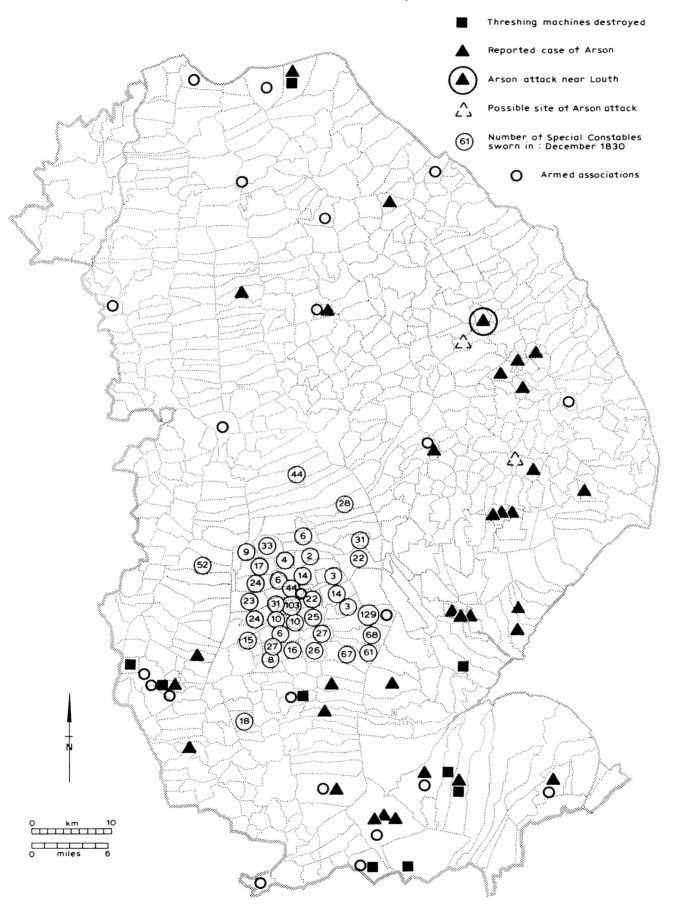

■ Threshing machines destroyed

▲ Reported case of Arson

Ⓐ Arson attack near Louth

△ Possible site of Arson attack

㊏ Number of Special Constables
sworn in : December 1830

○ Armed associations

The period from 1833 to the Forster Education Act of 1870 can be divided conveniently into two phases. The first, from 1833 to 1858, led to the Newcastle Commission, set up to investigate elementary education; the second, from 1859 to 1870, was a period of consolidation prior to the great changes that came about with the provision of Board schools, which classified all earlier schools as Non-Provided Public Elementary Schools, no matter how they had been established.

Parliament made the first grants towards education in 1833 and from then on the founding or re-establishment of schools gained momentum. In the 25 years to 1858, 176 schools were established, including 97 National Society schools, 60 Church of England, 10 Wesleyan, three parochial, three charity, one British, one Roman Catholic and one 'unspecified'. This variety reflects the opportunity for Catholics and Nonconformists to instigate education within their own tradition and beliefs. This was particularly strong in the western and coastal parts of the county.

Privately-owned schools continued to be built during both periods of the 19th century as it became clear that the landed gentry were to the forefront of innovation, readily providing land, grants and support in founding schools in their estate villages. The Marquis of Bristol at Anwick in 1868, the Earl of Londesborough at Blankney in 1848, the Countess of Winchelsea at Ewerby in 1840, the Earl of Ancaster at Rippingale in 1856 are just a few of those involved. It must be said, though, that they all insisted that the trust remained in their private hands.

Seven military gentlemen, with ranks from Captain to Colonel, also contributed, as well as 21 other individuals with no title. The clergy of course, as in earlier times, had glebe at their disposal and eight of them founded schools. The Lincoln Diocesan Board of Education had resources to establish a school at Tathwell in 1843. Charity trustees or governors were also involved–the Bridewell and Bethlem Hospital (Wainfleet St Mary, 1830), Browne's Hospital, Stamford (Swayfield, 1857) and the Governors of Charterhouse (Dunsby, 1855).

The Newcastle Commission Report indicated that only one in eight children was getting education. How far this was true of Lincolnshire is impossible to estimate but the foundation of more schools continued. Between 1859 and 1870 a further 93 new schools were started: 45 with the help of the National Society, 38 Church of England, three Wesleyan, two Roman Catholic, three parochial, only one charity and another one 'unspecified'. This brought the proportion of parishes with a school to 90 per cent. The Newcastle Commission was seeking sound and cheap education for all classes of people, not just the poor or labouring classes as in the past. The State really did not find the money to support this even at minimal cost. It continued to rely on self-help, on benefactors, on parish levy or rates. Public subscriptions were called for in some parishes even after a donor had provided the site. Burton Pedwardine, for example, was built in 1860 by the parish on land given by 'the late Mr. Handley'. Pinchbeck St Matthew (National) school was built on a site granted by Deeping Fen Trustees to the vicars of Pinchbeck and Pinchbeck West, but the building was put up, albeit first as a mission-room, by subscriptions of the church people. A few seemed to become schools almost incidentally, through the establishment of a building for religious worship: Moulton Seas End (1867) was really a place licensed or consecrated for the celebration of divine worship, subject to the Bishop of Lincoln's supervision and direction if any school therein was established. Crowle St Norbert (1869) was a conveyance on trust for a Roman Catholic chapel, with a dwellinghouse for the priest, and with permission for the remainder of the premises to be used for any other purpose which the Bishop might consider for the benefit of the Roman Catholics residing in Crowle. School establishment by the back door (!) but still at voluntary expense.

Most of the early schools had specified the number of pupils, whether it was two or twenty, but as the century progressed and grants were paid for the number attending, for the cost of buildings, for the salary of teachers, and for curriculum expansion, larger schools were built often well in excess of the places actually required. Attendances were notoriously low in rural areas anyway and the average attendance at Donington, with 530 places, was 257; at Carlton only 53 out of 107, even less at Cranwell with 20 out of 63, and less still at Belton with 16 attending for the 68 places. This may reflect the high infant mortality of Victorian times, though in rural areas it was unlikely to have been higher than a century earlier. No doubt illness, the vagaries of the weather and the demand for child labour especially at harvest time, kept numbers down.[1] In towns non-attendance was less of a problem, judging by the figures: 948 out of 991 at Gainsborough, 469 out of 510 at Grimsby National School. Spalding, in a very rural area, was an exception being half empty with 365 attending for the 605 places. It may be that the opportunities available to children in towns to be out of school earning a living were very few. Increasing urbanisation and industrialisation meant that people were leaving the rural settlements for the towns, abandoning rural school places and filling up those provided in the urban schools.

By the time state provision was introduced, many Non-Provided schools had become run-down, the charity provision failing to sustain the increasing expense of repairs, equipment and salaries. The £20 per annum left by Thomas Kitchen in 1711 to keep a free school in Bardney and a schoolmaster was hardly relevant to the late 19th century. However, the heritage established by churches, charities and benefactors in the previous two to three hundred years continued strongly into the post-1870 period. The partnership of Church and State has held firm for over another hundred years since the Forster Act of 1870.

Notes and further details on page 144.

Establishment of elementary schools
1833-1858 and 1859-1870

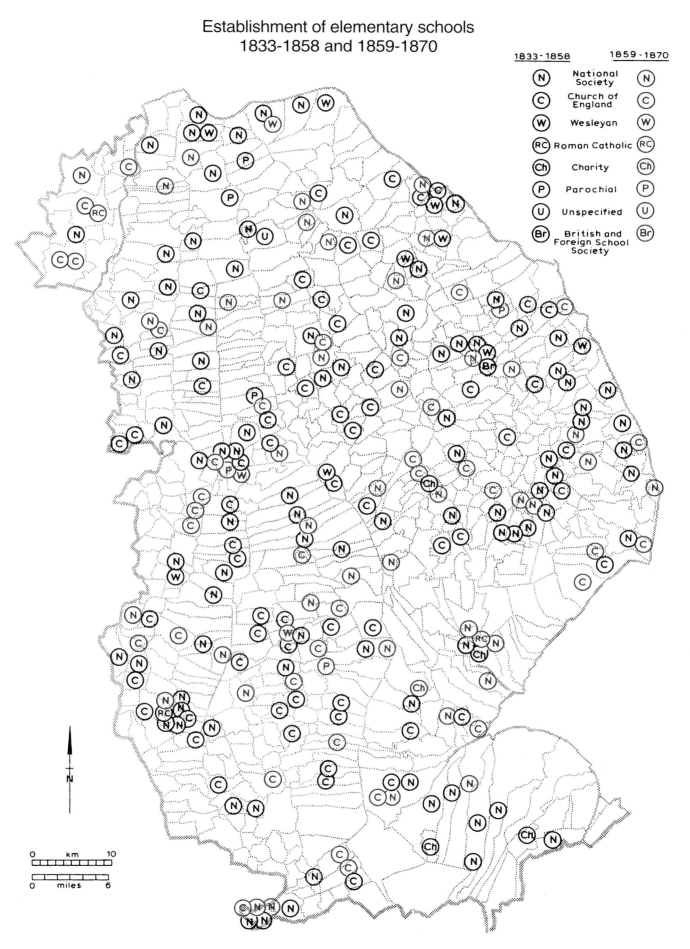

The 1834 Poor Law Amendment Act was one of the most controversial pieces of legislation in the 19th century. It marked a change from the independence and variation of the parochial system under the old Poor Law to the much more centralised uniformity of the new. In 1832 a Royal Commission was created to investigate the operation of the Poor Law. There was a strong feeling that the system was not only uneconomic but inadequate.

The Act of 1834 swept away the old system. It abolished outdoor relief for the able-bodied who now had to enter the workhouse. Here the principle of 'less eligibility' was to be enforced, whereby conditions in the workhouse were to be no better than those experienced outside–the theory being that this 'workhouse test' would act as a deterrent to all but the most destitute. Parishes were to be grouped together to form unions, governed by elected boards of guardians. The whole system was overseen by the poor law commissioners, based at Somerset House, in an attempt to impose some kind of uniformity. Undoubtedly one of the motives behind the Act was financial–an attempt to cut down on escalating expenditure. But Gulson, the assistant commissioner for Lincolnshire, argued that the moral benefits of the Act were as important as any financial ones. He claimed that, given the harshness of the workhouse test, the labouring classes would begin to realise the necessity of saving.

Between 1835 and 1837, 705 Lincolnshire parishes were allocated to 14 different unions. Their boundaries cut across county divisions and even counties. Lincoln union contained parishes in both the Kesteven and Lindsey divisions and Boston union included some districts in Lindsey as well as in the Holland division. Stamford union contained parishes in Northamptonshire and Rutland, Grantham included parishes from Leicestershire, and Gainsborough had some parishes from Nottinghamshire. Several parishes from Kesteven were included in the Newark union which had its workhouse at Claypole, a Lincolnshire parish. The Isle of Axholme parishes went to Goole and Thorne unions and Crowland went to that of Peterborough.

The reorganisation was relatively smooth, although a few parishes objected to being included in certain unions. The protests by the parishioners of Deeping St James were ignored and the parish included in the Bourne union. Welbourn refused to join the Sleaford union, preferring instead to be part of Lincoln, but despite boycotting the early meetings, and even refusing to elect a guardian, the parish remained in the Sleaford union. One problem was what to do with the old Gilbert unions. The old workhouse at Claypole could obviously be utilised, but as part of the Newark union. Caistor was chosen as the centre of an extensive union in preference to Grimsby or Market Rasen, because it was felt that no-one should be more than twelve miles from the workhouse. It was not until 1890 that Grimsby got its own union. The unions varied in size from Spalding with eight parishes to Lincoln with 86 and Louth with 88. This presented organisational difficulties. Each parish was to be represented on the board of guardians but, given such numbers, there clearly could not be a fair system of representation related to population size. Compromise was sought and the larger towns and villages were given more representatives. In Bourne union, for instance, Bourne had five guardians, Deeping St James three, Market Deeping and Billingborough two each and the remaining parishes one. The guardians were to be 'substantial persons', a point reinforced by property qualifications, both to be a guardian and to vote in the election for guardians. Few villages went to the trouble of having elections, some returning the same person annually, some adopting an unofficial rota. As might be expected, the vast majority of guardians were farmers with some professional people, especially clergymen, and a very small number of tradesmen. In addition, magistrates were *ex officio* guardians. Meetings of guardians were usually fortnightly and were rarely well attended. The problem was so acute in Bourne, especially in the summer, that the guardians suggested a monthly rota for parishes to attend.

Although the implementation of the Act was relatively smooth, there was sporadic opposition. Colonel Johnson, a Bourne magistrate, totally opposed the Act and was a thorn in the side of the Bourne guardians for several years. Grass roots opposition came at Gainsborough where the workhouse was destroyed during its construction in 1837 and at West Butterwick where the military were called out to protect officials. There were also disturbances at Horncastle and Spalding but none likely to threaten the implementation of the Act.

The desire to cut expenditure immediately bore fruit as the average expenditure on poor relief per head of the population was reduced by over thirty per cent in the first three years. The principle of less eligibility was enforced. In 1839 Grantham guardians reduced the quality of bread given on relief, on the grounds that labourers not receiving relief had to make do with poor quality bread due to the previous poor harvest. The Bourne guardians were severely reprimanded for providing a Christmas dinner for the inmates of the workhouse out of the poor rate. Such incidents demonstrate not just the desire to cut costs but also the central control exerted by the poor law commissioners.

Most unions built new workhouses. Although for many the material conditions inside were better than outside, the workhouses were disliked for their often harsh discipline, segregation and monotonous diet. The officials were not always honest or efficient. A relieving officer for Sleaford absconded with over £80. The workhouse master for Bourne was forced to resign due to 'excessive drinking'. All of this added to the stigma attached to poverty. Nevertheless the Act achieved its aim of cutting, or at least controlling, expenditure. Whether Gulson's hopes of a moral regeneration of the labouring classes was achieved is another matter.

Notes and further details on page 144.

Lincolnshire Poor Law Unions: 1835-1838

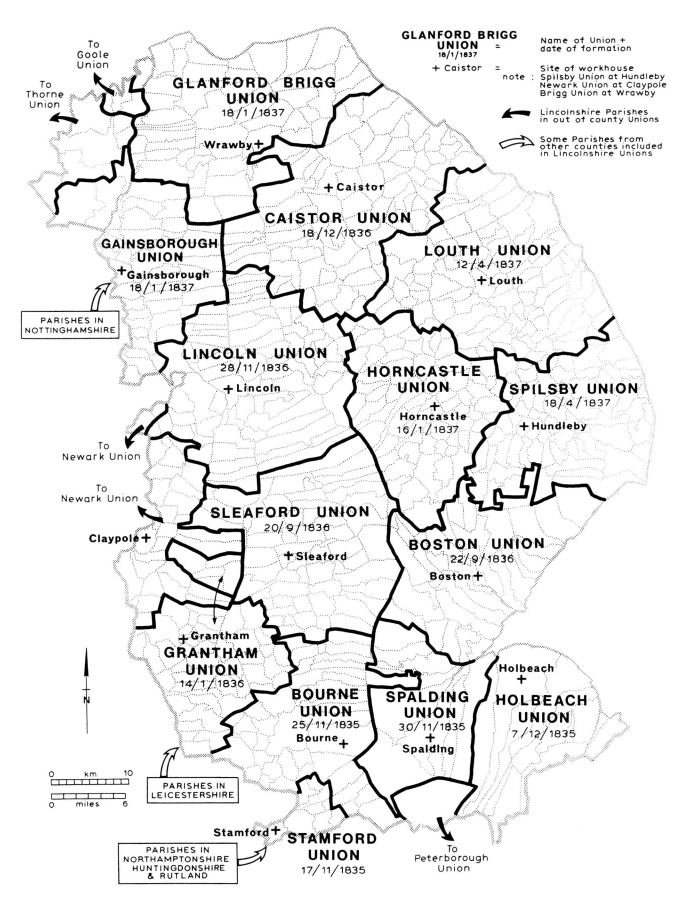

To Goole Union

To Thorne Union

GLANFORD BRIGG UNION
18/1/1837

Wrawby +

+ Caistor

CAISTOR UNION
18/12/1836

LOUTH UNION
12/4/1837
+ Louth

GAINSBOROUGH UNION
+ Gainsborough
18/1/1837

PARISHES IN NOTTINGHAMSHIRE

LINCOLN UNION
28/11/1836
+ Lincoln

HORNCASTLE UNION
+
Horncastle
16/1/1837

SPILSBY UNION
18/4/1837
+ Hundleby

To Newark Union

To Newark Union

Claypole +

SLEAFORD UNION
20/9/1836
+ Sleaford

BOSTON UNION
22/9/1836
Boston +

+ Grantham
GRANTHAM UNION
14/1/1836

BOURNE UNION
25/11/1835
Bourne +

SPALDING UNION
30/11/1835
+
Spalding

Holbeach
+
HOLBEACH UNION
7/12/1835

0   km   10
0   miles   6

PARISHES IN LEICESTERSHIRE

N

Stamford +   **STAMFORD UNION**
17/11/1835

PARISHES IN NORTHAMPTONSHIRE HUNTINGDONSHIRE & RUTLAND

To Peterborough Union

The 1841 General Election returned 13 Members of Parliament from Lincolnshire, two each from Boston, Grantham, Lincoln and Stamford and one from Great Grimsby. The remaining four were the 'Knights of the Shire': two from North Lincolnshire (Lindsey) and two from South Lincolnshire (Kesteven and Holland).

The map opposite shows the proportion of votes cast in each parish for the county members. Three candidates stood in each constituency. In Lindsey, Lord Worsley represented the Whig interests and R.A. Christopher and the Honourable C.H. Cust stood for the Tories. Worsley and Christopher had represented the region since the previous election in 1837. The fight in the southern division was between Sir John Trollope and Christopher Turnor for the Tories and Henry Handley representing Whig/Liberal interests. Handley had been M.P. since 1832 with the Whig Sir George Heathcote who had decided not to stand again. The votes cast are shown in the Table.[1] In the north, the voters supported the two existing members, while in the south Handley was defeated in favour of the two Tories.

Despite the passing of the 'Great Reform Act' in 1832, the franchise was still very limited. In the 1841 county election 16,738 people voted (9,722 in Lindsey and 7,016 in Kesteven Holland), a turn-out of approximately 85 per cent of those eligible. Sex and property were the principal qualifications. Voting was restricted to men over 21, who owned property with a rateable value of 40 shillings (£2) per annum, or who were leaseholders of land worth £50 per annum or £10 copyholders (tenants of farms which were traditionally passed from father to son). Such property qualifications excluded agricultural labourers.[2] Voting was open and was thus a matter of public record. This remained the case until the secret ballot was introduced in 1872. Individuals voted in the parish in which they had property. For example, of the 25 voters from Washingborough, 12 were resident elsewhere, one from outside Lincolnshire. At Reepham, eight of the 19 voters lived in other parishes. In rural parishes, not surprisingly, the majority of voters were farmers. For example all six voters at Scampton and at Minting all 16 resident voters were in this category. Shopkeepers and tradesmen formed the next largest group. At Barton upon Humber 74 of the 173 voters were tradesmen or in retail occupations.

The map opposite is based on the data contained in the two poll books[3] which give an account of all the votes cast in each parish. As each constituency returned two members, electors had two votes. As both had two Tories and one Whig candidate, it was not unusual to find electors casting their votes for candidates from each party. At Horncastle, for example, 145 electors cast 248 votes; 39 voted for Worsley (Whig) alone, 61 voted for Worsley and Cust or Christopher (Tory) and 45 for the Tory candidates alone. At Old and New Sleaford in the southern division, 120 individuals voted. Thirty-two voted for Handley (Liberal) alone, 50 for Handley and Turnor or Trollope (Tory) and 38 for the Tory candidates. Most parishes had few voters. Three hundred and forty-one (60 per cent) had no more than ten. Parishes with the largest number of voters tended to be in the recently-drained areas of the fens and the Isle of Axholme; Crowland had 123, Pinchbeck 158, Holbeach 216, Belton 159, Epworth 164, and Haxey 240 voters. It was in these multi-voter parishes where the electorate's allegiances were most diverse. At a time before national party machines, local issues and personalities played an important part in elections. In an agriculturally-based county such as Lincolnshire, one local issue coincided with one dominating the national scene—the protection of agriculture.

Voting was most uniform in parishes owned by a supporter of one particular candidate. Although outright bribery may not have taken place, landowners were able to influence their tenants to support a candidate of their choice. Parishes in which Sir George Heathcote was dominant showed substantial support for the Liberal Handley. At both Ingoldsby and Rippingale, for example, 15 of the 16 voters cast a vote for Handley. At Folkingham, 14 of the 15 voters cast their votes for Handley and only four votes were cast for the Tories. In parishes dominated by the Whig Sir Robert Heron there was a similar pattern. At Stubton (Heron's seat) the electors each used only one of their votes to vote for Handley; at Dry Doddington, 17 of the 23 voters cast a single vote for Handley, two voted for Handley and Turnor and four non-resident voters cast their votes for both Tory candidates. Not surprisingly in Handley's home parish of Burton Pedwardine, where he 'owned most of the soil', each of the eight voters cast a single vote in his favour.

Supporters of the Tory candidates were equally influential. At Charles Chaplin's seat at Blankney he was able to deliver all the votes for the Tory cause. At Metheringham, too, a parish where he was dominant, the Tories achieved 109 of the 112 votes. At Leadenham, the seat of the Tory supporter Colonel Reeve, 45 of the 46 votes cast were for the Tory cause. At Uffingham (near Trollope's seat of Casewick) and at Stoke Rochford (Turnor's seat) they had total support.

In Lindsey the situation was similar. Brownlow's interests did not extend north of Lincoln and therefore Cust was unable to obtain the kind of support he would have got in Kesteven. The opposite was true of Lord Worsley. He was supported by the Earl of Yarborough, the largest landowner in the county. In the 15 parishes in which Yarborough was dominant the 108 voters could have cast 216 votes. In fact they cast only 113 votes of which 101 were for Worsley.

The county therefore returned three of its four 'Knights of the Shire' to support a Tory government under the leadership of Sir Robert Peel.

Notes and further details on page 144.

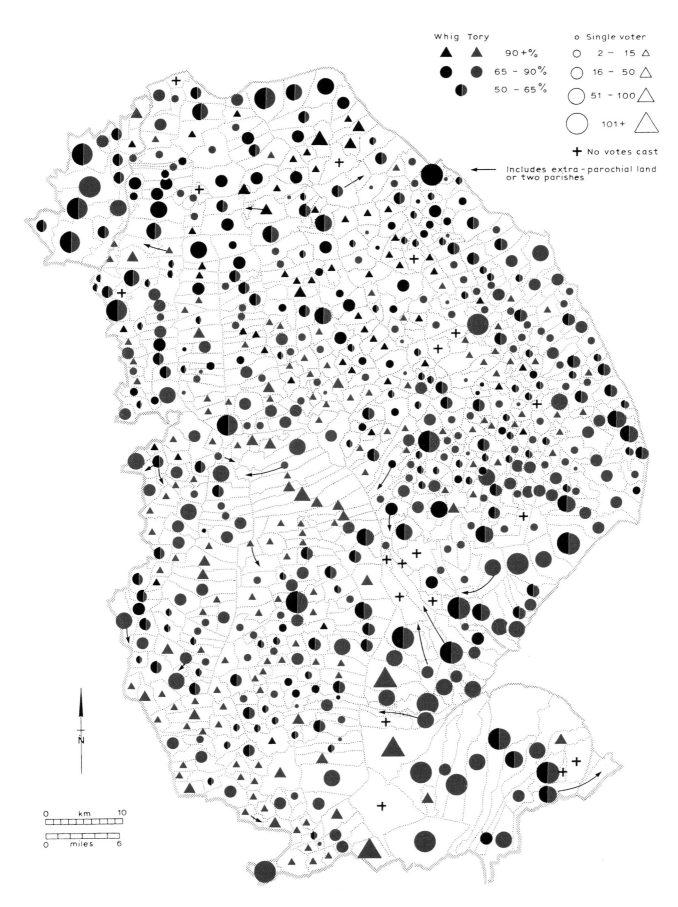

Whig Tory
▲ ▲ 90 +%
● ● 65 - 90%
◖ 50 - 65%

o Single voter
○ 2 - 15 △
○ 16 - 50 △
○ 51 - 100 △
○ 101+ △

✛ No votes cast

← Includes extra-parochial land
or two parishes

km
0   10
miles
0   6

103

The Census of Religious Worship, which was carried out on Sunday 30 March 1851, provides the basis for a study of religious adherence in the county at that date. This unique exercise used the machinery of the population census, taken at the same time, to gather figures for attendance at religious worship in England and Wales. The minister or an official from each place of religious worship made its return and the Census enumerators attempted to make up any deficiencies.[1] The tables from the published Census Report, which present the results of the census returns by registration district, have been used to map attendance at religious worship.[2]

Two measures of religious adherence have been plotted for Sunday, 30 March 1851. These are the proportion of the total population present at worship, including Sunday scholars (the index of attendance), and the percentage share of these worshippers attending three main denominations or groups of denominations: the Church of England, the various branches of Methodism, and other places of worship.[3] The largest of the churches and denominations included in the third group were the various branches of the Baptists, the Independents, and the Roman Catholics, but this group also included Lady Huntingdon's Connexion, the Mormons, the Society of Friends, and the Unitarians. Indexes of attendance and the percentage share of worshippers are shown for the morning, afternoon and evening services on Census Sunday. The material for the whole of Lincolnshire is at the bottom left of the map.

The highest index of attendance for the whole of the county—just over 22 per cent of the total population—was for morning worship, although those for the afternoon and evening services were only a little lower. However, the figures for individual registration districts show that in seven the highest indexes were achieved in the afternoon and in six in the morning. These were the two times of the day when the Church of England had its best attendances and in the county as a whole it achieved its highest percentage of total attendances—56.8 per cent—in the morning. The time when the Anglican percentage share was highest did not, however, always coincide with the times when the index of attendance was greatest, which in the Caistor, Horncastle and Gainsborough registration districts was in the evening, when the various branches of Methodism had the majority of attendants. In Caistor, Gainsborough, Louth and Thorne districts, Church of England attendances were less than those of the other churches and denominations at all three times of the day, although this was by relatively narrow margins in the morning and afternoon in all of the districts except Thorne which included only eight Lincolnshire parishes.

The Church of England achieved its highest percentage shares of attendances in the south-west of the county. These occurred at both morning and afternoon services in the Bourne, Grantham and Stamford districts. To the immediate north of this area of relative Anglican strength there were also high percentages of worshippers attending the Church of England, either in the morning or afternoon, in Newark and Sleaford districts. It also had a relatively high percentage share of attendances at these times in the Spilsby and Lincoln districts.

No single religious body had larger attendances in the morning or afternoon than the Church of England in any district except Thorne. The next largest were usually at Wesleyan Methodist services where the largest percentage share of worshippers was in the evening. The Primitive Methodists were frequently, but not invariably, next but at some services in the Bourne, Holbeach, Spalding and Stamford districts, the Baptists or Independents occupied that position. In Grantham district the Wesleyan Reform movement had more than double the percentage share of the Primitives at evening worship and were just under five per cent less than the Wesleyan Methodists from whom they had recently broken away.

In the fenland districts of Holbeach and Spalding, the Baptists had a quarter of the total attendances at their best attended services which were in the evening, while in Boston and Bourne districts their share was 14.3 per cent and 15.8 respectively. The Independents achieved some of their highest percentage share of attendances—19.3 at their evening service—in the Stamford district. There was a relatively small number of people living in the Lincolnshire part of this district, most of whom were in the town of Stamford. All the Independent attendances related to their Stamford church. Indeed there were no nonconformist places of worship in the villages of the district apart from a Primitive Methodist chapel in Tallington.

The Roman Catholic church achieved its highest percentage share of attendance in the Stamford district. This was also based entirely on the town where the Catholic chapel had 7.5 per cent of all the district's worshippers at morning service. The next highest was in Bourne district. The usual attendance at its one Catholic chapel, which was in the village of Irnham, was said to be about 200—a 5.2 per cent share of morning attendances. The district with the greatest number of Catholic places of worship was Caistor with one in each of the towns of Grimsby and Market Rasen, and one in the village of Osgodby. They had a total of 4.8 per cent of the morning attendances.

It was, however, in the evening, except in Stamford district, that the nonconformist churches predominated throughout Lincolnshire. After allowance is made for the Baptists in some areas, this was the time when Methodist chapels and meetings, often two and sometimes three in a village, came into their own. Of the 20 per cent of the county's total population who attended religious worship on the evening of Census Sunday, nearly 50 per cent were at Wesleyan Methodist and nearly 30 per cent at Primitive Methodist services.

Notes and further details on page 144.

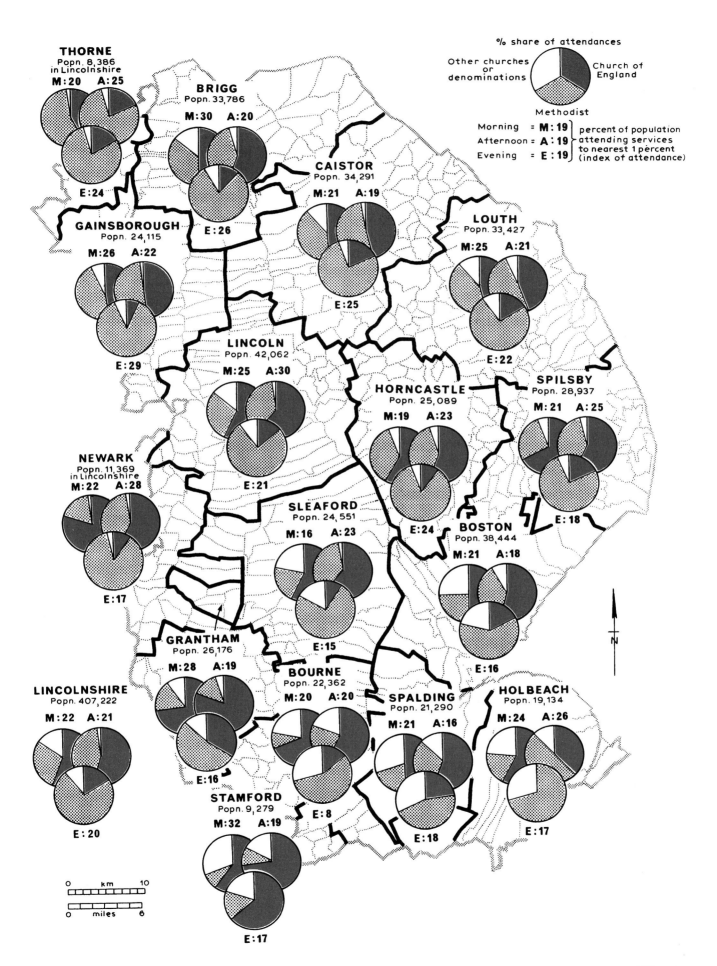

THORNE
Popn. 8,386
in Lincolnshire
M:20   A:25

E:24

BRIGG
Popn. 33,786
M:30   A:20

E:26

GAINSBOROUGH
Popn. 24,115
M:26   A:22

E:29

CAISTOR
Popn. 34,291
M:21   A:19

E:25

LOUTH
Popn. 33,427
M:25   A:21

E:22

LINCOLN
Popn. 42,062
M:25   A:30

E:21

HORNCASTLE
Popn. 25,089
M:19   A:23

E:24

SPILSBY
Popn. 28,937
M:21   A:25

E:18

NEWARK
Popn. 11,369
in Lincolnshire
M:22   A:28

E:17

SLEAFORD
Popn. 24,551
M:16   A:23

E:15

BOSTON
Popn. 38,444
M:21   A:18

E:16

GRANTHAM
Popn. 26,176
M:28   A:19

E:16

BOURNE
Popn. 22,362
M:20   A:20

E:8

SPALDING
Popn. 21,290
M:21   A:16

E:18

HOLBEACH
Popn. 19,134
M:24   A:26

E:17

LINCOLNSHIRE
Popn. 407,222
M:22   A:21

E:20

STAMFORD
Popn. 9,279
M:32   A:19

E:17

% share of attendances

Other churches
or
denominations

Church of
England

Methodist

Morning = **M:19**
Afternoon = **A:19**
Evening = **E:19**

percent of population
attending services
to nearest 1 percent
(index of attendance)

0 km 10

0 miles 6

N

105

The two main purposes of the map are to demonstrate the broad distribution of country seats in relation to physical features and to indicate which parishes contained one or more seats and which had none. While it is possibly true that there were more gentry resident in the countryside during the Victorian period than ever before or since, the presence of a gentleman of substantial means in any particular parish could not be taken for granted. Thus only 124 seats are shown on the map, against a number of parishes exceeding 600.

Much, of course, depends on how the terms 'substantial means' and 'country seats' are used. Any definition is bound to be in some measure arbitrary. The main basis of the map is the list of the nobility, gentry and clergy published in 1856 by William White in his *History, Gazetteer and Directory of Lincolnshire.* As White must have taken some pains not to give offence, this is a good starting point.

From his list all parsonage houses were removed, regardless of the fact that some of them were very substantial dwellings and some of their occupants were members of the gentry. Evidence for the remaining seats was then sought in the parish entries of the directory, in respect of their impact on the landscape and whether or not their occupants held positions of influence in their parishes. Extensive ownership of land and influence exercised within the community (for example, by being a patron of the living, or lord of the manor) were particularly noted. The first edition of the Ordnance Survey one-inch maps was of some help in identifying parks. A seat in White's list was excluded from the map if its occupant was found to be a farmer, or a man engaged in a profession or in commerce (with the exception of the Hon. A.L. Melville of Branston Hall, who was a Lincoln banker). Other sources consulted include a selection of maps, Pevsner's *Buildings of England: Lincolnshire,* earlier and later directories, and Edward Willson's notes of *c.*1830 on the Lincolnshire section of Britton's *Beauties of England and Wales, 1807.*[1] These cross-references led to the inclusion of four seats which were temporarily unoccupied when White collected his data and were thus omitted by him: Aswardby near Spilsby, Culverthorpe, Harrington and Norton Place.

Although other investigators would doubtless have produced a map differing in detail, there are no doubts as to the general patterns shown. It will not surprise a Lincolnshire reader to find only four seats marked in the Holland division of the county, and relatively few in other low-lying areas. Height above sea-level was not important in itself—indeed, the tops of the Wolds and the crests of the limestone Cliff were shunned by all seats except Fillingham 'Castle'. Rather, the landed owner looked for a well-drained but sheltered spot where the house could be seen against rising ground with woods and parkland, while its occupants could take in distant views downslope.

These criteria help to explain the popularity of sites part way up the limestone escarpments, on the hills south of Gainsborough looking over the Trent, in the pleasant valleys of south Kesteven and along the foothills of the Wolds, especially in Spilsbyshire. The presence of very large estates, particularly Brocklesby, Grimsthorpe and Belton, reduced the number of available sites in some attractive areas, because wide tracts of land belonged to their aristocratic owners. Indeed, it should be remembered that even relatively modest seats needed the rents from more than one parish to provide their upkeep.

An attempt has been made to represent certain aspects of the hierarchy of seats by giving distinctive symbols to those of the nine peers, not that all of these men had estates of the largest size. The Bishop's Palace at Riseholme has been included with them as a special case. A further 18 seats occupied by persons with the titles Honourable, Right Honourable, Knight or Baronet have also been distinguished, along with the anomalous case of Stoke Rochford (Lady and Christopher Turnor). The remaining 96 seats were occupied by plain esquires, with a sprinkling of clergy and army officers.

Finally, Lincolnshire needs to be seen within the national context (see Table, below). In the late Victorian period, both small and very large estates took up larger proportions of land in the county than in England and Wales as a whole. Consequently, estates of a medium size, between 1,000 and 10,000 acres, were less important here than elsewhere. These figures suggest that Lincolnshire probably had fewer country seats per unit area than the national average, since estates of under 1,000 acres were too small to sustain country seats, and very large estates reduced the number of medium-sized estates. Furthermore, there is some evidence to suggest that Lincolnshire had more than its share of absentee landowners.[2]

TABLE

National Comparisons, 1883[3]

	Great estates over 10,000a	Gentry estates 1,000-10,000a	Small owners under 1,000a
Lincolnshire:			
Rank out of 39 counties ...	12th	35th	equal 16th
Percentage of total area ...	28%	23.0%	41.0%
England and Wales:			
Percentage of total area ...	24%	29.5%	38.5%
Nearby counties:	(Notts)	(Leics)	(Cambs)
Rank out of 39 counties ...	3rd	17th	3rd
Percentage of total area ...	38%	30.0%	51.0%

Notes and further details on page 144.

Country Seats: 1856

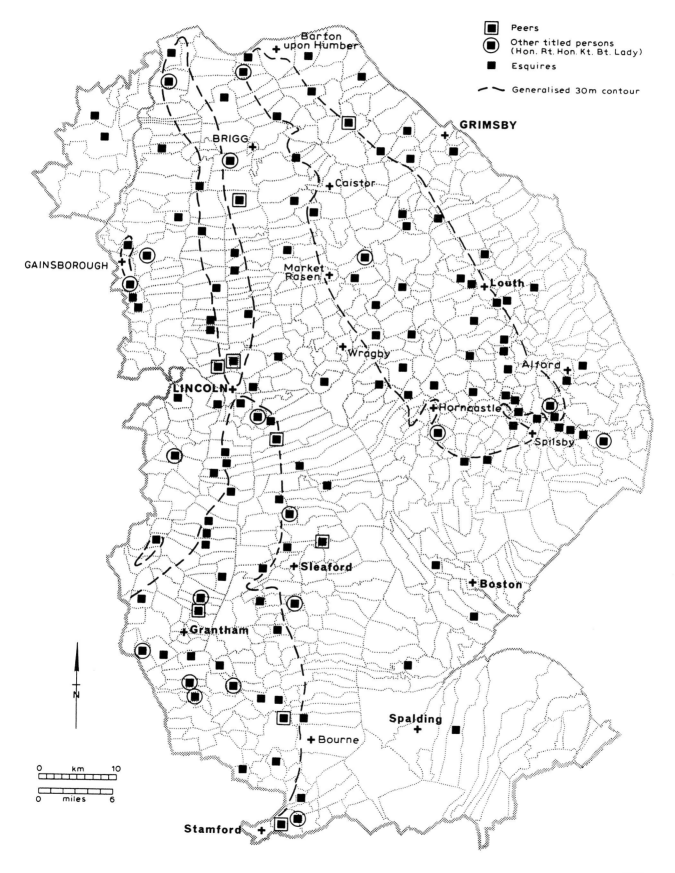

■ (boxed)	Peers
● (circled square)	Other titled persons (Hon. Rt. Hon. Kt. Bt. Lady)
■	Esquires
‿ ⁓	Generalised 30m contour

Barton upon Humber

GRIMSBY

BRIGG

Caistor

GAINSBOROUGH

Market Rasen

Louth

Wragby

Alford

LINCOLN

Horncastle

Spilsby

N

Sleaford

Boston

Grantham

Spalding

Bourne

0 km 10

0 miles 6

Stamford

The County: Until 1832 Lincolnshire was a single two-member county, polling at Lincoln in the Castle Yard. (The castle, bail and close of Lincoln were part of the shire but not of the city of Lincoln, which was a county of itself.) In 1832, under the Reform Act of that year, the shire was divided into two constituencies, each returning two members to parliament. Lindsey formed one division, and Kesteven and Holland the other. The city of Lincoln and its liberty (Bracebridge, Canwick, Waddington and Branston) were to vote, insofar as their inhabitants qualified for the county franchise, in Lindsey, and they continued to do so even when, in the mid-1830s, the liberty was abolished and its parishes returned to Kesteven. Instead of polling only at Lincoln, the county divisions were subdivided into polling districts centred where possible on market towns.

The second Reform Act, passed in 1867, redivided Lincolnshire into three two-member constituencies (North, Mid and South) corresponding respectively with northern Lindsey, south Lindsey with north Kesteven, and the remainder of Kesteven with Holland. This made less sense in terms of pre-existing local boundaries than the previous arrangement, but in drawing their lines the boundary commissioners made use of the old divisions of the administrative counties into wapentakes, hundreds and sokes. North Lincolnshire, for instance, was to comprise the wapentakes of Aslacoe, Bradley Haverstoe, Corringham, Ludborough, Manley, Walshcroft and Yarborough, plus the hundred of Louth Eske and so much of the hundred of Calceworth as lay within Louth Eske.

The Boroughs: Before 1832 Lincolnshire had five parliamentary boroughs: the city of Lincoln, and the boroughs of Boston, Grantham, Great Grimsby and Stamford. All survived into the age of reform, but Grimsby lost one member in 1832 and Stamford one in 1867. The parliamentary boundaries after 1832 did not always match the municipal ones. At Lincoln and Stamford they marched together: at Lincoln, the bail and the close came into the city, and at Stamford, the borough was enlarged to embrace part of the suburban parish of St Martin, Stamford Baron, which lay not in Lincolnshire but in Northamptonshire. At Boston and Grantham, on the other hand, the parliamentary boundaries were now somewhat larger than the municipal, the aim (as at Stamford) being to include areas whose interests were judged to be urban rather than rural. At Grimsby the parliamentary boundary was considerably enlarged, with the aim this time of diluting the corrupt electorate of the town with pure country voters. From 1832 it included the parishes or townships of Bradley, Great and Little Coates, Laceby, Scartho, Waltham, Clee with Cleethorpes and Weelsby.[1]

Notes and further details on page 145.

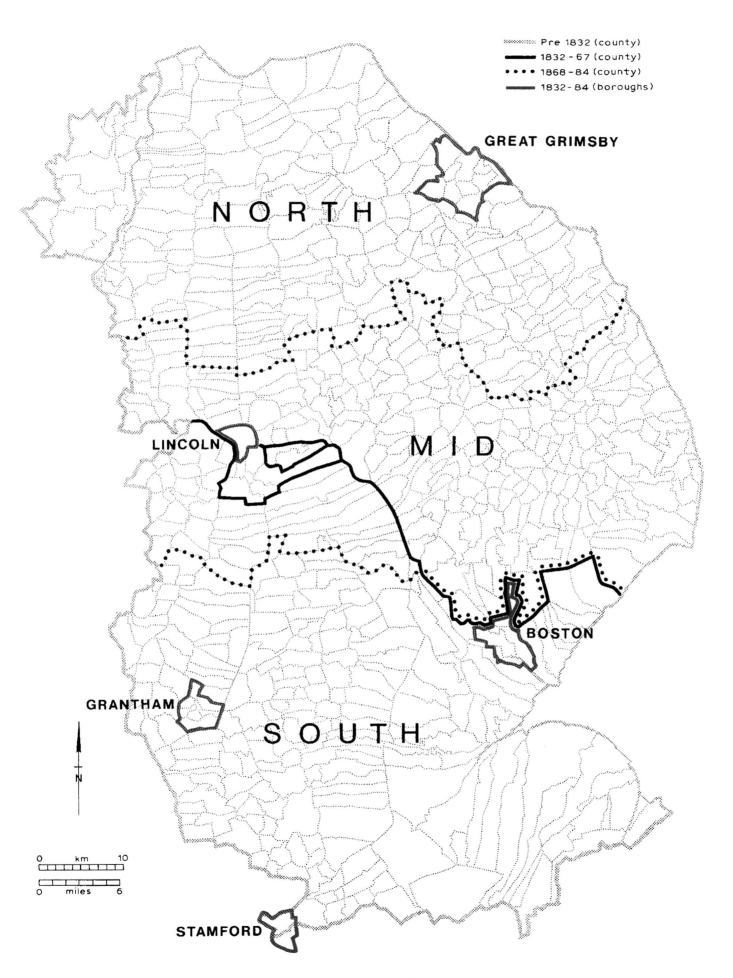

NORTH

GREAT GRIMSBY

MID

LINCOLN

BOSTON

SOUTH

GRANTHAM

STAMFORD

Pre 1832 (county)
1832 – 67 (county)
1868 – 84 (county)
1832 – 84 (boroughs)

N

0   km   10

0   miles   6

The Third Reform Act and Redistribution of Seats, 1884-5: The recommendations of the boundary commissioners were confirmed by a Boundary Act in 1885, and marked a radical change as far as the county constituencies were concerned. Lincolnshire was to have seven single-member county divisions, to be known as West Lindsey or Gainsborough, North Lindsey or Brigg, East Lindsey or Louth, South Lindsey or Horncastle, North Kesteven or Sleaford, South Kesteven or Stamford, and Holland or Spalding.

The boundaries for the most part followed petty-sessional areas rather than wapentakes and hundreds. The Gainsborough division, for instance, comprised the city of Lincoln and the petty-sessional areas of Lincoln (Lindsey), Gainsborough and Epworth. But this was only one stage removed from the older units, since the petty-sessional divisions were themselves founded on wapentakes. Lincoln (Lindsey), for instance, comprised Aslacoe, Lawress and part of Well, whilst Epworth was the western part of Manley, a large wapentake spanning the Trent. The petty-sessional areas, however, were not consistently followed. The new Louth division had to share parts of the Grimsby, Horncastle and Alford areas with neighbouring divisions. The Lindsey boundary was adhered to, but the Kesteven divisions both took small bites from Holland.

In 1885 the boroughs of Lincoln, Boston and Grantham were reduced to single-member constituencies. Grimsby retained its member, but Stamford was disfranchised. The main boundary change was at Lincoln, where the parish of Bracebridge was added to the city.

The Representation of the People Act 1918: The next major review of boundaries took place in 1918, when rural and urban districts (which had not existed as such in 1885) were taken as the basis of the county divisions. These districts were essentially a creation of the 1834 Poor Law, and owed nothing to the ancient administrative divisions of the county. The four new Lindsey divisions roughly followed the pattern of the old, and retained their names, but adjustments were necessary to equalise the population. The Brigg division, for instance, shrank in geographical size to match the increase in its population. In southern Lincolnshire, Boston and Grantham ceased to have separate representation. The boundary between Kesteven and Holland was followed for the first time in its entirety, resulting in a Holland division coterminous with the administrative county. Kesteven was less tidy: the southern half was joined with Rutland, and the rural district of Grantham had to be divided between the new Grantham and Stamford constituencies.

The Representation of the People Act 1948: No radical change occurred in 1948, either in the representation of Lincolnshire by two boroughs and seven county divisions, or in the principles of boundary-drawing, which continued to follow local government areas. In Lindsey, the Caistor rural district was transferred from the Louth to the Gainsborough division. In Kesteven, there was a minor modification to the boundary between the Grantham and Stamford divisions. The parliamentary boundaries of Lincoln and Grimsby now matched the municipal ones. Thus, although Lincolnshire had lost three of its five parliamentary boroughs since 1884, the two that remained were recognisably the descendants of their medieval ancestors. In the county divisions, however, repeated modifications and changes of criteria had, except in Holland, all but obliterated the importance of the shire in rural politics.

Notes and further details on page 145.

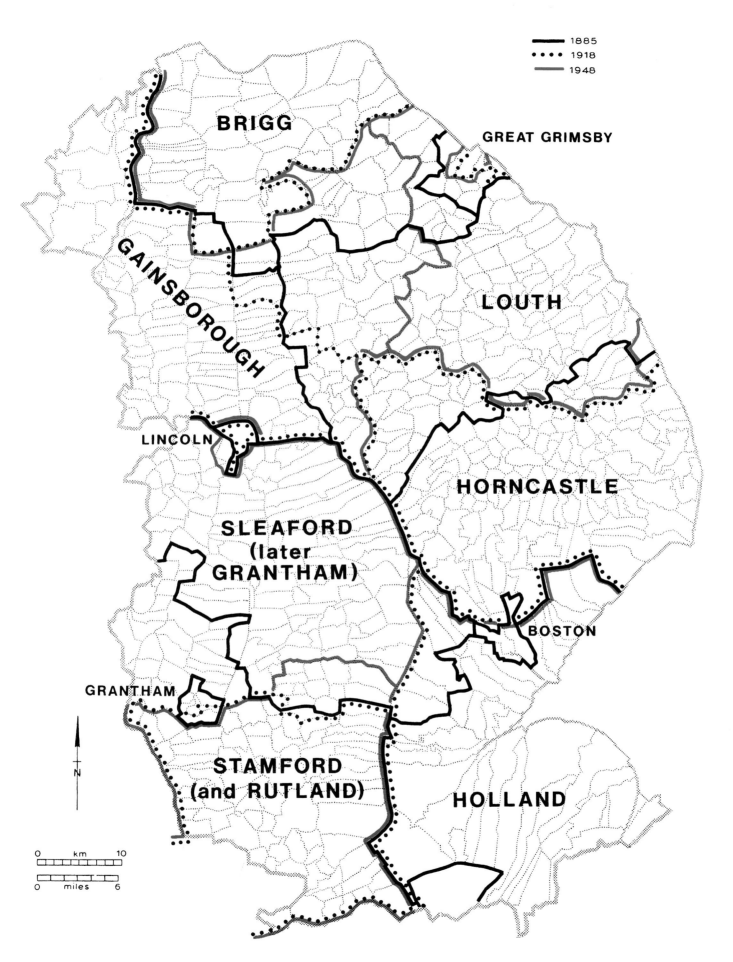

BRIGG

GREAT GRIMSBY

GAINSBOROUGH

LOUTH

LINCOLN

HORNCASTLE

SLEAFORD
(later
GRANTHAM)

BOSTON

GRANTHAM

STAMFORD
(and RUTLAND)

HOLLAND

1885
1918
1948

N

0   km   10

0   miles   6

111

The first railway service between London and Yorkshire was an indirect route via Birmingham and Derby. Proposals for railways through Lincolnshire had been made in the 1830s but nothing came of them. In the mid-1840s, however, a number of separate schemes were united as a Great Northern Railway project for a direct line from London to York via Lincolnshire and this was eventually approved by Parliament. A number of alternative schemes were put forward, resulting in the Midland Railway branches from Peterborough to Stamford and from Nottingham to Lincoln. These were opened in 1846 and provided the first railways into the county.

The Great Northern Railway (GNR) was to have a main line from London to a point north of Doncaster, running through the western edge of Lincolnshire (with stations at Grantham and a few villages) rather than along the fenland route through the centre of the county. To serve the other main towns in the county a 'Lincolnshire Loop Line' was planned, from Peterborough to Doncaster via Boston, Lincoln and Gainsborough, joining the main 'Towns Line' at each end. Also under the control of the GNR was the East Lincolnshire Railway (ELR) which would run from Boston to Grimsby via Alford and Louth.

The first section to be opened was part of the ELR, from Grimsby to Louth, on 1 March 1848. By October, trains were running all along the ELR and from Lincoln to Peterborough on the Loop. From Peterborough the GNR's main line to London was opened in August 1850. For a few years Lincolnshire was the main base of the GNR's operations, and its engineering offices and workshops were located in Boston until they moved to Doncaster in 1853. The Loop was extended from Lincoln to Gainsborough in 1849 and in 1852 the remainder of the main line was opened from Werrington (near Peterborough) to Retford. Until 1867, when the Loop Line north of Gainsborough was completed, the GNR ran a service to Retford (at first from Gainsborough but later from Sykes Junction) on tracks belonging to the Manchester, Sheffield and Lincolnshire Railway (MSLR).

The MSLR was an extension of a railway across the Pennines from Manchester to Sheffield which had been opened by the early 1840s. A scheme was put forward to extend it east to the port of Grimsby, and build a huge new dock there. The MSLR scheme also included a line north to New Holland, whence a ferry ran across the Humber to Hull, and a branch south from Barnetby to Lincoln where it would join end-on to the Midland Railway branch from Nottingham. The first Lincolnshire section of the MSLR to be opened was from New Holland to Grimsby, on the same day as the first part of the ELR. The rest of the MSLR was opened in stages over the following 13 months.

The MSLR had taken over the old Dock Company at Grimsby and proceeded to create a large new dock on land reclaimed from the Humber. The Royal Dock was opened in 1852 but commercial traffic did not reach the levels anticipated. It was the growth of a new fishing industry which was to transform the town of Grimsby and lead over the next 80 years to the construction and extension of three fish docks on reclaimed land east of the Royal Dock. Even though the fishing industry at Grimsby ended in the 1980s, the town is still one of the main centres in the UK for the processing of fish and other foods. Space for further commercial traffic at Grimsby was provided by the opening of the Alexandra Dock in 1880, and by a completely new dock at Immingham which was opened in 1912.

The GNR and MSLR (the latter later called the Great Central Railway) dominated the railways of Lincolnshire for 80 years, the MSLR in the north and the GNR in the centre and south. Ambitions by the Great Eastern Railway and the Midland Railway respectively for two cross-country routes were only achieved as Joint Lines in which the GNR was involved. The GN & GE Joint Line went diagonally across the county from East Anglia to Yorkshire, and the M & GN Joint Line took over a number of short lines in south Lincolnshire and Norfolk.

A number of branches to small market towns or to the coast were created by local companies, the train services being operated by the GNR which eventually took over nearly all of these short lines. The few additions to the MSLR lines in Lincolnshire included the Trent, Ancholme and Grimsby Railway built to serve the new town of Scunthorpe, and the lines to Immingham Dock. The company also built the short extension to Cleethorpes and spent large sums on the development of that resort. Almost the only public line independent of the two dominant companies was the small light railway built in the Isle of Axholme between 1902 and 1909. Private lines operated for a number of years to serve the Grimsthorpe Estate, potato estates at Nocton, Fleet and Dawsmere, and Cranwell airfield.

A scheme for a dock and harbour of refuge on the Lincolnshire coast at Sutton on Sea came to nothing. A new dock at Sutton Bridge was built in running silt and had to be abandoned within a month of its opening in 1881, but the dock opened at Boston in 1884 was operated profitably by Boston Corporation until 1990 when it was sold to a local consortium.

From the early 20th century, as motor buses, lorries and cars became more efficient they started to take traffic away from the railways. In 1922 the GNR and MSLR both became part of the London and North Eastern Railway which in 1948 was absorbed in British Railways. From 1939, when the Spilsby branch was closed to passengers, sections of line were gradually abandoned, but the major change occurred on 5 October 1970 when most of the East Lincolnshire line and the 'Lincolnshire Loop' line were closed. Even where lines are still in use, nearly all of the village stations have been closed or reduced to unmanned halts. Changes in more recent times have included the replacement of steam by diesel power in the early 1960s, and in 1989 the East Coast main line (the GNR 'Towns Line') through Grantham was electrified.

Notes and further details on page 145.

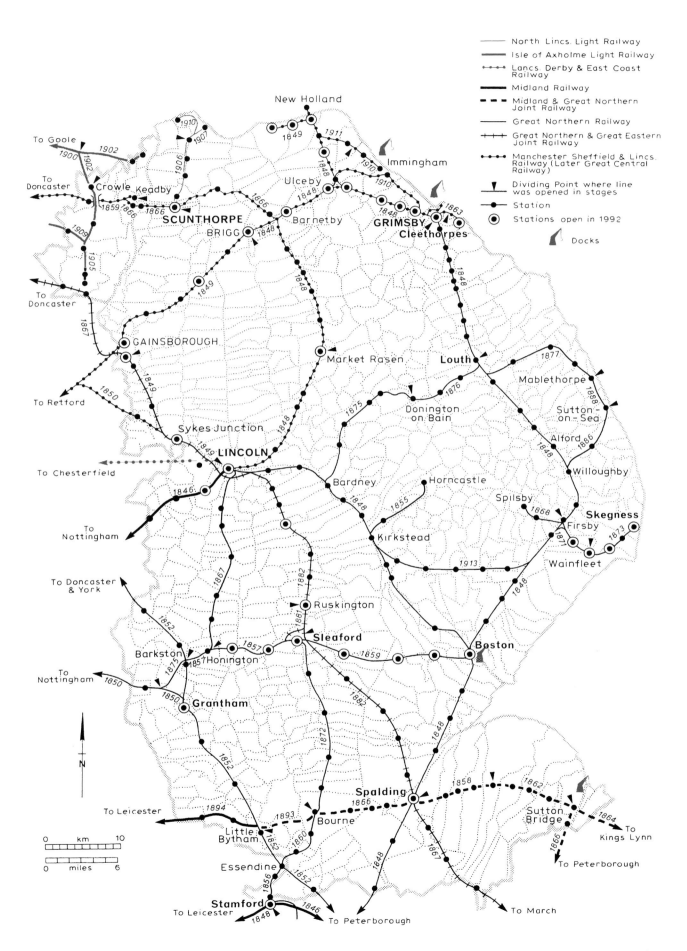

New Holland

1910
1907
1906 *1911*

To Goole
1902
1900 *1902*

To Doncaster
Crowle Keadby
1859 *1866*
SCUNTHORPE
BRIGG
1848 *1849* *1849* Barnetby Ulceby *1848* *1848* *1910* *1910* *1863* Immingham
1866 *1846* *1848* GRIMSBY
1909 *1905* Cleethorpes

To Doncaster
1867
GAINSBOROUGH
1850 *1849* Market Rasen Louth *1877*
Mablethorpe *1888*
1876 Donington on Bain Sutton-on-Sea
To Retford Sykes Junction *1875* Alford *1866*
1849 LINCOLN Willoughby
To Chesterfield *1846* Bardney Horncastle
Spilsby
1848 *1855* *1866* Skegness
Firsby
To Nottingham Kirkstead *1871* *1873*
1913 Wainfleet
1867 *1882* *1848*

To Doncaster & York
1852 Ruskington *1881*
1875 *1857* Sleaford
Barkston *1857* Honington *1859* Boston
1850 *1852* *1881*
To Nottingham Grantham *1882*
1852 *1848*
1858 *1862*
Spalding
To Leicester *1894* *1866* Sutton *1864*
1893 Bourne Bridge To Kings Lynn
Little *1860* *1866*
Bytham *1852* *1852* To Peterborough
Essendine *1856*
Stamford *1846*
1848 To Leicester To Peterborough To March

North Lincs. Light Railway
Isle of Axholme Light Railway
Lancs. Derby & East Coast Railway
Midland Railway
Midland & Great Northern Joint Railway
Great Northern Railway
Great Northern & Great Eastern Joint Railway
Manchester Sheffield & Lincs. Railway (Later Great Central Railway)
Dividing Point where line was opened in stages
Station
Stations open in 1992
Docks

km
miles

N

Ironstone is found in a strip of land passing through or near Grantham, Lincoln and Scunthorpe, part of the broad geological band of Lias and Oolites which extends from Dorset to the mouth of the Tees. Since the middle of the 19th century this band has come to be the main source of British iron ore, and in Lincolnshire it led to the creation of a completely new industrial town in the north-west corner of the county with open-cast ironstone mines, blast furnaces and steel mills. Ironstone has also been mined in the south of the county around Grantham, but that was sent elsewhere for processing.

Lincolnshire iron was apparently known and worked in Roman and medieval times but its value was forgotten until 1859 when Rowland Winn, then living at Appleby Hall, had some of the local ironstone analysed. The results were favourable and Winn became the driving force behind the development of the iron industry on his family estates in Appleby, Scunthorpe, Frodingham and Brumby.

Land was leased to the Dawes Brothers, ironmasters of Barnsley, who began mining ironstone in 1860, sending it for processing at their works in Yorkshire. A railway was built to take the ore from the quarry to the east bank of the Trent, from whence it was conveyed by water. In 1859 the South Yorkshire Railway had opened a branch line to the opposite bank of the Trent and plans were made for the construction of a bridge and railway to exploit the new iron field. The Manchester, Sheffield and Lincolnshire Railway eventually acquired both the SYR and the new line built through the ironfield. The bridge over the Trent was opened in April 1866 and the line east to Barnetby in October of that year.

The Trent Iron Works was built for the Dawes Brothers in 1862-4 and was quickly followed by the Frodingham Iron Works, built for Joseph Cliff, where the first blast furnace was blown in during 1865. By 1880 there were 21 furnaces, of which 15 were in blast. In 1888 the Cliff brothers decided to build a steel works next to their iron works, and the first steel furnace was tapped in 1890. After 1900 firms from outside the district started taking over the various works, and in 1912 the Normanby Park Works was opened by John Lysaght Ltd. of Newport. The industry was nationalised in 1967 and Scunthorpe became one of the British Steel Corporation's five main steel production centres. But from 1979 there have been extensive cut backs, including the closure and demolition of the Normanby Park Works.

The original Trent and Frodingham companies mined ore from land they leased adjacent to their works but the others were supplied by Winn from his own open-cast mines. Winn also granted mineral leases to companies which had blast furnaces elsewhere. The first mines were located where the railway crossed the sandy warrens of Scunthorpe and Frodingham; as they were worked out the excavations spread north and south. The North Lincolnshire Light Railway was opened in stages in 1906-7 partly to give access to the area north of Scunthorpe and most subsequent mines adjoined this line.

In the early days the work in the mines was done by hand but in 1885 Winn, now Lord St Oswald, introduced grab cranes and these were later replaced by larger machines. Skilled workers came from other iron areas of the country but most of the labourers were from local agriculture and worked seasonally. By 1917 Lord St Oswald's Lincolnshire mines were supplying one-twelfth of the nation's total output of iron ore and he was the largest single producer in the kingdom. Ironstone mining continued to grow until 1961 when over 5.5 million tons were extracted, but it then declined as more foreign ore was used in the steelworks.

Frodingham parish contained the townships of Brumby, Frodingham, Scunthorpe and Crosby which before 1860 were thinly inhabited. The iron works and housing for the new community grew up first in Frodingham and Scunthorpe and later spread north and south into the adjoining townships including Ashby in Bottesford parish. Winn planned a new town and laid out streets on his land in Frodingham but many people preferred to build on other land in Scunthorpe. Winn built a school, a 'town hall' with a reading room and library, and also provided allotments and a cricket ground. As the independent townships developed there was strong hostility to amalgamation, but eventually in 1919 they united to form the borough of Scunthorpe.

The developments at Scunthorpe generated interest in mineral working in other parts of Lincolnshire. A mineral railway was laid to an open-cast mine on Lord Yarborough's land at Appleby, and another one to an underground mine at Claxby near Caistor which was operated from 1868 to 1885. Another underground mine was operating at Nettleton from 1929 to 1969. The ironstone mine at Greetwell near Lincoln, worked from 1873 until 1939, was probably the longest-lived underground system in the county. Ore was also excavated from a small mine at Coleby south of the city.

The Coleby mine was close to a railway opened in 1867 by the Great Northern Railway, running along the base of the escarpment south of Lincoln, to join the Boston to Grantham line at Honington. It passed the home of the GNR chairman, George Packe, and within ten years the first open-cast mine in south-west Lincolnshire had been opened on his property at Caythorpe. Other mines were started in several parishes towards the southern end of the Honington Branch, and the area continued to produce ironstone until 1946.

Another ironstone district straddled the county boundary between Lincolnshire and Leicestershire. The GNR built mineral railways to open up the parishes west of Grantham in the hills behind Belvoir Castle, including Woolsthorpe, Denton and Harlaxton. The mines in this area continued in use until the 1930s and the area was reopened in the mid-1970s. The Holwell iron works near Melton Mowbray was built in 1878-81 but the exploitation of iron ores in the area around Colsterworth had to await the opening of the railway between Bourne and Saxby in 1894.

Notes and further details on page 145.

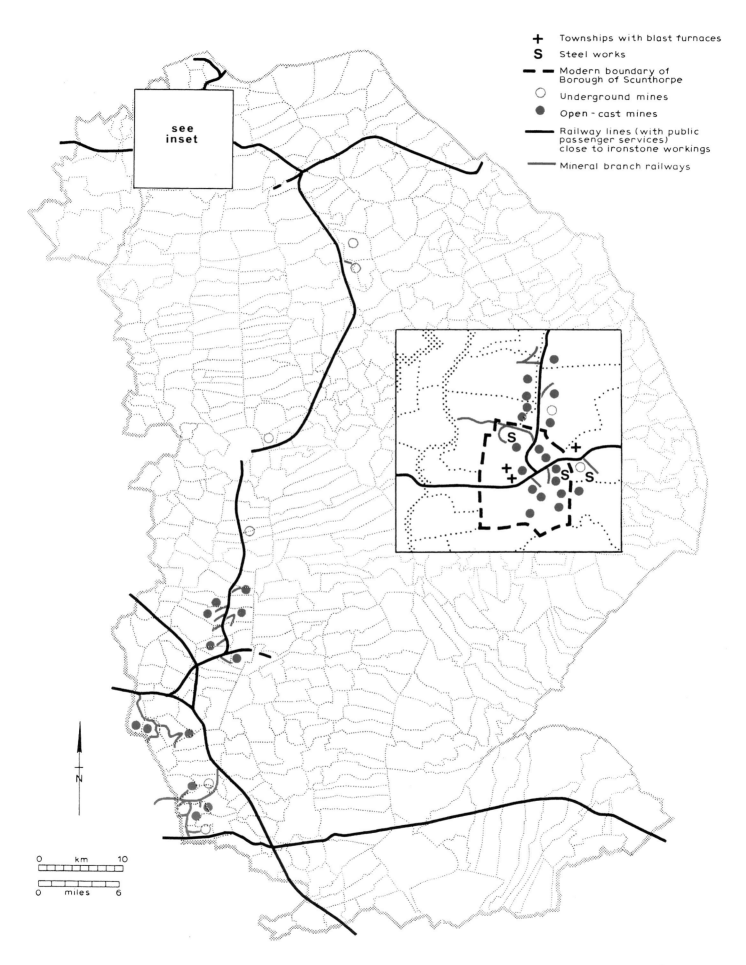

Townships with blast furnaces

S Steel works

Modern boundary of Borough of Scunthorpe

○ Underground mines

● Open - cast mines

Railway lines (with public passenger services) close to ironstone workings

Mineral branch railways

see inset

S

S

S

km
0   10

miles
0   6

N

Much of the surface of Lincolnshire is of clays and silts, easily exploited for brickmaking. There is scattered evidence for tile making in the Roman period, but use of clay in succeeding centuries was confined to making pottery where only shallow diggings were required. Not until Lincolnshire came under Flemish influence, principally through Boston and across the Humber from Hull from the 13th and 14th centuries, did brickmaking begin to flourish in the county. Bricks could be imported from Hull for the gatehouse of Thornton Abbey (1360s-80s) and for Gainsborough Old Hall in the mid-15th century, but kilns in Boston and on Edlington Moor supplied the bricks for Tattershall Castle (1430s-40s); those for the chancel of Bardney church (1430s) and the Magdalen School at Wainfleet (1484) probably came from similar sources. Soft plastic clays were mixed with sand, glacial clays were sifted of stones, tempered by turning and treading, kneaded into a 'clot' and hand-pressed into a wooden mould, stacked on a 'hack' to dry and finally fired in a temporary clamp using brushwood and timber. A clamp could take from three to six weeks to burn. The bricks nearest the fire were often overburned, with dark vitrified headers, while those on the outside were lighter in colour. The darker ones could be used to make diaper patterns, or later a chequerboard of light headers in Flemish bond.

Brickmaking spread further into Lincolnshire in the 16th century (Halstead Hall and Doddington Hall) and in the 17th (Red Hall at Bourne, Goltho church, Alford Manor House and Harrington Hall). For the rebuilding of South Ormsby Hall in 1660, bricks were made on site,[1] although finishing bricks for the front of the hall came from Hull. Even in the 1730s bricks were imported through Boston, but by the 1770s brick was being used for cottages as well as big houses and public buildings. Clay Holland or 'pann tyles' were first imported and then from the late 18th century made along the Humber bank, with a continuous history to the present day.

When East, West and Wildmore Fens were drained and enclosed at the beginning of the 19th century there was a requirement for some eleven million bricks for sluices, locks and bridges and all were burned locally near the new drains. By the mid-1820s there were 35 brick and tile works in the county, mainly along the Humber bank, but as places like Lincoln and Grimsby grew, major brickworks were established with permanent Scotch kilns using coal for fuel, brought in by water or rail.[2] Towns such as Louth and Horncastle were largely built with bricks made in pits within the town boundaries; at Louth, Dale's Brickyard off Brackenborough Road was opened to build the town hall (1854). By 1849 the number of brickworks had increased to 94, with further expansion to 130 brickyards in the next decade, after the removal of the Brick Tax in 1850. By the second half of the 19th century, almost every town and large village had its brickpit. It also seems that architects, such as James Fowler of Louth helped to make brick fashionable by his use of it in churches and parsonage houses. Wet autumns in the 1870s increased the demand for land drainage pipes, particularly on the heavier clay lands of west Kesteven, which extended the life of some pits where immediate local requirements for bricks declined with rural depopulation.

The distribution of brickworks was related to the outcrops of suitable clays. In the west is the orange-red Keuper Marl of the low, flat-topped hills in the Isle of Axholme, the Lower Lias in the Trent vale and the Middle Lias exposed along the foot of the Cliff–where the small amount of lime in the clay acted as a flux and also reduced contraction of the raw brick when drying. In the central clay vale are the Oxford-Kimmeridge clays and derived boulder clays, and the localised Tealby and Hundleby clays were exploited in some southern Wolds valleys. East of the Wolds are the glacial clays of the Middle Marsh, and small brickworks existed on the silts of the Outmarsh behind the coastal dunes where seaborne coal was readily available. The silts and clays were extensively used in the central and southern Fens, under the early influence of Boston, but the heaviest concentration was along the warplands of the Humber bank from North Killingholme to Barton and specialising in pantiles for export. Most Lincolnshire bricks are medium-dark red, although those from the Isle of Axholme are more brown, but some yards, as at Ewerby, Farlesthorpe and Hatton, were noted for a grey-white or yellowish product, achieved by an admixture of lime; these bricks are well seen at Sausthorpe and Wragby churches.

Small brickworks continued to produce hand-made bricks through most of the 19th century, but large firms used extrusion and wire-cutting machines from the 1880s. The maker's name could be impressed into one face of the brick with a die using a hand-operated machine. Other bricks had holes, from three to 21 using brass dowels on a ram.[3] The number of brickworks in the county rose to a peak of 187 in the early 1880s, but the next decade saw a decline to 126, and that included 30 on the Humber bank, some exporting fancy bricks and tiles, finials and chimney pots to London. The cause of the decline was the ready availability through rail transport of cheap Flettons which could be burned more easily because of the oil fuel content of the clays. By the First World War, the number of Lincolnshire brickworks had fallen to 80; by 1920 this was halved and by 1969 the number was sixteen. Brickmaking ceased at Barton in the 1960s. Some specialised, for example at Skegness in decorative interior bricks, at Mablethorpe in drainage pipes. There are four–at Barton and Barrow/Goxhill (tileries), Belton in the Isle of Axholme and Stamford.

Apart from the universal evidence of local brick and the occasional remaining Scotch kiln as at Baumber (now restored), East Halton, Farlesthorpe, Stixwould and Sutton on Sea, the only traces of a once extensive industry are water-filled pits now nature reserves or used for fishing, and names like Brickfield, Brick Close and Brickyard Lane.

Notes and further details on page 145.

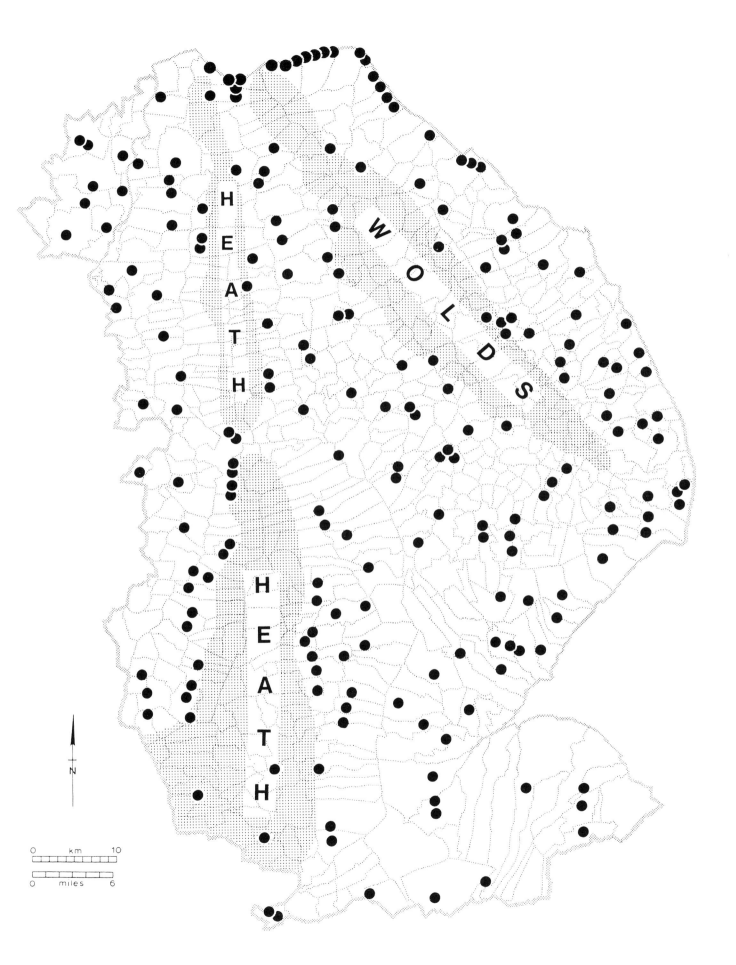

HEATH

WOLDS

HEATH

N

0   km   10

0   miles   6

Malting and brewing are both ancient industries that are inextricably linked. Lincolnshire was a great centre for growing barley from which is produced malt, an essential ingredient of beer. After the Welland was made navigable to Stamford in the 17th century a flourishing malt trade developed in the town. During the 18th and 19th centuries small maltings were established in other towns and in many villages. Some maltings were built beside navigable waterways so that the bulky malt could be easily moved to breweries in the midlands and north. By 1856 there were 163 maltsters in Lincolnshire, mostly located in the towns and in several villages in Kesteven and the northern and western parts of Lindsey, with very few on the Wolds or in the fens. Maltings had a distinctive architecture to reflect the processes carried on within. Early maltings were small buildings scattered among houses but during the 19th century there was a tendency for brewers to erect large maltings of their own and these, like the breweries, became centralised.

Brewing was for many centuries carried on in small undertakings, often just a brewhouse attached to an inn or tavern. A few breweries of this type still survived in Lincolnshire in the early years of the 20th century. Buildings with the distinctive louvred windows can still be seen behind some of the older public houses in the county, though none are still used as brewhouses. Brewing companies grew large by the ownership of large numbers of public houses which were tied to sell their beer. Dawber & Co. of Lincoln, founded in 1826, had by 1904 over sixty public houses. By 1856 there were 166 brewers in the county, situated in all of the main towns as well as in several villages, particularly (in contrast to maltings) in the fens and the fen-edge areas of eastern Kesteven and the southern Wolds.

The map shows that 83 towns and villages had at least one maltster or brewer. By 1856 nearly half of all brewers in the county had both a malting and a brewery. Of those breweries without a malting, nearly one third were attached to beerhouses or public houses. The largest numbers of maltsters and brewers were to be found in the towns. In the villages it was usually combined with some other occupation, such as victualling, farming, milling, or brickmaking.

During the late 19th and early 20th centuries these industries were transformed as maltings and breweries were closed or taken over by larger concerns. This started locally, as firms in the main towns grew at the expense of the smaller ones in the county, but later on firms from outside entered Lincolnshire. By 1913 nearly sixty of the villages which had a brewery or malting in 1856 had lost it, although there were a further 11 places where new breweries or maltings had been established. There had also been a separation between the two trades, as in 1913 only six firms or individuals were listed as both brewers and maltsters. Besides these, there were a further 32 brewers in the county and another 26 maltsters.

The reduction in numbers of maltings was due partly to local firms taking over others in the county, but others collapsed in the face of competition from breweries who built their own maltings in the county. The Truswell Brewery of Sheffield built maltings beside the railway line at Barnetby le Wold in 1875 and Bass, Ratcliff & Gretton of Burton on Trent erected the huge multiple maltings at Sleaford in 1899-1905. The building of such

maltings led to the decline of the smaller firms. By 1913 all the village maltings in Kesteven had closed, except Helpringham, and the industry was concentrated in the towns and a few new railside maltings such as Ancaster, Bracebridge and Gonerby. In north Lindsey there were still maltings in six places and new ones had been built in a couple of villages.

In 1856 there were over fifty brewers listed in the 10 main towns of the county but by 1913 the number had been halved. In the countryside it was even more drastic as practically every village brewery had closed. In 1913 beer was brewed in 24 communities in the county compared with 62 in 1856, and malting was done in 28 places compared with 61 before. Individual brewers gave way to brewing companies which took over other breweries to acquire their tied houses. By 1913 at least nine Lincolnshire brewers had taken over premises in other towns, in some cases keeping them as separate breweries but in others using them simply as stores and distribution centres. Village breweries remained at places like Moulton Chapel and Dogdyke and even some attached to public houses in places such as Boston (the *Robin Hood*), Market Rasen (the *Aston Arms*) and elsewhere but they were the last of a dying trade. During the course of the 20th century, all but one of the local brewers and maltsters had been absorbed in larger concerns. In the 1960s Melbourne's Brewery in Stamford was taken over and was converted into a museum, and since then Bateman's of Wainfleet has been the only remaining independent commercial brewery in Lincolnshire.

During the 19th century the growing Victorian concern about the problem of drunkenness led to the temperance movement. One response was the commercial brewing of non-alcoholic drinks, like dandelion and burdock, and the production of artificial 'mineral waters' such as lemonade and ginger beer. Some were produced by chemists and druggists such as J.H. Thomas and Sons of Boston and others by companies such as the Grantham Soda Water Manufactory established in 1835. The firm of Mills and Baxter, founded in 1864, was by 1913 one of Bourne's largest employers. Few such concerns existed in 1856, but in 1913 there were four 'botanical beer brewers' and 45 mineral water manufacturers.

By the late 20th century all of the small maltings and mineral water manufacturers had closed, like the local breweries before them, but several maltings had been converted to other uses. The huge Bass Maltings at Sleaford are no longer used for their original purpose but remain as one of the outstanding industrial monuments of Lincolnshire.

Notes and further details on page 145.

Maltings and breweries: 1856 and 1913

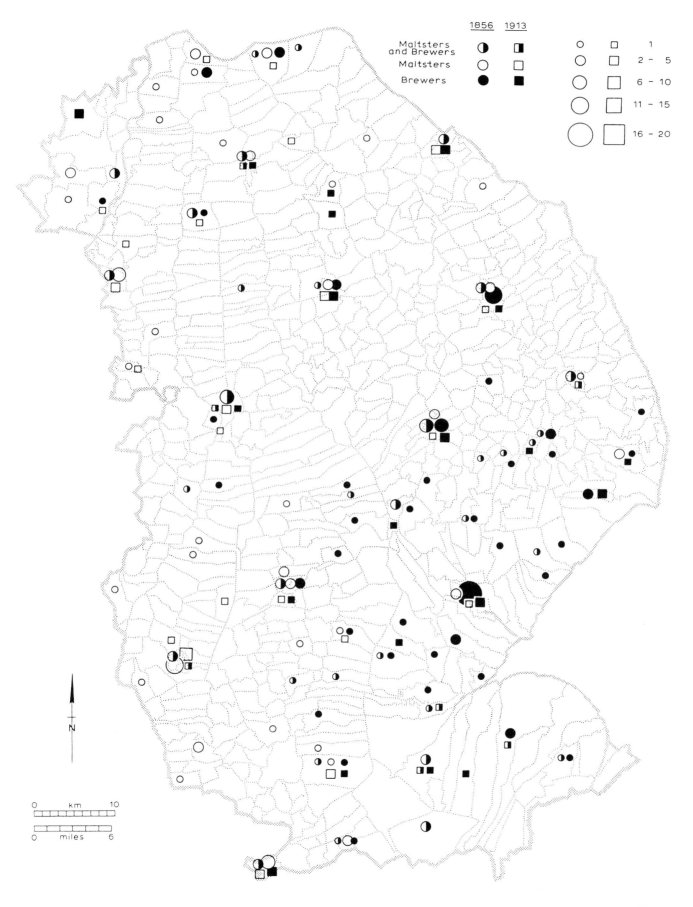

	1856	1913
Maltsters and Brewers	◐	◧
Maltsters	○	▢
Brewers	●	■

1856	1913	
○	□	1
○	□	2 - 5
○	□	6 - 10
○	□	11 - 15
○	□	16 - 20

0 km 10

0 miles 6

Lincolnshire's main role in the industrial revolution was as a supplier of agricultural produce, particularly food, to the populations of London and the industrial centres of Yorkshire and the east midlands. This brought wealth to many people involved–farmers, merchants and professional men–but it also needed the investment of money in enclosures, drainage works, turnpikes, waterways and harbour improvements. This led some Lincolnshire merchants to set up as bankers in the late 18th and early 19th centuries.

The first bank in Lincolnshire was opened in 1754 by William Garfit, a Boston merchant. In the same year Joseph Pease of Hull opened the first bank in Yorkshire, convenient for people in north Lincolnshire. The second bank in the county was opened in Lincoln in 1775 by Ellison, Smith and Brown. Richard Ellison of Thorne had already founded a bank in Doncaster and Abel Smith had previously established a bank in Nottingham. John Brown of Lincoln was the resident partner. Bartholomew Claypon was taken in as a partner by William Garfit in 1774 and the firms of Garfit, Claypon & Co. (the Boston Bank) and Smith, Ellison & Co. (the Lincoln Bank) remained as the main banks in Lincolnshire throughout the 19th century. Like all provincial private banks they published their own bank notes; in 1799 the Lincoln Bank had notes worth £116,000 in circulation.

Some small banks were opened in the 1780s and 1790s including Charles Wigelsworth in Louth and Clarke & Gee in Boston. Henry Gee had arrived in Boston in 1781 and joined Henry Clarke to trade as merchants and brewers and, from 1783, as bankers. Later they owned a fleet of sailing ships in partnership with William Ingelow, who opened his own bank in 1805. It was a reflection of Boston's vigorous commercial activity at this period that by 1790 there were four banks in the town and six between 1805 and 1814, a greater number than in any other Lincolnshire town.

In the 1790s banks were opened in Grantham, Stamford, Sleaford, Gainsborough and other towns. Peacock, Handley & Co. opened their first office in Sleaford in 1792; in 1806 they started a separate bank in Newark and by 1826 had a branch in Bourne. In their later years Peacocks built a Lincoln branch with a magnificent terracotta façade and this is now the East Midland Electricity Company's showrooms in the High Street. Other private banks which operated for most of the 19th century were Eaton, Cayley & Co. of Stamford and Hardy & Co. of Grantham.

Several Lincolnshire merchants went into banking during the Napoleonic Wars but collapsed in the face of economic difficulties. There were failures in Gainsborough in 1803, Grantham in 1811 and Barton on Humber in 1812, but worse occurred in 1814 when several banks in Lincolnshire and adjacent counties went down like dominoes. Most of the firms which survived through the rigours of 1815 continued in business for most of the 19th century until they were respectably amalgamated with other banks after 1890. In fact between 1825 and 1844 only one bank failed in Lincolnshire which was the county with the second highest note circulation in England.

After 1817 trustee savings banks were established in many towns so that working men and small tradesmen could safely bank their takings and earn a little interest,

The Lincoln TSB had been established in 1816 and by 1819 there were others in 10 Lincolnshire towns. These all continued as independent banks until the 20th century when they gradually amalgamated into larger groupings such as the East Midlands TSB centred on Boston. Finally in the 1980s the TSB became a single national bank, no longer controlled by local trustees.

Private banks were limited by law to a maximum of six partners. Only after 1826 did it become legal to set up joint stock banks which could raise capital by the issue of shares in the company. Within ten years two such banks had been established with their head offices in Lincolnshire. The Stamford, Spalding and Boston Banking Co. had opened branches in those towns by 1836, and the Lincoln and Lindsey Banking Co. was launched in Lincoln in 1835 and soon had branches in Louth, Horncastle, Gainsborough and Brigg. The Hull Banking Co. opened some branches in the north of the county but had withdrawn by 1839. The fourth joint stock bank in the county was the National Provincial which established branches in Boston, Spalding and Long Sutton at this time.

In later years banks in adjacent counties opened branches in border towns such as Stamford, Grantham and Grimsby but it was not until the end of the 19th century that others penetrated deep into the county. The bank which had the most steady growth during the century was the Stamford, Spalding and Boston Banking Co. which established or took over branches in a number of Lincolnshire towns and in the adjacent counties of Leicestershire, Rutland and Northamptonshire.

Until 1891 most of Lincolnshire's banking needs were met by banks with headquarters in the county, the main exception being the National Provincial. The Lincoln and Lindsey had 15 branches in the county and Garfits and Ellisons also opened branches. The two main private banks each had some agents and branches in the county at different times, Garfits mainly in south and east Lincolnshire (plus Gainsborough where one of the family was a merchant) and Smith, Ellison & Co. in north and west Lindsey; in 1890 Garfits had nine and Smiths had seven.

All of the Lincolnshire banks were largely dependent on the prosperity of one industry–agriculture–and they were very vulnerable when that industry went into depression in the closing decades of the century. Salvation lay in amalgamation with other banks that were strong in non-agricultural districts, and the lead was taken by Garfit, Claypon & Co. which amalgamated with the Capital & Counties Bank in 1891. Smith, Ellison & Co. united with others in 1902 and the remaining three Lincolnshire banks joined other outside groups between 1911 and 1913.

Notes and further details on page 145.

Banking: 1750-1890

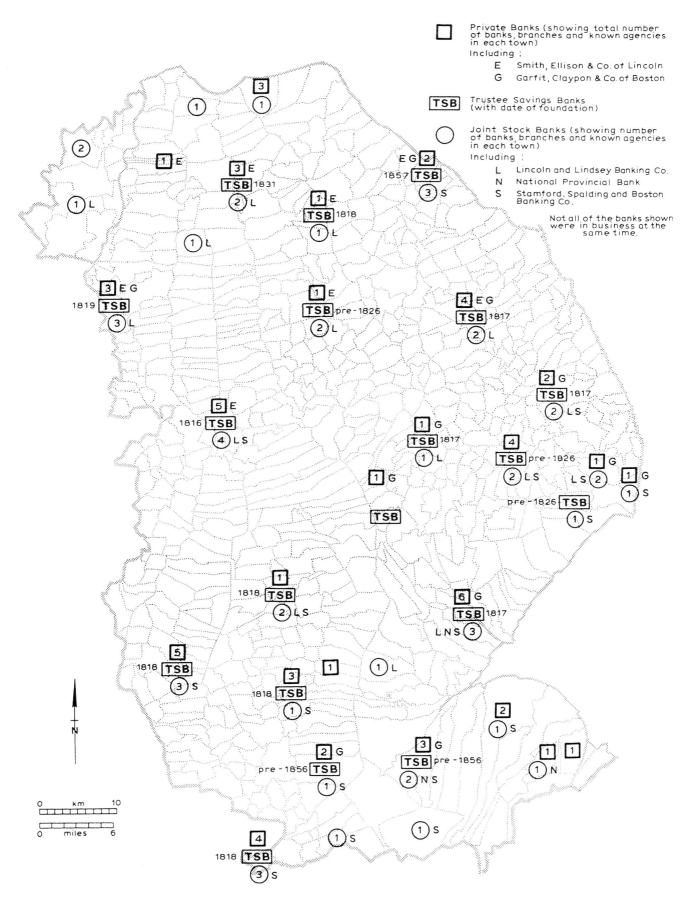

Private Banks (showing total number of banks, branches and known agencies in each town)
Including :
E   Smith, Ellison & Co. of Lincoln
G   Garfit, Claypon & Co. of Boston

TSB   Trustee Savings Banks (with date of foundation)

○   Joint Stock Banks (showing number of banks, branches and known agencies in each town)
Including :
L   Lincoln and Lindsey Banking Co.
N   National Provincial Bank
S   Stamford, Spalding and Boston Banking Co.

Not all of the banks shown were in business at the same time.

David Robinson

The cult of sea bathing, and drinking Neptune's Ale on doctor's orders, came relatively late to Lincolnshire because of the remoteness of the coast and lack of decent roads. By the second half of the 18th century a number of sea-bathing hotels were in business: the *Ship Inn* at Fosdyke on the sandy Welland estuary, *Neptune Inn* and *Pudding-pie House* at Skirbeck on the Witham estuary, and the *New Inn* at Saltfleet. A turnpike extension was built from Boston to Freiston Shore because of the popularity of the two hotels there, the *Plummers* and the *Marine*. It became 'the Brighton of the middle classes of Lincolnshire', but sea bathing ceased as saltmarsh replaced sand from the 1880s.[1] These early inns attracted visitors from Nottinghamshire and Leicestershire.

The first inn at Cleethorpes was the *Dolphin*, built about 1760.[2] By the mid-19th century there were two more inns (*Leeds Arms* and *Cliff House*) and 106 lodging houses. In 1842 part of the sea front was laid out for recreation. Visitors came from Yorkshire, Derbyshire and Lancashire, some by steamboat to Grimsby. The well-established *Vine Hotel* near Skegness claimed 'as clean a shore as any in England'. By the early 19th century there was also the *New (Hildred's) Hotel* (it too had a warm sea-bath) and 23 houses in Skegness took lodgers. The *Mablethorpe Hotel*, later *Book in Hand*, had 10 bedrooms, new houses were built to provide summer lodgings, and the village attracted day visitors long before the railway arrived. The original *Sutton Hotel* was replaced by the *Jolly Bacchus* about 1805 and offered hot and cold baths. Similar facilities were soon on offer at the *New Bathing Hotel* at Ingoldmells, just behind the sea bank near Vickers Point.[3]

The arrival of the railways promoted change. Grimsby was reached in 1848 and Cleethorpes in 1863; branches from the East Lincolnshire line reached Skegness in 1873, Mablethorpe in 1877 and Sutton in 1886. With the railways came the trippers: 30,000 to Cleethorpes (population 1,400) on 3 August 1863, and 10,000 to Skegness (population 500) on August Bank Holiday 1874. At Cleethorpes the railway company built sea defences to protect the cliff (1883-5), and the local council built the Kingsway Promenade and gardens (1902-6), the bathing pool and boating lake in the 1920s, and the Marine Embankment to the dunes at Humberston Fitties in 1930. Consequently all the amenity developments have been behind the sea defences.

The new town of Skegness, laid out to a grid pattern[4] by the Earl of Scarbrough in 1878, gained land from the sea after the building of the promenades. There the Marine Gardens were laid out (1887-8) and a Figure-Eight railway built (1908); the boating lake opened in 1924, the swimming pool in 1928, Butlin's Amusement Park and the Embassy Ballroom in 1929, and the Sun Castle in 1932. The pier, the fourth longest in Britain, opened in 1881, eight years after that at Cleethorpes.[5] Hotels sprang up along the Parades, including the large *Seacroft Hydro* (1908-9), together with convalescent homes such as the National Deposit Friendly Society (1927, now the Town Hall), and golf courses were laid out at either end of the resort—at Seacroft (1892-5) and North Shore (1911).

The Seaside Convalescent Home at Mablethorpe had opened in 1871, and the Leicester Poor Boys' and Girls' Summer Home in 1906. Plans in the 1880s for a fish dock at Sutton on Sea failed, but it gained The Park

as a piece of speculative building. Sutton was a 'select holiday resort', with a sea-wall promenade (1885), whereas Mablethorpe was more for the trippers, with amusements and concert parties on the sands and later Butlin's amusement park on the dunes.

By the time Billy Butlin opened his Luxury Holiday Camp (the first in Britain) at Ingoldmells in 1936, the age of the motor car had already given a new mobility to explore the remoter sandy seaside. Shacks appeared among the dunes, with iron huts at Bohemia near Sutton (by 1921), and there were plans for Rimac on Sea at Saltfleetby (1928) and the Tennyson Glen estate at Gibraltar Point (1930).[6] Chapel St Leonards was transformed from three farms and an inn to a seaside-orientated centre, and houses appeared on the dune top at Anderby Creek. The 1908 dream of a new garden village by the sea—Woldsea between Sandilands and Anderby Creek—was not to be, but today Lincolnshire has more caravans than any other maritime county, around 22,000, one-third of them at Ingoldmells.

Woodhall became a spa because of a failed attempt to sink a coal mine. Started in 1811, it was taken over by John Parkinson in 1821 but abandoned at a depth of 1,020 feet in 1823-4. The shaft filled with water and overflowed, and lord of the manor Thomas Hotchkin found it beneficial for his gout. Analysis showed the water to have more iodine and bromine than any other known mineral water, so Hotchkin built a pump room and bath house in 1838. The following year the *Victoria Hotel* (150 bedrooms) was built nearby. The branch railway (1855) brought more visitors. In the 1880s a syndicate bought 100 acres to lay out a new township planned by architect R.A. Came. By 1890 there were 100 dwellings in tree-lined avenues, with a shopping mall which developed into the 120-bedroom *Royal Hotel* (1897). In its Edwardian heyday (population 1,500) there could be 500 residents in the three hotels as well as those in the 65 boarding houses.[7] Woodhall Spa never recovered after the Great War. The *Victoria Hotel* burned down in 1920, the *Royal Hotel* was largely destroyed by a parachute mine in 1942, the railway closed in 1954, the well water ceased to be used in hydrotherapy, and the final blow came in 1983 when the buildings over the spa well collapsed into the shaft.

There was a smaller spa at Braceborough, where a bath house was established near his house by Dr. Francis Willis in 1841. The spring water was noted for its quality.[8] From 1860 the Spa was served by a halt on the Bourne to Essendine railway, but visitors were always small in number because of lack of accommodation. Despite attempts to revive the spa after the First World War,[9] it finally ceased in 1939.

Notes and further details on page 145.

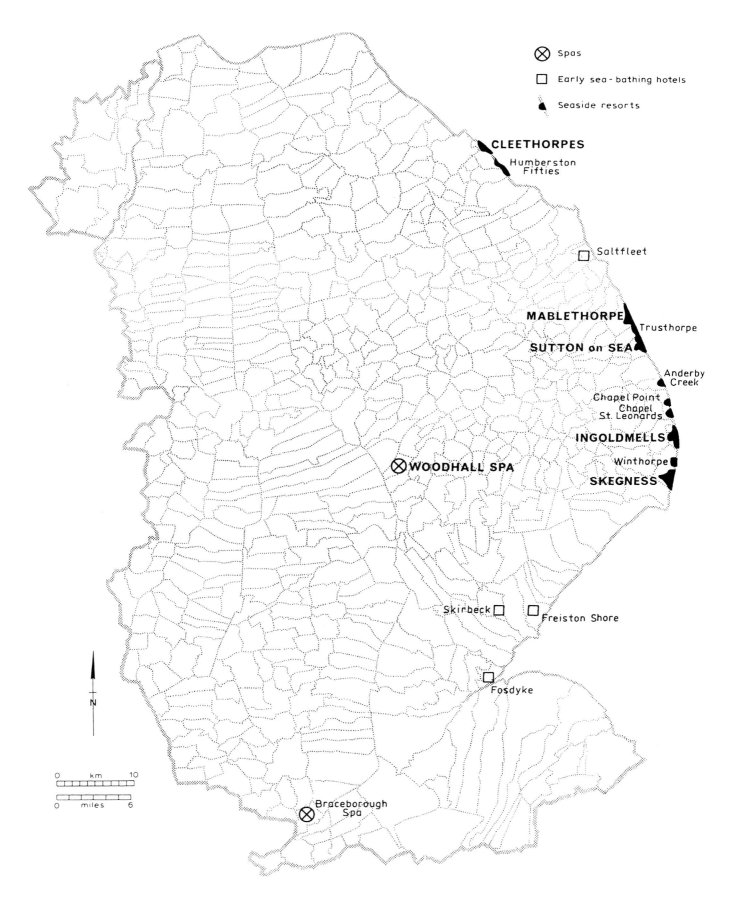

Spas

Early sea-bathing hotels

Seaside resorts

CLEETHORPES

Humberston
Fifties

Saltfleet

MABLETHORPE

Trusthorpe

SUTTON on SEA

Anderby
Creek

Chapel Point
Chapel
St. Leonards

INGOLDMELLS

Winthorpe

WOODHALL SPA

SKEGNESS

Skirbeck

Freiston Shore

Fosdyke

N

0 km 10

0 miles 6

Braceborough
Spa

During the 17th and 18th centuries strolling bands of players or 'comedians' came under official disapproval but theatrical performances were part of the social life of the aristocracy and during the 18th century the first theatres in Lincolnshire were erected at Stamford and Lincoln which were the main social centres in the county. The Stamford theatre was built sometime after 1718 and about 1731 Erasmus Audley erected the Lincoln theatre in Drury Lane in the city. In other towns players had to perform in warehouses or other impromptu settings for many more years. Until 1745 the courtroom in Spalding town hall was used regularly for that purpose.

In the late 18th century this situation changed dramatically and by 1820 theatres had proliferated. Some were still warehouses or primitive sheds in inn yards but others had been specially built as theatres. These included ones in Spalding (about 1760), Gainsborough (1772 and 1787), Boston (1777, replaced on a new site 1806), Grantham (also 1777, rebuilt 1800), Louth (by 1798) and Sleaford (1824). The Lincoln theatre was also rebuilt in 1806. These Georgian theatres were generally plain functional red brick buildings on the exterior, though the old theatre at Gainsborough was in the then fashionable Egyptian style. Inside the theatre the audience was on three levels, with the most discerning in boxes, and the rest either on a gallery above them or in the pit in front of them. Some theatres had an annual season of five or six weeks but other performances took place to coincide with events such as fairs, race meetings and assizes when the county gentry and their families would be in town. Out of season the theatres could be used for other purposes such as public dinners or political meetings.

The leading patrons of the Georgian theatres were the urban middle class, a small group of lawyers, merchants, doctors and clergy, but the entertainment also had to appeal to the unsophisticated mixed audience who filled the pit and the gallery. An evening's performance in such a theatre might well consist of a short comedy, two songs, a farce, and an extract from Shakespeare, or tumblers, slack-wire walkers and similar skills we now associate with the circus.

The construction of permanent theatres was associated with the creation of 'circuits' served by regular companies. The main circuit in the county was based on Lincoln, and included up to eleven theatres in Lincolnshire and adjacent counties. Stamford became part of the main circuit in the midlands. Early in the 19th century other companies were established in Gainsborough and Sleaford and served the neglected areas of north and east Lincolnshire. These circuits were not rigidly fixed and over the years towns could be visited by different companies.

The basis of the main circuit was established by William Herbert who became manager of the Lincoln theatre in 1750. In 1768 he moved the theatre downhill from Drury Lane to buildings which he adapted in Kings Arms Yard, where the present Theatre Royal now stands. Later the management was taken over by his son Nat Herbert in partnership with James Whitely of the largest midland circuit. Whitely had been visiting Stamford since at least 1752. His company performed on the opening night of the new theatre there and though Whitely died in 1781 his company continued until at least 1808. For many years the Lincoln circuit was run

by the Robinson family. In about 1806 James Smedley set up a new circuit in the northeast of the county, and managed it until 1841. From before 1807 until about 1830 there was also a company led by William Huggins based on the theatre in Gainsborough Old Hall, and they also visited Louth, Horncastle and Spalding.

The opening of railways made it easier for the gentry to travel to London or major provincial centres for more sophisticated theatre, and the audience left in a county like Lincolnshire could not provide a living for the local companies of actors. During the first half of Victoria's reign nearly all the theatres in Lincolnshire closed, and for a time most drama was again presented in sheds or other structures temporarily converted for the purpose. The theatre in Gainsborough Old Hall was removed in 1849 and the Boston theatre closed the same year. By 1856 the Grantham theatre had become a Methodist chapel and the Sleaford one was about to become an infant school, as did the Horncastle theatre in 1859. Stamford theatre closed in 1871 and became a billiard hall but the Lincoln one survived through to the theatrical revival at the end of the century.

Theatrical revival came through the growth of the Music Hall of the late Victorian period. This popular type of entertainment flourished in the new seaside resorts as well as in the larger towns such as Grimsby and Lincoln, and numerous large and gaudy theatres were built. The variety format of Music Hall provided a convenient way of showing early cinematic films which could be inserted as items in a bill of live entertainment. Early films were also shown in fairground booths, but gradually special 'Cinematograph Halls' were built in which film was the only or main entertainment. By 1913 there were 14 cinemas in the county, of which four were in Grimsby and two in Scunthorpe. In the 1920s and 1930s larger and grander cinemas in the Odeon and Regal style were erected in most Lincolnshire towns, but after only thirty or forty years they went into decline as television and later video became available to bring films directly into people's homes. In 1937 there were over 54 cinemas, in small towns such as Long Sutton, Market Rasen and Crowle as well as the main centres (there were 10 in Grimsby alone) but by 1991 there were only 12 left in the whole of Lincolnshire.

Popular theatre of the variety form, or featuring actors from television programmes, continues during the summer in the seaside resorts, and pantomime remains traditional during the Christmas period. The sessions house at Spilsby has been converted into a privately owned theatre but most theatres are now run by local authorities, and there are subsidised Arts Centres in the county at Stamford, Boston, Gainsborough and Grantham.

Notes and further details on page 146.

Public entertainment

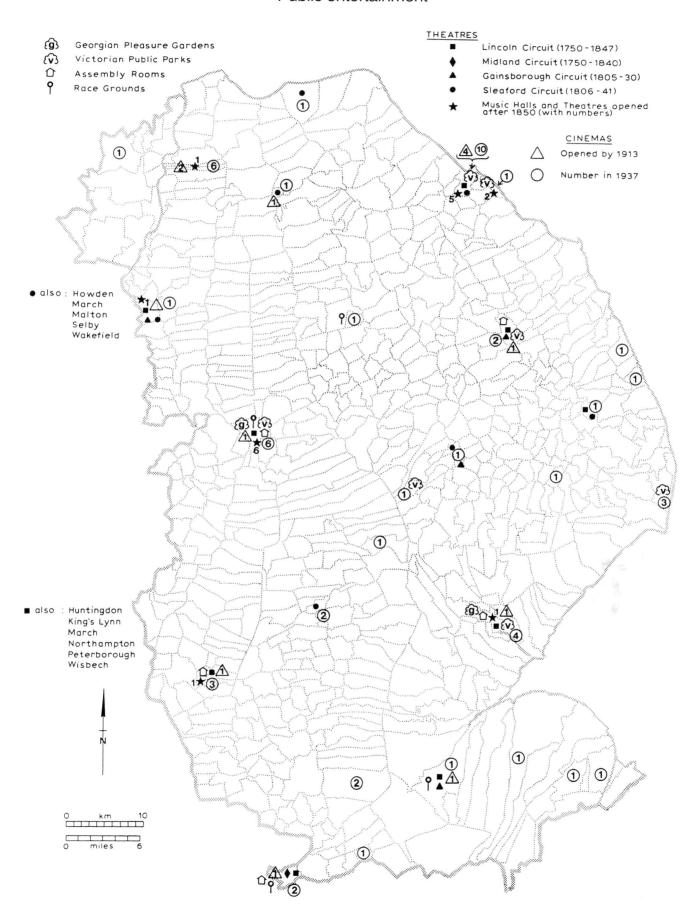

Georgian Pleasure Gardens

Victorian Public Parks

Assembly Rooms

Race Grounds

Lincoln Circuit (1750-1847)

Midland Circuit (1750-1840)

Gainsborough Circuit (1805-30)

Sleaford Circuit (1806-41)

Music Halls and Theatres opened after 1850 (with numbers)

CINEMAS

Opened by 1913

Number in 1937

● also : Howden
March
Malton
Selby
Wakefield

■ also : Huntingdon
King's Lynn
March
Northampton
Peterborough
Wisbech

0   km   10

0   miles   6

N

125

Lincolnshire is not a natural political unit; it is more realistically part of a wider East Midlands region. Nevertheless, for the purposes of this study, the nine constituencies show some interesting patterns. The Liberal decline nationally took place between 1906, when with 400 seats the Liberals formed a majority government, and 1935, when the Liberals returned a mere 21 seats in the General Election and were not even the official opposition. This decline was uneven, and the Liberals had moments of hope, but the crucial year was 1924. In retrospect this year, with the formation of the first Labour government, was the great divide. Many potential Liberal voters from now on voted Conservative to 'keep Labour out' and a much smaller number moved over to Labour as the only way of preventing perpetual Conservative government. The Liberals from that time onwards have been the confirmed third force in the Commons.[1]

In 1906, Lincolnshire had returned eight Liberals out of the 11 MPs then sent from the county. In 1935, not one genuine Liberal was returned out of the nine MPs who now represented the county. In Boston, the MP was a 'National Liberal', but he was part of a group of breakaway Liberals who were now welded to the Conservatives. The decline in Lincolnshire as elsewhere had been uneven both in time and location. In 1910, six out of 11 MPs had been Liberals; out of nine MPs in 1918, none. A by-election gain was made in Louth in 1920 and the seat was held in a second by-election in 1921. In the 1922 election, the Liberals rose to three out of the nine, and with one gain and one loss remained at three in 1923 but, in the great divide of 1924, in that year's General Election Lincolnshire Liberals did badly everywhere losing all of their three seats, and coming poorer seconds or thirds everywhere else. A modest revival led to a by-election gain in Boston in 1929, and this was held in the 1929 General Election, but it was to be the only Liberal seat this time. This MP was to follow Sir John Simon in 1931 and to become therefore a 'National Liberal', soon to sit with and support the Conservatives.

Of parallel interest between 1918 and 1929 is the rise of Labour.[2] Lincolnshire is not assumed to be fertile ground for the Labour Party, yet Brigg went to Labour in 1929, as did Boston in 1918, 1922 and 1923, and Lincoln in 1924 and 1929. By looking beyond the straight wins, however, at the shares of each poll gained by second and third candidates, and by comparing these with national averages, we can begin to see whether Lincolnshire is typical of the whole of the country, whether there are local variations, and, by scouring local newspapers, whether local factors seem to make much impact.

The graphs show the Liberal vote in general elections, constituency by constituency, from 1918 to 1931. In each case the constituency vote is compared with the national average per opposed candidate (the average vote gained by Liberal candidates in every constituency where they stood). The 1918 general election is too complicated for a national average per opposed candidate, since the Liberals were split between supporters of Lloyd George and those of Asquith, with a further complication that generally the Conservatives did not field candidates against Lloyd George supporters. This was the famous 'coupon election', with

interesting implications for Lincolnshire Liberals, where none stood bearing Lloyd George's and Bonar Law's endorsement. However in Grantham, for instance, the Liberal dilemma was revealed by R. Pattinson, who in his campaign felt compelled to sing the praises of Lloyd George as a war leader, and committed to support him as a Liberal, yet it was his opponent, Colonel Edmund Royds, who had Lloyd George's endorsement as a 'Coalition Conservative'.[3]

Where no Liberal candidate stood in a particular election, the graphs naturally leave a space, but this itself is often indicative of the state of the local Liberal Association. The pattern throughout the 1920s is of declining membership and finances.[4]

A special word needs to be said about Boston in the 1929 and 1931 general elections. J. Blindell, by-election victor in March 1929, proceeded to hold the seat, as a Liberal, in the General Election of May.[5] In 1931, the Liberals split for the third time since 1886, this time into three parts. Blindell aligned himself with that faction closest to the Conservatives (called 'National Liberals'). He therefore faced no Conservative opponent in 1931, hence the very high (over seventy per cent) vote for him. For this election in Boston he is compared not with other Liberals, but with National Liberals.

What conclusions can be tentatively drawn from this preliminary exercise? The nine constituencies divide themselves into three groups. The first group is of constituencies where the Liberals occasionally contested elections, and then performed below the national average. Brigg, Grimsby and Rutland-and-Stamford fall into this category. The second category includes those seats where the Liberals contested elections more often than not, and with mixed results, sometimes better than the national average, sometimes not. Lincoln is one of these, as are Grantham (with a victory in 1922), Gainsborough (with a victory in 1923) and Boston (with a victory in 1929, but see above for 1931). The final group of two constituencies, Louth and Horncastle, showed a Liberal vote consistently ahead of the national average in every election in this period, with victories both in 1922 and 1923. These two seats with their remarkably similar patterns clearly need further study for an explanation.[6]

One final conclusion vindicates Baldwin's tactics in 1924 of letting Labour form a minority government; in Lincolnshire it is noticeable that as the Liberal vote declined Labour hardly benefited. The Conservatives picked up the lion's share of ex-Liberal voters. Whereas in 1906 the Liberals won eight out of the then 11 Lincolnshire seats, Labour in 1945 managed only three out of nine.

Notes and further details on page 146.

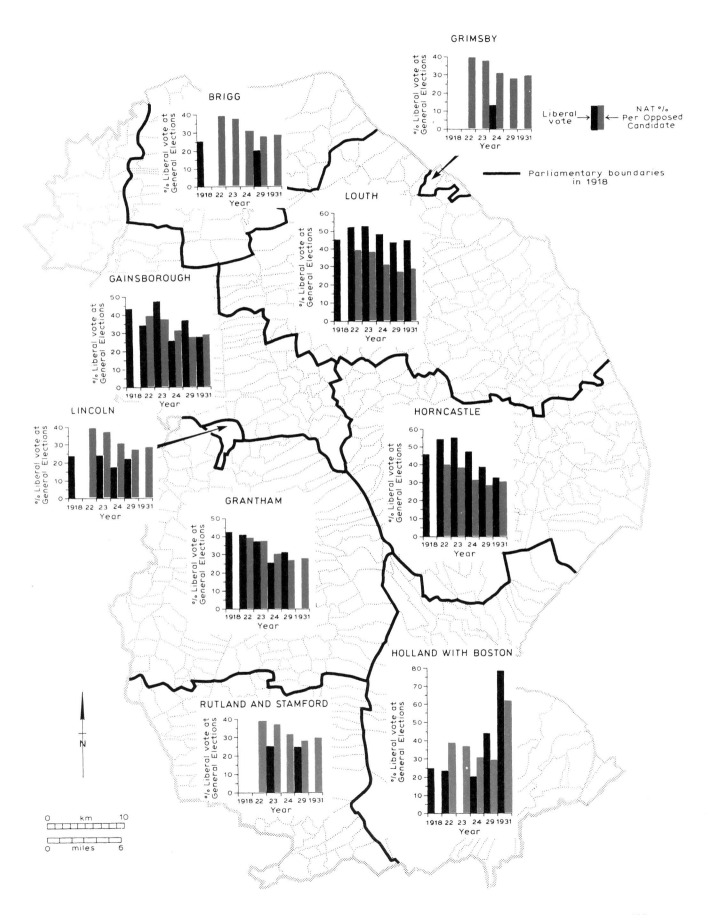

A rudimentary geography of dispensaries and hospitals has been put together from the wide range of directories published in the century 1826-1937 by William White and Kelly's, with some supplementation from local sources. The dates of establishment have not been exactly ascertained for some of the local authority hospitals. This is due to the inferior treatment they received from directory editors, presumably because these hospitals had not emerged from the charitable and public-spirited sentiments which were supposed to have been responsible for the setting-up of the voluntary hospitals. Nevertheless, local authority hospitals fared better than the infirmary sections of workhouses, about which little has been found in directories.

Disregarding medieval 'hospitals', the County Hospital in Lincoln was the first hospital to be established in the county. In 1769 a house on Waterside was taken for this purpose, but was replaced in 1777 by a new building in Drury Lane, which is now the Theological College. It was not until 1828 that a second hospital appeared–at Stamford, then a much bigger town in relative terms than it is now, and the Lincolnshire town situated nearest to London, from which new ideas often flowed. The table (see Notes and further details) gives the establishment dates for general voluntary hospitals, with population figures for appropriate dates.

Clearly there was only a very rough correspondence between a town's population and the date at which a hospital was opened. Why, for example, did Market Rasen acquire one long before Spalding, Bourne and, most particularly, Gainsborough? The solo effort of Mrs. C.A. Reynard, the rector's wife at Willingham by Stow, who built a 14-bed cottage hospital in a village with less than 500 people, probably has some bearing on the late provision in Gainsborough, only six miles away.

Woodhall Spa was another special case, as the hospital was part of the town's economy. Frodingham and Skegness came late because population growth was also late, and the disparity between Grimsby and Stamford is partly related to Grimsby's small population early in the century (4,048 in 1831 for example). Some towns, of course, served wide hinterlands, but Spilsby and Horncastle were late appearing on the scene despite their importance in this respect. In 1901 there were several substantial places without hospitals: Long Sutton (4,629), Sleaford (3,824), Barton (5,671) and Brigg (2,827).

An important element in early medical facilities was the establishment of dispensaries for the sick poor. In this respect Horncastle in 1789 was exceptionally forward-looking by national standards, the first dispensary being founded in London only in 1770. The idea caught on in nearby Boston in 1795 and Louth in 1803. In Horncastle and Louth the dispensaries served as the direct launch pads for the promotion of hospital schemes. Conversely, where a hospital was already in existence, with the exception of Lincoln, no general dispensary was subsequently set up. The tuberculosis dispensaries at Louth, Brigg and Horncastle were due to the initiative of the Lindsey County Council after the First World War.

This initiative should be seen alongside other local authority establishments of the late 19th and early 20th centuries: isolation, tuberculosis, smallpox and maternity hospitals and sanatoria. These specialised institutions came about to fill gaps in the facilities available in voluntary hospitals or in poor law infirmaries. Frequently this occurred because central government was laying down minimum standards of provision which had to be made available in each local government area by one means or another.

Workhouses have been left off the map owing to the difficulty in ascertaining the extent of their medical facilities; but it should be appreciated that these could be used by non-paupers who were willing to agree to a legal fiction that they could not afford treatment elsewhere.

The former workhouses at Bourne, Holbeach, Spilsby and Louth are still in use as hospitals.[1] That at Louth became the County Hospital and superseded the voluntary hospital in Crowtree Lane, recently turned into a boarding house for the Grammar School. At Grimsby the Scartho Road Hospital was set up as a Poor Law Infirmary in 1892, when the Grimsby Union was formed out of the urban part of the Caistor Union. It was increasingly used as a general hospital and was taken over by the Borough Council in 1930 on the abolition of the Poor Law Guardians.[2] This Poor Law hospital is marked on the map.

Special arrangements had to be made at the two main ports to cope with the quarantining of persons with foreign, often tropical diseases. A variety of arrangements was made at Grimsby from about 1880, including the use of a hospital ship at one stage in the 1890s. At Boston the Port Sanitary Authority called its institution in Skirbeck the Cholera, Yellow Fever and Plague Hospital, but as at Grimsby the letter P has been used to designate it.

The map also shows the three main mental hospitals, but no attempt has been made to trace doctors' residences which were used as small private asylums, as at Greatford (Dr. Willis) and Horncastle (Dr. Harrison).

Notes and further details on page 146.

Establishment dates of hospitals and dispensaries

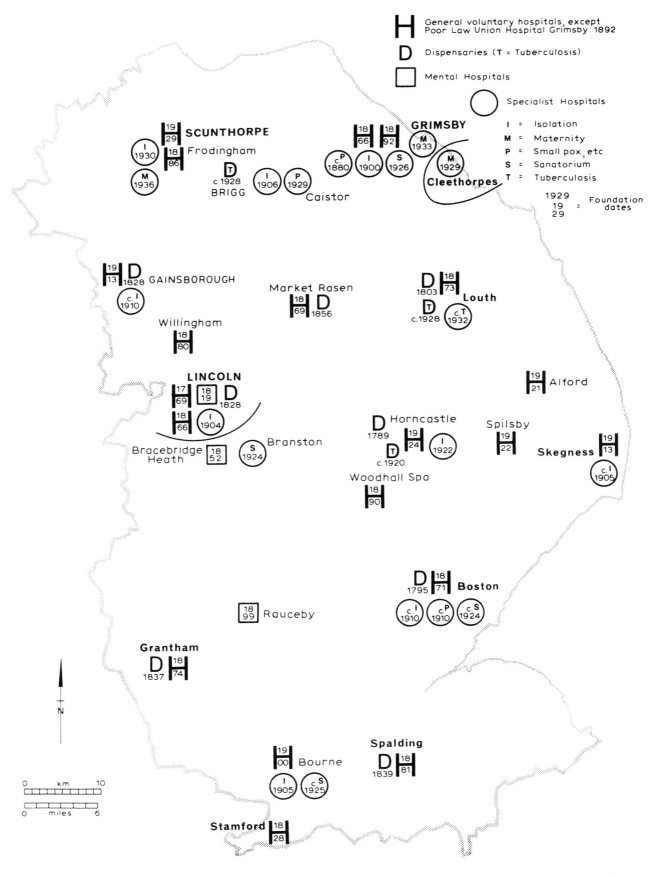

Military aircraft were first based in Lincolnshire on the outbreak of the First World War, when a squadron of the Royal Naval Air Service (RNAS) arrived just outside Skegness to patrol the coast. Killingholme quickly took over this role and by 1918 grew into a major flying base, patrolling out over the North Sea as far as the Heligoland Bight. In 1915, the RNAS also opened a large airfield at Cranwell to train its aircraft and airship pilots who went on to Freiston for bombing and gunnery training.

Zeppelin attacks caused great public outcry and from 1916 the Royal Flying Corps (RFC), the army's air branch, established a chain of Home Defence fighter airfields along the east coast. Six were built in Lincolnshire, along the cliff north and south of Lincoln, but despite constant patrols no Zeppelins were attacked. Emergency Landing Grounds were also dotted around the county so that the Home Defence fighters could land to refuel. The huge losses of RFC aircrew on the western front meant a great increase in flying training and Lincolnshire's flat countryside, sparse population and lack of industrial haze attracted the airfield surveyors. Several training airfields opened from 1916 on and were kept very busy; there were many accidents due to the frailty of these early aircraft and the inexperience of the trainees. In 1918 German submarines were torpedoing merchant ships close to the British coast, causing coastal patrol flights to be formed, particularly near to ports. North Coates and Greenland Top housed two of these.

The Royal Air Force was formed by amalgamating the RFC and the RNAS on 1 April 1918 but the work of the 35 Lincolnshire airfields was little affected and carried on until the war ended, when most of them closed. The end of the war also affected Lincoln's engineering firms which had built several thousand aircraft, these being flight tested from the West Common.

France was then regarded as the only country strong enough to pose a threat so the RAF's operational units were in the south. However, Lincolnshire's suitability for flying training had been amply demonstrated so that in 1920 the RAF College was sited at Cranwell. Grantham and Digby also trained pilots, the three stations producing two-thirds of the RAF's needs in the 1920s. Waddington reopened in 1926 to house Lincoln's Auxiliary Air Force Squadron, and in 1927 North Coates and Sutton Bridge became armament training camps. The RAF's squadrons came to one of these for a week each year, using the ranges at Donna Nook and Holbeach.

By the early 1930s, peace was no longer secure and by 1935 Nazi Germany was a definite threat. Lincolnshire was now in range of the Luftwaffe's bombers and, conversely, RAF bombers had to be in eastern England to reach Germany. The training units started to move west, fighters flew into Digby and some new airfields opened. When war broke out, Waddington, Scampton and Hemswell housed six squadrons of Hampden bombers comprising 5 Group, Bomber Command. The Hampdens were in action immediately and bore the brunt of operations until 1941 when they were replaced by the Manchester (briefly) and then by the Lancaster. In the north of the county, Wellingtons served with 1 Group until they were also replaced by the 'Lanc'. New airfields opened almost monthly until 1943 and by April 1945 21 bomber airfields could dispatch a force of 700

Lancasters against the Third Reich. Losses were severe, however. Some 20,000 airmen lost their lives flying from Lincolnshire bases, not all falling to enemy flak or fighters; over 300 Lancasters crashed in the county due to damage, mechanical problems, bad weather or pilot error.

The bomber operations were so large in scale that they overshadowed the RAF's other activities in the county but these were also helping the war effort. Day and night fighters operated from Digby, Kirton in Lindsey, Coleby Grange, Wellingore and Hibaldstow, directed by the radar stations at Stenigot, Orby, Langtoft, Skendleby and Humberston, aided by the Royal Observer Corps. Training increased dramatically at Cranwell, Grantham and other stations, whilst North Coates and, for a time, Strubby operated a dangerous war against enemy shipping off the north European coast. The U.S. Army Air Force took paratroops and gliders to the major airborne operations from three airfields around Grantham. On the ground, bomb stores supplied the airfields, Rauceby hospital cared for the injured, Grimsby's high-speed launches rescued ditched airmen and the radio stations listened to, and confused, German transmissions. Thousands of airmen and women from many countries served in the county and many acres of farmland were covered by concrete.

Many stations closed down in 1945-6 but Stalin's Russia posed a new threat and Lincoln bombers remained at five airfields in the county; other bases, notably Cranwell and Swinderby, continued to train future pilots. The first jet bombers, Canberras, arrived at Binbrook in 1951 and by the late 1950s the Vulcan formed the main nuclear deterrent. Thor ICBMs, also part of the deterrent, were based at several former airfields for a few years, Bloodhound anti-aircraft missiles protected these deterrent forces, later supplemented by Binbrook's Lightnings, and Coningsby's Phantoms.

In the twilight of its service the Vulcan dropped bombs in anger during the Falklands War, but was then withdrawn from service, leaving Lincolnshire no longer 'Bomber County'. The end of the Cold War saw several stations close, whilst others changed roles, Scampton housing the Central Flying School and the famous Red Arrows, before closure in 1995. Swinderby's School of Recruit Training closed in 1993. The remaining stations expanded to house units from closed stations around the county. Cranwell, still the RAF College, is also home to the Central Flying School and the non pilot aircrew training unit, plus the East Midlands University Air Squadron Air Experience Flight. The Red Arrows moved back to a small reopened part of Scampton in 2000, whilst Barkston Heath is the civilian-run Joint Elementary Flying Training School where pilots are trained for all three services. Also catering for all three services, and Americans, is the Joint Services Signals Unit at Digby. Two airfields are still in the front-line. Coningsby with its Tornado fighters, soon to be replaced by the Eurofighter, and home of the Battle of Britain Memorial Flight, and Waddington, with the Sentry flying radar stations and Nimrod 'ears in the sky', to be joined in 2005 by a new squadron operating a new radar system.

Notes and further details on page 146.

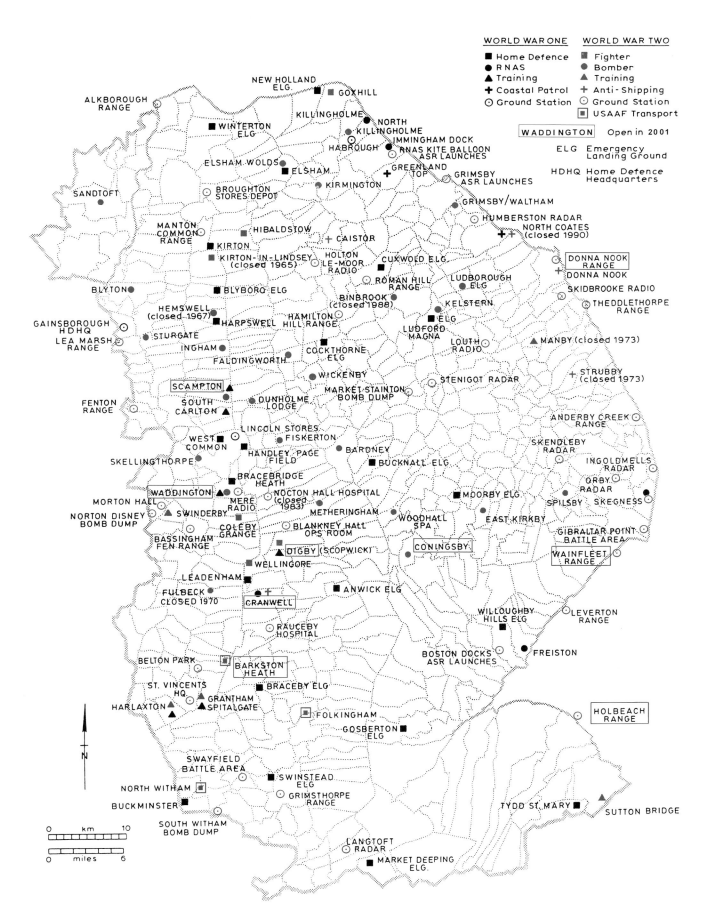

WORLD WAR ONE
- ■ Home Defence
- ● RNAS
- ▲ Training
- + Coastal Patrol
- ⊙ Ground Station

WORLD WAR TWO
- ■ Fighter
- ● Bomber
- ▲ Training
- + Anti-Shipping
- ⊙ Ground Station
- ▣ USAAF Transport

WADDINGTON   Open in 2001

ELG   Emergency Landing Ground

HDHQ   Home Defence Headquarters

ALKBOROUGH RANGE

NEW HOLLAND ELG.   GOXHILL

KILLINGHOLME   NORTH KILLINGHOLME
IMMINGHAM DOCK
HABROUGH   RNAS KITE BALLOON ASR LAUNCHES

WINTERTON ELG

ELSHAM WOLDS   ELSHAM   GREENLAND TOP   GRIMSBY ASR LAUNCHES

KIRMINGTON   GRIMSBY/WALTHAM

SANDTOFT   BROUGHTON STORES DEPOT

HUMBERSTON RADAR
NORTH COATES (closed 1990)

MANTON COMMON RANGE   HIBALDSTOW   CAISTOR

KIRTON   HOLTON LE-MOOR RADIO   CUXWOLD ELG   LUDBOROUGH ELG   DONNA NOOK RANGE
KIRTON-IN-LINDSEY (closed 1965)   DONNA NOOK

BLYBORO ELG   ROMAN HILL RANGE   SKIDBROOKE RADIO

BLYTON   BINBROOK (closed 1988)   KELSTERN   THEDDLETHORPE RANGE

HEMSWELL (closed 1967)   HAMILTON HILL RANGE   ELG
HARPSWELL   LUDFORD MAGNA
GAINSBOROUGH HDHQ   STURGATE   LOUTH RADIO   MANBY (closed 1973)
LEA MARSH RANGE   INGHAM   COCKTHORNE ELG
FALDINGWORTH   STRUBBY (closed 1973)

WICKENBY   STENIGOT RADAR

SCAMPTON   MARKET STAINTON BOMB DUMP

FENTON RANGE   DUNHOLME LODGE   ANDERBY CREEK RANGE
SOUTH CARLTON

LINCOLN STORES   SKENDLEBY RADAR

WEST COMMON   FISKERTON   INGOLDMELLS RADAR
HANDLEY PAGE FIELD   BARDNEY   ORBY RADAR
SKELLINGTHORPE   BUCKNALL ELG   SPILSBY   SKEGNESS

BRACEBRIDGE HEATH   MOORBY ELG

WADDINGTON   NOCTON HALL HOSPITAL (closed 1983)   EAST KIRKBY   GIBRALTAR POINT BATTLE AREA
MORTON HALL   MERE RADIO   WOODHALL SPA
NORTON DISNEY BOMB DUMP   SWINDERBY   METHERINGHAM
COLEBY GRANGE   BLANKNEY HALL OPS ROOM   CONINGSBY   WAINFLEET RANGE
BASSINGHAM FEN RANGE
DIGBY (SCOPWICK)

WELLINGORE

LEADENHAM   LEVERTON RANGE
FULBECK CLOSED 1970   ANWICK ELG
CRANWELL   WILLOUGHBY HILLS ELG

RAUCEBY HOSPITAL
BOSTON DOCKS ASR LAUNCHES   FREISTON

BELTON PARK   BARKSTON HEATH

ST. VINCENTS HQ   BRACEBY ELG
GRANTHAM
HARLAXTON   SPITALGATE   FOLKINGHAM   HOLBEACH RANGE

GOSBERTON ELG

SWAYFIELD BATTLE AREA

NORTH WITHAM   SWINSTEAD ELG
BUCKMINSTER   GRIMSTHORPE RANGE   TYDD ST. MARY   SUTTON BRIDGE
SOUTH WITHAM BOMB DUMP

LANGTOFT RADAR

MARKET DEEPING ELG.

N

0   km   10

0   miles   6

Urban evolution is rarely a smooth process. A brief glance at Lincoln's development shows that this city is no exception. The long-term trend of urban growth has been punctuated by peaks and troughs in the city's social and economic fortunes. Over two millennia Lincoln has undergone several metamorphoses in its development from a pre-Roman lakeside settlement ('lin' meaning lake) to the 21st-century city we know today. Most of those earlier phases have left enduring remnants. Walls and other remains of the Roman colonia are still in evidence, as are medieval and later buildings, including, of course, the Minster and other ecclesiastical buildings.

Cycles of prosperity and decline were such that, for much of the period after the establishment of the Roman settlement, the overall growth of the urban area was relatively modest. Although there was significant growth in medieval times (Lincoln being second in population size to London at the time of the Conquest), the greatest expansion started only in the 19th century. The roots of modern Lincoln are bedded deep in the heavy engineering industry which spread the city's name far across the globe in the 19th and early 20th centuries, stamped indelibly on steam-engines, cranes and other products of the works which dominated Lincoln's economy for so many decades. The impact on the evolution of the urban fabric can be seen not only in the remnants of the works themselves, but also in the streets of terraced houses east and west of High Street and north and south of Monks Road, terraces built to house the thousands of people employed in the nearby works.

The coming of the railway (1846) was, of course, crucial to the industrial development of Lincoln, and had significant and lasting effects on the city's urban form. Like the waterways, it followed the line of least resistance, the Lincoln Gap, which gives the city its distinctive uphill/downhill form. Thus the railways and most of the heavy industrial works dominated a broad band of land running west/east through the Lincoln Gap alongside the waterways: the Fossdyke navigation, Brayford Pool and the River Witham. The bulk of the historic core (based on the Roman colonia and dominated by the cathedral) lay to the north, while to the south the built-up area stretched southwards in a thin line alongside the old Roman road, Ermine Street. The terraced houses alongside the works had started to give the southern extension more depth. Although much of this part of the city was still contained within the limits of the medieval settlement, which had terminated at the South Bar (south end of the High Street) with the River Witham and Sincil Dyke forming western and eastern boundaries respectively, the workers' houses had now spread into the area east of Sincil Bank.

Suburbs for the affluent (and personally mobile) middle classes had already started to grow up in areas like St Catherine's and parts of the West End. The advent of public transport then began to have a marked effect on the city's form. Trams and buses enabled larger numbers of people to live further from their places of work. As a result, the city spread further south along Newark Road, east along Monks Road and west along Carholme Road. This linear extension of the urban area was less marked uphill, but expansion later took a new form in that part of the city when the first 'edge-of-town' local authority housing estate was established at St Giles. Others followed–Ermine to the north, and

Westwick Gardens and The Manse in the south. This led to the characteristic hour-glass shape which was a feature of Lincoln for most of the 20th century, amplified by the effects of increasing car-ownership. North/south traffic flows were constrained by both the waterways and the railways. Until recently there were within the City Centre two bridges over the water for vehicles– Wigford Way (opened 1972) and Thorn Bridge (Broadgate)–High Bridge having been effectively closed to traffic when High Street was pedestrianised in 1974. The new university road bridge has had an enormous impact on traffic flow and with Pelham Bridge (1957) provides north/south routes through the City Centre which does not involve a level crossing.

What, then, can this idiosyncratic gallop through Lincoln's past suggest about future changes? One clear pointer is the past impact of changes in transport technology. Increasing access to public and then private transport had stimulated the expansion of towns and cities during the 20th century. Until recently, continuation of that trend seemed inevitable. However, mounting concerns about environmental, social and economic effects of car-dependency have started to influence political decisions and a significant change of direction can now be expected. The need to reduce dependence on cars and to promote efficient public transport, together with walking and cycling, is already changing attitudes among those with responsibility for planning urban areas. Such changes take time, but will affect the future form of cities such as Lincoln. Already the next major housing area, Skewbridge, is being planned with increased emphasis on the needs of pedestrians and cyclists. Ways of making more effective use of Lincoln's railways for local journeys are being examined. Extension of the by-pass around the city's eastern side will give new opportunities to exclude from central parts of the city all but essential traffic. There may be several 'Park and Ride' sites, linked to the city centre by bus, train, and perhaps even boat.

The educational face of the city has been transformed by the university which with the retail redevelopment of the old St Mark's railway station has regenerated derelict land within the built-up area. The conventional approach of segregating land uses will probably become outdated with the realisation that carefully planned, but mixed, patterns of land use can help to minimise the need for car travel. Similarly, the damaging side-effects of the almost total displacement from many parts of the city of housing by shops and offices are now widely appreciated (desertion after the shops close, crime, vandalism) and houses and flats will become an increasingly important part of the mixture of city centre uses.

Notes and further details on page 146.

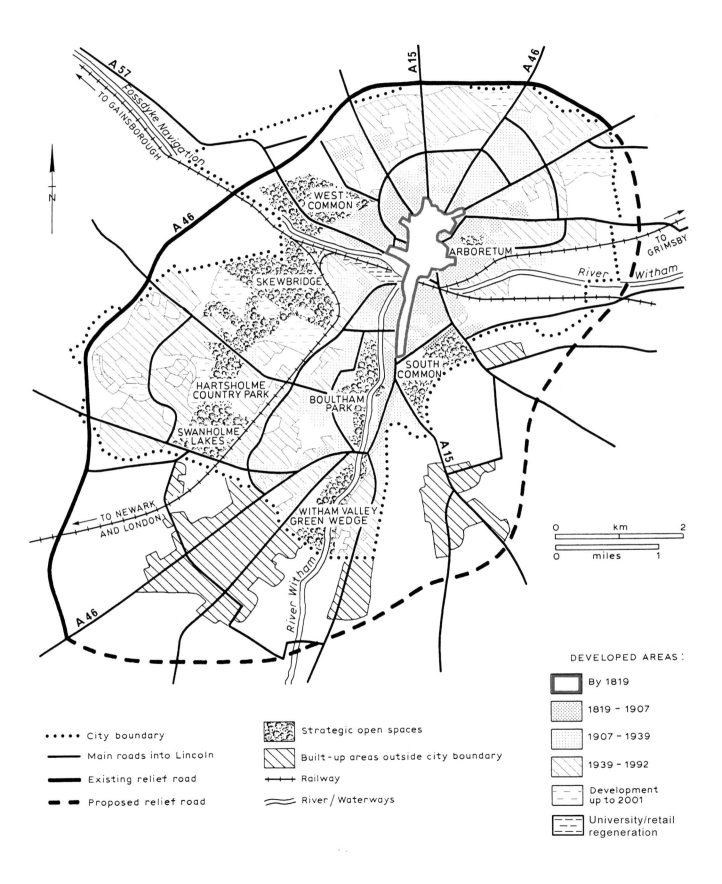

A 57

Fossdyke Navigation

TO GAINSBOROUGH

A 46

A 15

A 46

WEST COMMON

ARBORETUM

TO GRIMSBY

River Witham

SKEWBRIDGE

HARTSHOLME COUNTRY PARK

BOULTHAM PARK

SOUTH COMMON

SWANHOLME LAKES

A 15

TO NEWARK AND LONDON

WITHAM VALLEY GREEN WEDGE

River Witham

A 46

| 0 | km | 2 |
| 0 | miles | 1 |

DEVELOPED AREAS :

☐ By 1819

▦ 1819 - 1907

▦ 1907 - 1939

▧ 1939 - 1992

☐ Development up to 2001

☐ University/retail regeneration

• • • • • City boundary

—— Main roads into Lincoln

━━ Existing relief road

━ ━ Proposed relief road

▨ Strategic open spaces

▨ Built-up areas outside city boundary

+ + + Railway

〜〜 River / Waterways

133

Peter Raspin

As a result of the Local Government reorganisation of 1996 the County of Humberside, which had since 1974 administered both the north and south banks of the Humber, was replaced by new unitary authorities. Lincolnshire remained as it had since 1974 with its administrative centre at Lincoln; North Lincolnshire's administrative centre is at Scunthorpe and the much smaller North East Lincolnshire at Grimsby.

In the last ten to fifteen years of the 20th century Lincolnshire experienced a period of change. In many parts of the county, but particularly in the south, population and associated development increased significantly as new migrants recognised the advantages of the Lincolnshire environment. Elsewhere, most notably in the south Humber area, change occurred as declining traditional industries, such as steel, heavy engineering and fishing, were gradually replaced by more modern employment enterprises. For the future, the planning authorities of Lincolnshire are determined to take advantage of the opportunities offered by this period of change. Their policies will essentially be positive and also fully aware of the need to protect all that is best and most attractive in the county. Lincolnshire's diversity is one of its advantages and this must be both protected and further promoted in the future.

The first image people have of Lincolnshire is still that of an extensive agricultural county, and this remains true with over 1.5 million acres of farming land, much of which is of the highest quality. Whilst the farming industry is currently experiencing problems, it is almost certain that, in the national interest, the majority of Lincolnshire land will remain in agricultural production. In future, however, Central Government and other EU measures could lead to greater diversification and the introduction of more sustainable and environmentally acceptable methods of production. Closely associated with agriculture, food processing is also a large industry, particularly in the south of the county and around Grimsby, and it is important that it continues to develop as a significant source of local employment.

The next twenty years could see the population of 'historic' Lincolnshire rise to nearly one million people, a seven per cent increase. Many new homes will be needed to house this population, but the county will not be transformed into endless suburbia. On the contrary, Lincolnshire will still remain one of the most sparsely populated counties in England, but this new growth provides the opportunity to consolidate the major urban centre, regenerate the many market towns and also help to sustain many rural communities and their vital local facilities such as the school, shop and Post Office.

As Lincolnshire develops, the communications network must be further improved. As for roads, the M180 runs through the north of the county, and the A1 skirts the western edge, but elsewhere there is very little dual carriageway. Lincoln will soon have a dual carriageway link to the A1 at Newark and major improvements are programmed from the south to Peterborough and along the east-west link to the coast, but further road building is still needed. Unnecessary travel by private car and lorry is perceived as being less supportable, so the rail and bus networks are likely to be developed. A direct rail connection to London from Lincoln is a distinct possibility, as are local station re-openings and an extensive Inter-Connect bus service linking the market towns with the villages in their hinterlands will be greatly expanded. The county's main ports of Immingham, Grimsby, Boston, Sutton Bridge and wharfage facilities along the Humber, Trent and

Welland are also likely to be developed further, as connections and water-borne trade with Europe continue to be consolidated. Kirmington airport is also likely to offer an enhanced service to Lincolnshire residents and visitors.

Improved communications play a key role in attracting new industry and employment into many parts of Lincolnshire. The perception of peripherality and isolation must be overcome before the county can fulfil its potential and successfully market itself. Larger urban centres with their modern business parks have much to offer prospective developers, whilst the new high-technology, 'footloose' enterprises are ideally suited to attractive rural but accessible locations. The establishment and rapid expansion of the University of Lincolnshire and Humberside in Lincoln during the late 1990s have a key role to play in the county's future development. Not only will the university make Lincolnshire better known in the national context, but it can also act as a major catalyst for future growth and investment.

As Lincolnshire becomes better known, its already significant tourist industry must develop and prosper. The traditional popularity of the holiday coast, based around Skegness, Ingoldmells, Mablethorpe and Cleethorpes, needs to be maintained, but it is hoped that the wider attractions of the county will also become increasingly appreciated. These include the Lincolnshire Wolds Area of Outstanding Natural Beauty, gems such as Stamford and Woodhall Spa, and of course Lincoln with its famous cathedral and historic uphill area. Lincoln has the potential to become one of the major tourist attractions of the future. Tourism should generally be encouraged, but this should not be at the expense of the county's attractive and peaceful character. The county's historic towns and buildings will continue to be preserved and enhanced, and the unique and extensive countryside protected from adverse development. In this context, small scale or 'green' tourism is likely to assume more importance, perhaps linked to Lincolnshire's internationally recognised areas of nature conservation, notably the Wash and Humber estuaries.

One often forgotten aspect of Lincolnshire is its involvement in the minerals industry. The expanding port of Immingham is of national importance as an oil terminal and refining centre. Theddlethorpe has a large natural gas terminal, and the county itself is the second largest producer of on-shore oil in England. The derricks and nodding donkeys are already familiar parts of the landscape to the north of Lincoln. About 180 million tons of coal reserves are also located in the Witham prospect, between Lincoln and Newark and, whilst there are no immediate plans to develop this resource, its future exploitation would be both a major challenge and a significant change for Lincolnshire.

Lincolnshire's future prospects depend on how successfully it can adapt to and harness the opportunities for change. Planned and co-ordinated development and re-generation have already, in the 1990s, shown the way forward. A successful future for the county and its inhabitants lies not in resisting change but in understanding, guiding, and taking advantage of it. This is the key challenge facing the county planner in the future—shaping a modern Lincolnshire well equipped for the 21st century, but a Lincolnshire still retaining its unique character that is so much a product of its distinguished history.

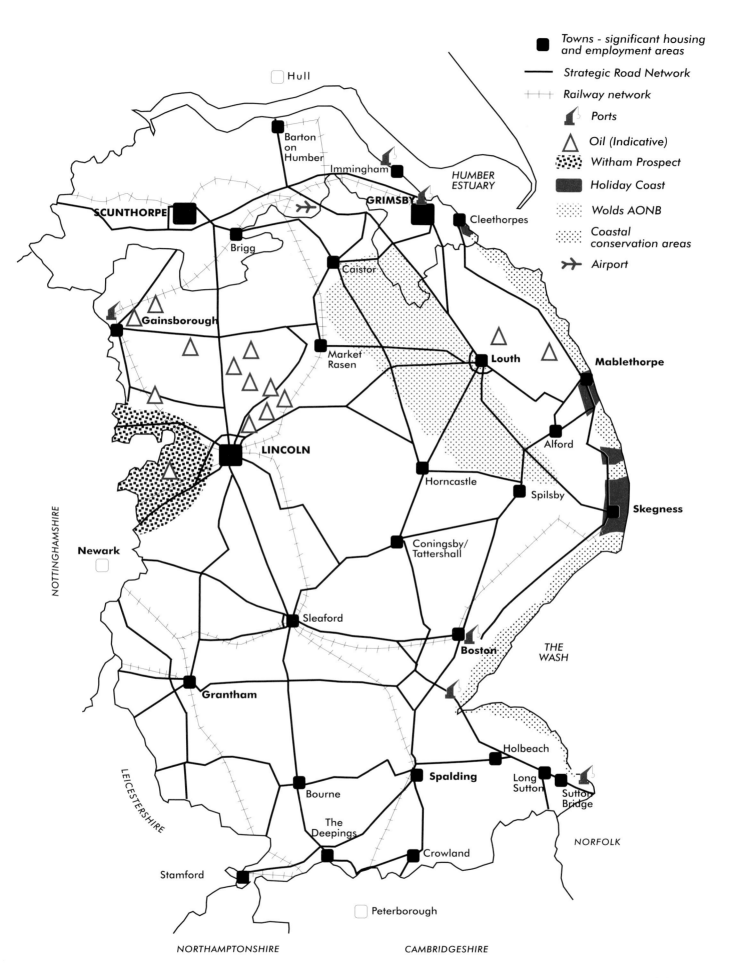

Map Legend

- **Towns** - significant housing and employment areas
- **Strategic Road Network**
- **Railway network**
- **Ports**
- **Oil (Indicative)**
- **Witham Prospect**
- **Holiday Coast**
- **Wolds AONB**
- **Coastal conservation areas**
- **Airport**

Hull

Barton on Humber

Immingham

HUMBER ESTUARY

GRIMSBY

Cleethorpes

SCUNTHORPE

Brigg

Caistor

Gainsborough

Market Rasen

Louth

Mablethorpe

Alford

LINCOLN

Horncastle

Spilsby

Skegness

Newark

Coningsby/Tattershall

Sleaford

Boston

THE WASH

NOTTINGHAMSHIRE

Grantham

Holbeach

Spalding

Long Sutton

Sutton Bridge

LEICESTERSHIRE

Bourne

The Deepings

Crowland

NORFOLK

Stamford

Peterborough

NORTHAMPTONSHIRE

CAMBRIDGESHIRE

FURTHER INFORMATION

ABBREVIATIONS

AASRP   *Associated Architectural Societies Reports and Papers*
HL   History of Lincolnshire
LAASRP   *Lincolnshire Architectural and Archaeological Society Reports and Papers*
LAO   Lincolnshire Archives Office
LHA   *Lincolnshire History and Archaeology*
LNQ   *Lincolnshire Notes and Queries*
LRS   Lincoln Record Society
PRO   Public Record Office

1. THE MAKING OF THE LANDSCAPE
Note

TABLE 1: Geological Succession

Stage	Age (years B.P.)	Climate
	up to 10,000	
Flandrian		Temperate
Devensian		Cold: glacial ice reached Lincolnshire
	100,000	
		Warm temperate
	130,000	
Wolstonian		Cool-cold: no glacial ice in Lincolnshire
	180,000	
Hoxnian		Warm temperate
	250,000	
Anglian		Cold: glacial ice covered Lincolnshire
	300,000	
Cromerian		Warm temperate
	350,000	

Bibliography
J.D. De Jong, 'The Quaternary of the Netherlands', *The Quaternary* 12 (1967), 301-426.
R.W. Gallois, 'Geological investigations for the Wash Water Storage Scheme', *Institute of Geological Sciences Report* 78/19 (1979), 22-3.
'The Pleistocene in Great Britain', *Geofile* 109 (1988).
J. Rose, 'Status of the Wolstonian Glaciation in the glaciation in the British Quaternary', *Quaternary Newsletter* 53 (1987), 1-9.
I. Shennan, 'Flandrian sea level changes in the Fenland', *Journal of Quaternary Science* 1 (1986), 155-79.
I. Shennan, 'Holocene sea level changes in the North Sea region', in *Sea Level Changes,* eds. M.J. Tooley and I. Shennan (Oxford, 1987), pp. 109-51.
A. Straw, 'Pre-Devensian glaciation of Lincolnshire (Eastern England) and adjacent areas, *Quaternary Science Review* 2 (1983), 229-60.
A. Straw and K. Clayton, *The Geomorphology of the British Isles: Eastern and Central England* (1979).
P. Worsley, 'Pre-Devensian glaciation of Lincolnshire' in *The Wolstonian,* ed. A. Bilham-Boult (Lincoln, 1988), 1-4.

2. SOLID GEOLOGY
Notes
1   This effect is emphasised by a progressive thinning of many Lower Cretaceous beds towards the north-west and the successive overlap of Upper over Lower Cretaceous beds in the same direction.

2   Oil and gas found within these deep strata are currently being extracted near Corringham, Gainsborough, Glentworth and Welton.
3   Local names are often attached to these beds, such as 'Kirton Cementstones' and 'Collyweston Slate'.
4   The Middle to Upper Jurassic stratigraphic boundary within this thin deposit is based upon the different species of fossils found within its lower and upper beds.
5   A local variation is formed in their lower part by the 'Elsham Sandstone', a seven metres thick lens of cemented sandstone.
6   Recent work on rare fossils shows that they cross the Jurassic-Cretaceous boundary.
7   Only the lower part of the Burnham Formation (Middle to Upper Chalk) is now present in the county, although higher zones may have been present pre-glacially.

3. DRIFT GEOLOGY
Notes
1   In north-west Lincolnshire, the Mercia Mudstone (Triassic) gives the tills a dark red matrix, while other areas have blue, grey or yellowish tills due to the different clays involved.
2   For example 'Rhomb Porphyry' from southern Norway and 'Borrowdale Volcanics' from the English Lake District.
3   For example the 'glacial clays' near Killingholme that were investigated for a nuclear waste disposal site.
4   The similarity of their rock type constituents to those of the parent till less the more soluble materials should provide confirmation.
5   No extensive deposits of this type indicating large lakes have been recorded, the known deposits all being too small to show on this map and located in areas close to postulated ice-front positions from other evidence.

4. NATURAL REGIONS
Bibliography
H.H. Swinnerton and P.E. Kent, *The Geology of Lincolnshire* (Lincoln, 1976).
D.N. Robinson, 'Geology and Scenery' (9-16) in E.J. Gibbons, *The Flora of Lincolnshire* (Lincoln, 1975).
D.L. Linton, 'Landforms of Lincolnshire', *Geography,* 1954 (67-78).
J.W. Blackwood, 'The distribution of nature reserves in the natural regions of Lincolnshire', *Transactions Lincolnshire Naturalists' Union,* 1972 (1-7).

5. THE BEGINNINGS OF FARMING: THE NEOLITHIC PERIOD
Note
The map does not aim to show every site and object attributed to the Neolithic period in Lincolnshire but rather to select significant finds in order to demonstrate certain general aspects of the period, such as economic, funerary and ceremonial activities. Too few sites are known even to begin to reconstruct settlement patterns.

Bibliography
W.A. Cummins and C.N. Moore, 'Petrological identification of stone implements from Lincolnshire, Nottinghamshire and Rutland', *Proceedings of the Prehistoric Society* 39 (1973), 219-55.

W.A. Cummins, 'Stone axes as a guide to Neolithic communications', *Proceedings of the Prehistoric Society* 46 (1980), 45-60.

N. Field, 'A multi-phased barrow and possible henge monument at West Ashby, Lincolnshire', *Proceedings of the Prehistoric Society* 51 (1985), 103-36.

J. May, *Prehistoric Lincolnshire* (HL 1, 1976).

C.W. Phillips, 'The excavation of the Giants' Hills Long Barrow, Skendleby, Lincolnshire', *Archaeologia* 85 (1936), 37-106.

P. Phillips (ed.) *Archaeology and Landscape Studies in North Lincolnshire*, British Archaeological Reports British Series 208, 1989). In two parts: (i) long barrows; (ii) aerial and surface surveys, and excavations at Newton Cliffs.

D.N. Riley, 'Neolithic and Bronze Age pottery from Risby Warren and other occupation sites in north Lincolnshire' *Proceedings of the Prehistoric Society* 23 (1957), 40-56.

J.G. Evans and D.D.A. Simpson, 'Giants' Hills 2 long barrow, Skendelby, Lincolnshire, *Archaeologia* 109 (1991) 1-45.

6. THE LATER IRON AGE
Note

The map does not aim to show the location of every site and artefact of the period but rather to select the most significant discoveries in order to demonstrate social and economic structure, as far as we know it at present, in relation to the geographical environment. Our present evidence is biased towards the end of the Iron Age (1st century BC and early 1st century AD). There is less evidence for the middle centuries of the period (3rd-2nd centuries BC) and very little yet for the early Iron Age (*c.*6th-4th centuries BC).

Bibliography
P. Chowne, M. Girling, J. Greig, 'Excavation at an Iron Age defended enclosure at Tattershall Thorpe, Lincolnshire', *Proceedings of the Prehistoric Society* 52 (1986), 159-88.

B.W. Cunliffe, *Iron Age Communities in Britain* (3rd revised edition, London, 1991).

N. Field, 'An Iron Age timber causeway at Fiskerton, Lincolnshire', *Fenland Research* 3 (1985-6), 49-53.

P.P. Hayes and T.W. Lane, *Lincolnshire Survey: the south-west Fens* (East Anglian Archaeology 55, 1992).

J. May, *Prehistoric Lincolnshire* (HL 1, 1976).

J. May, 'Dragonby: an interim report on excavations on an Iron Age and Romano-British site near Scunthorpe, Lincolnshire, 1964-9', *Antiquaries Journal* 50 (1970), 222-45.

B. Simmons, 'Iron Age and Roman coasts around the Wash', in *Archaeology and Coastal Change,* ed. F.H. Thompson (London, 1980).

T.J. Wilkinson, 'Palaeoenvironments of the upper Witham Fen: a preliminary view', *Fenland Research* 4 (1986-7), 52-6.

7. ROMAN LINCOLNSHIRE
Bibliography
B.C. Burnham and J. Wacher, *The Small Towns of Roman Britain* (London, 1990).

R. Goodburn, 'Winterton: Some Villa Problems' in M. Todd *Studies in the Romano-British Villa* (Leicester, 1978).

P.P. Hayes and T.W. Lane, The Fenland Project No. 5: *Lincolnshire Survey, the south-west Fens* (East Anglian Archaeology 55, 1992).

M. Todd, *The Coritani* (revised edition) (Stroud, 1991).

J.B. Whitwell, *The Coritani: some aspects of the Iron Age tribe– the Roman Civitas* (British Archaeological Reports 99, Oxford, 1982).

J.B. Whitwell, *Late Roman settlements on the Humber and Anglian Beginnings* (British Archaeological Reports 193, Oxford, 1988).

J.B. Whitwell, *Roman Lincolnshire* (HL 2 revised edition, 1992).

8. ROMAN LINCOLN
Bibliography
M.J. Darling and M.J. Jones, 'Early Settlement at Lincoln', *Britannia* 19 (1988), 1-56.

M.J. Jones, 'Lincoln', in G. Webster (ed.), *Fortress into City* (London, 1988), 145-66.

M.J. Jones, 'The Latter Days of Roman Lincoln', in A.G. Vince (ed.), *Pre-Viking Lindsey* (1993).

J.B. Whitwell, *Roman Lincolnshire* (HL 2, revised edition, 1992).

11. LINCOLNSHIRE IN THE ANGLO-SAXON PERIOD, *c.*450-1066
Note

1 A small number of rich burials are known. One at Caenby Corner was marked by a round barrow situated prominently at the junction of two routeways. At St Paul in the Bail, one important burial was accompanied by a seventh-century copper alloy hanging bowl, a vessel type found in several of the apparently pagan Anglo-Saxon cemeteries in the county.

Bibliography
B.N. Eagles, *The Anglo-Saxon Settlement of Humberside* (2 vols., British Archaeological Reports (British Series) 68, 1979).

B.N. Eagles, 'Lindsey', in *The Origins of the Anglo-Saxon Kingdoms,* ed. S.R. Bassett (Leicester, 1989), 202-12.

K.A. Leahy, 'Late Roman and early Germanic metalwork from Lincolnshire', in *A Prospect of Lincolnshire*, eds. N. Field and A. White (Lincoln, 1984), 23-32.

C. Mahany and D. Roffe, 'Stamford: the development of an Anglo-Scandinavian borough', *Anglo-Norman Studies* 5 (1983), 197-219.

A. Meaney, *A Gazetteer of Early Anglo-Saxon Burial Sites* (London, 1964).

J.N.L. Myres, *A Corpus of Anglo-Saxon Pottery of the Pagan Period,* 2 vols. (Cambridge, 1977).

D. Roffe, 'The seventh century monastery of Stow Green, Lincolnshire', *LHA* 21 (1986), 31-2.

P. Stafford, *The East Midlands in the Early Middle Ages* (Leicester, 1985).

Pre-Viking Lindsey, ed. Alan Vince (CLAU, 1993), including:
   Mark Blackburn, 'Coins and coin circulation in Lindsey *c.*600-900'.
   Rupert Bruce-Mitford, 'Late Celtic hanging bowls in Lincolnshire and South Humberside'.
   Simon Esmonde Cleary, 'Late Roman towns in Britain and their fate'.
   Paul Everson, 'Pre-Viking settlement in Lindsey'.
   Sarah Foot, 'The Kingdom of Lindsey'.
   Richard Gem, 'The episcopal churches of Lindsey in the early ninth century'.

M.J. Jones, 'The latter days of Roman Lincoln'.

K. Leahy, 'The Anglo-Saxon settlement of Lindsey'.

Peter Sawyer, *Anglo-Saxon Lincolnshire* (HL3, 1998).

Kate Steane and Alan Vince, 'Post-Roman Lincoln: archaeological evidence for activity in Lincoln in the 5th-9th centuries'.

David Stocker, 'The early church in Lincolnshire'.

Barbara Yorke, 'Lindsey: the lost kingdom found?'

12. ANGLO-SAXON LINCOLN
Bibliography

S.R. Bassett, 'Lincoln and the Anglo-Saxon kingdom of Lindsey', *Anglo-Saxon England* 18 (1989), 1-32.

Current Archaeology 129 (1992) [special issue on Lincoln].

B.N. Eagles, 'Lindsey', in *The Origins of the Anglo-Saxon Kingdoms*, ed. S.R. Bassett (Leicester, 1989), 202-12.

M.J. Jones, 'St Paul in the Bail, Lincoln: Britain in Europe', in *The Archaeology of the Early Church*, ed. K.S. Painter (Society of Antiquaries Occasional Paper, 1993).

D. Perring, *Early Medieval Occupation at Flaxengate* (Lincoln, 1981). [See also other related reports in the series *The Archaeology of Lincoln*.]

Pauline Stafford, *The East Midlands in the Early Middle Ages* (Leicester, 1985).

A.G. Vince (ed.), *Pre-Viking Lindsey* (Lincoln, 1993).

13 and 14. SALT MAKING I AND II: IRON AGE AND ROMAN, SAXON AND MEDIEVAL
Bibliography

F.T. Baker, 'The Iron Age salt industry in Lincolnshire', *LAASRP* 8 (1960), 26-34.

P. Chowne, 'Bronze Age settlement in south Lincolnshire', in *The British Later Bronze Age,* eds. J. Barrett and R. Bradley (British Archaeological Reports (British Series) 83, 1980), 295-305.

K.W. De Brisay and K.A. Evans (eds.), *Salt—The Study of an Ancient Industry* (Colchester, 1975).

A.J. Fawn, K.A. Evans, I. McMaster and G.M.R. Davies, *The Red Hills of Essex* (Colchester, 1990).

S. Mandson Grant, 'Ancient pottery kilns', *LNQ* 8 (1904-5), 33-8.

D. Gurney, 'A salt production site at Denver: excavations by Charles Green, 1960', in *Settlement, Religion and Industry on the Fen-edge: three Romano-British sites in Norfolk,* East Anglian Archaeology 31, (1986), 93-146.

H.E. Hallam, *Settlement and Society; A Study of the Early Agrarian History of South Lincolnshire* (Cambridge, 1965).

P.P. Hayes and T.W. Lane, *Lincolnshire Survey: the south west Fens* (East Anglian Archaeology 55, 1992).

R.H. Healey, 'Medieval salt-making', in *South Lincolnshire Archaeology* (1977), 4-5.

B. Kirkham, 'The excavation of a prehistoric saltern at Hogsthorpe, Lincolnshire, *LHA* 16 (1981), 5-10.

T.W. Lane, 'Pre-Roman origins for settlement on the fens of south Lincolnshire', *Antiquity* 62 (1988), 314-21.

J. May, *Prehistoric Lincolnshire* (HL 1, 1976).

E.H. Rudkin, D.M. Owen and H.E. Hallam in *LAASRP* 8 (1960), 76-112.

B.B. Simmons, 'The Lincolnshire Car Dyke: Navigation or Drainage?', *Britannia* 10 (1979), 183-96.

B.B. Simmons, 'Iron age and Roman coasts around the Wash', in F.H. Thompson, ed. 'Archaeology and Coastal Change', *Soc. Antiq. Occas. Pap.* 1 nos. 1, 56-73, (1980).

H.H. Swinnerton, 'The Prehistoric pottery sites of the Lincolnshire coast', *Antiquaries Journal* 12 (1932), 239-53.

15. THE DISTRIBUTION OF SILVER STREET KILN-TYPE POTTERY IN LINCOLNSHIRE
Notes

1 Kilns have also been found at Torksey, then possibly a small urban centre.

2 D. Perring, *Early medieval occupation at Flaxengate, Lincoln* (Archaeology of Lincoln 9/1, 1981).

3 P. Miles, J. Young and J. Wacher, *A late Saxon kiln-site at Silver Street, Lincoln* (Archaeology of Lincoln 17/3, 1989).

4 A. Vince and J. Young, 'East Midlands Anglo-Saxon pottery project' *(Lincoln Archaeology,* 1990-1).

5 D. Selling, *Wikingerzeitliche und frümittelalterliche keramik in Schweden* (Stockholm, 1955).

16. MEDIEVAL LINCOLN, 1066-*c*.1500
Bibliography

B.J.J. Gilmour and D.A. Stocker, *St Mark's Church and Cemetery* (Archaeology of Lincoln, 1986).

Sir Francis Hill, *Medieval Lincoln* (Cambridge, 1948; reprinted with new introduction, Stamford, 1990).

R.H. Jones, *Medieval Houses at Flaxengate* (Archaeology of Lincoln, 1980).

S.R. Jones, K. Major and J. Varley, *Survey of Ancient Houses in Lincoln* (3 fascicules, Lincoln, 1984-90).

Medieval Art and Architecture at Lincoln Cathedral (British Archaeological Association Conference Transactions for 1982, 1986).

T.P. O'Connor, *Animal Bones from Flaxengate* (Archaeology of Lincoln, 1982).

D.M. Owen, *Church and Society in Medieval Lincolnshire* (HL 5, 1971).

N. Pevsner and J. Harris, *The Buildings of England: Lincolnshire* (2nd edition revised by N. Antram, 1989).

G. Platts, *Land and People in Medieval Lincolnshire* (HL 4, 1985).

D.A. Stocker, *St Mary's Guildhall* (Archaeology of Lincoln, 1991).

A.G. Vince, 'Late Medieval Lincoln—a suitable case for treatment', *Lincoln Archaeology* 4 (1991-2), 41-6.

17. DOMESDAY SETTLEMENT
Notes

demesne—that part of a manor over which a lord had propriety rights; the home farm.

bordar—a paid labourer on the lord's demesne with little or no land of his own.

king's thegn—a pre-Conquest lord who owed services directly and personally to the king.

geld—a tax on land.

carucate—notionally the amount of land that could be ploughed by an eight-ox team; in reality a fiscal unit for the purposes of assessing geld.

hundred—in Lincolnshire, the equivalent of the vill (see Medieval Administration).

Bibliography

H.C. Darby, *The Domesday Geography of Eastern England* (Cambridge, 1952).

G. Fellows-Jensen, *Scandinavian Settlement Names in the East Midlands* (Copenhagen, 1978).

P. Morgan (ed.), *Domesday Book: Lincolnshire* (Chichester, 1986).

D.R. Roffe, 'Place-naming in Domesday Book', *Nomina* 14 (1990-1), 47-60.

18. DOMESDAY ESTATE STRUCTURE
Bibliography

John Morris (gen. ed.), *Domesday Book: Lincolnshire* (Chichester, 1986).

D.R. Roffe, 'Domesday Book and northern society: a reassessment', *English Historical Review* 105 (1990), 310-36.

D.R. Roffe, 'From thegnage to barony: sake and soke, title and tenants-in-chief', *Anglo-Norman Studies* 12 (1990), 157-76.

F.M. Stenton, *Types of Manorial Structure in the Northern Danelaw* (Oxford, 1910).

19. MEDIEVAL ADMINISTRATION
Bibliography

H. Cam, *The Hundred and the Hundred Rolls* (London, 1930).

D.R. Roffe, 'The Lincolnshire Hundred', *Landscape History* 3 (1981), 27-36.

D.R. Roffe, 'Hundreds and Wapentakes', *The Lincolnshire Domesday,* eds. A. Williams, G.H. Martin (London, 1992) 32-42.

F.M. Stenton, 'Introduction' in *The Lincolnshire Domesday and the Lindsey Survey,* eds. C.W. Foster and T. Longley (LRS 19, 1924), ix-xlvi.

F.M. Stenton, 'Lindsey and its Kings' in *Preparatory to Anglo-Saxon England,* ed. D.M. Stenton (Oxford, 1970), 127-35.

J. Varley, *The Parts of Kesteven: Studies in Law and Local Government* (Sleaford, 1974).

20. CASTLES
Bibliography

R.A. Brown, *Castles* (Princes Risborough, 1985).

D.J. Cathcart King, *Castellarium Anglicanum: an Index and Bibliography of the Castles in England, Wales and the Islands* (London, 1983), vol. 1, 258-69.

M.W. Thompson, *The Decline of the Castle* (London, 1990).

21. TOWNS AND MARKETS IN THE MIDDLE AGES
Bibliography

P. Dover, *The Early Medieval History of Boston* (Boston, 1972).

J.W.F. Hill, *Medieval Lincoln* (Cambridge, 1948; reprinted Stamford, 1990).

G. Platts, *Land and People in Medieval Lincolnshire* (HL 4, 1985).

A. Rogers (ed.), *The Making of Stamford* (Leicester, 1965).

22. DOMESDAY WATERMILLS IN LINCOLNSHIRE
Notes

1 The figures used to produce this map differ from the aggregated ones compiled by H.C. Darby in *The Domesday Geography of Eastern England* (Cambridge, 1971). Darby counted all mill fractions as separate entries and also rounded up any fractional remainders in other entries. On the current map, these have been assigned as they stand to the relevant settlements, in the hope of producing a more accurate local picture. Where doubt exists as to the correct settlement in which to place a mill, the location most obviously suited by virtue of geography or known milling clusters has been preferred: the mill in either Osgodby or Tealby, for example, is assigned to Tealby. Mills at 'Nongetune' (probably Spittlegate) and Houghton are included in the Grantham figure to accommodate them to the scale of the map. The common error of assigning 'Eslaforde' entries to Old Sleaford rather than to New Sleaford has also been corrected.

2 See D.M. Owen, 'The beginnings of the port of Boston' in A *Prospect of Lincolnshire,* eds. N. Field and A. White (Lincoln, 1984), 42.

Bibliography

H.C. Darby, *The Domesday Geography of Eastern England* (Cambridge, 1971).

C.W. Foster and T. Longley (eds.), *The Lincolnshire Domesday and the Lindsey Survey* (LRS 19, 1924).

R. Holt, *The Mills of Medieval England* (Oxford, 1988).

R. Lennard, *Rural England 1086-1135* (Oxford, 1959).

S. Pawley, 'Grist to the mill: a new approach to the early history of Sleaford', *LHA* 23 (1988), 37-41.

23. PARISH CHURCHES
Bibliography

C.W. Foster (comp.), 'Index of Institutions' (MS in LAO).

C.W. Foster (ed.), *The State of the Church in the Reigns of Elizabeth and James I,* i (LRS 23, 1926).

W.E. Lunt, *The Valuation of Norwich* (Oxford, 1926).

D.M. Owen, *Church and Society in Medieval Lincolnshire* (HL 5, 1971).

*Taxatio Ecclesiastica Angliae et Walliae Auctoritate P. Nicholai IV, c.*1291, eds. T. Astle, S. Ayscough and J. Caley (Record Commission, 1802).

The Clergy List for 1848 (London, 1848).

N. Pevsner and J. Harris, *The Buildings of England: Lincolnshire* (2nd edition, revised by N. Antram, 1989).

The Diocese of Lincoln: Handbook and directory, 1992.

24. RELIGIOUS HOUSES
Bibliography

D. Knowles and R.N. Hadcock, *Medieval Religious Houses, England and Wales* (2nd edition, London, 1971).

D.M. Owen, *Church and Society in Medieval Lincolnshire* (HL 5, 1971).

Victoria County History, Lincolnshire, ii (London, 1906).

25. ECCLESIASTICAL BOUNDARIES
Bibliography

A. Hamilton Thompson, 'Diocesan Organisation in the Middle Ages: Archdeacons and Rural Deans', *Proceedings of the British Academy* 29 (1943), 153-94.

W.E. Lunt, *The Valuation of Norwich* (Oxford, 1926).

K. Major, 'The archdeacons of Stow', in *Registrum Antiquissimum ix* (LRS 62, 1968), 255-62.

D.M. Owen, *Church and Society in Medieval Lincolnshire* (HL 5, 1971).

*Taxatio Ecclesiastica Angliae et Walliae Auctoritate P. Nicholai IV. c.*1291, eds. T. Astle, S. Ayscough and J. Caley (Record Commission, 1802).

26. DESERTED MEDIEVAL VILLAGES
Notes

1 'This day I took my horse and went to a place called Gainstrop which lies in a hollow on the right hand, and about the middle way as you come from Kirton to Scawby. Tradition says that the aforesaid Gainstrop was once a pretty large town, though now there is nothing but some of the foundations. Being upon the place I easily counted the found-ations of about two hundred buildings and beheld three streets very fair ... Tradition says that the town was, in times of yore, exceeding infamous for robberies, and that nobody inhabited there but thieves; and that the country

having for a long while endured all their villanies they at last, when they could suffer them no longer, rose with one consent, and pulled the same down about their ears.'

2 C.W. Foster, 'Extinct villages and other forgotten places', in *The Lincolnshire Domesday and the Lindsey Survey,* eds. C.W. Foster and T. Longley (LRS 19, 1924), *xlvii-lxxii.*

Bibliography

M.W. Beresford, *The Lost Villages of England* (London, 1954).

M.W. Beresford and J.G. Hurst, *Deserted Medieval Villages* (Lutterworth, 1971).

G. Platts, *Land and People in Medieval Lincolnshire* (HL 4, 1985).

T. Rowley, *Villages in the Landscape* (London, 1978).

T. Rowley and J. Wood, *Deserted Villages* (Princes Risborough, 1978).

C. Taylor, *Village and Farmstead* (London, 1983).

27. MARKETS AND FAIRS, 1086-1792
Notes

1 C.W. Foster and T. Longley (eds.), *The Lincolnshire Domesday and the Lindsey Survey* (LRS 19, 1924), 21, 53, 86, 106, 109, 114.

2 R.H. Britnell, 'The proliferation of markets in medieval England, 1200-1349', *Economic History Review,* 2nd series, 34 (1987), 209.

3 R.W. Ambler, 'The small towns of South Humberside', in *Humber Perspectives: A Region through the Ages,* eds. S. Ellis and D.R. Crowther (Hull University Press, 1990); G. Platts, *Land and People in Medieval Lincolnshire* (HL 4, 1985), 229.

4 T. Duffus Hardy (ed.), *Rotuli Literarum Clausarum, i,* 1204-1224 (London, 1833), 398; D.M. Stenton (ed.), *The Earliest Lincolnshire Assize Rolls, A.D. 1202-1209* (LRS 22, 1926), xl; Platts, *Land and People,* 139.

5 Listed in Platts, *Land and People,* Appendix I. Details of earlier markets in *The First Report of the Royal Commission on Market Rights and Tolls, i* [*C. 5550*] (London, 1889), Appendix XIX.

6 Ambler, 'Small towns', 294.

7 H.E. Hallam, *Settlement and Society: A Study of the Early Agrarian History of South Lincolnshire* (Cambridge, 1965), 182.

8 E.W. Moore, *The Fairs of Medieval England: An Introductory Study* (Toronto, 1985), 1, 10-11; Ambler, 'Small towns', 294; Platts, *Land and People,* 143-4.

9 Platts, *Land and People,* 143.

10 Alan Everitt, 'The marketing of agricultural produce' in *The Agrarian History of England and Wales, iv, 1500-1640,* ed. H.P.R. Finberg (Cambridge, 1967), 474; *Royal Commission on Market Rights and Tolls,* 180-3.

11 *The Diary of Abraham de la Pryme, the Yorkshire Antiquary,* ed. Charles Jackson (Surtees Society 54, 1870), 128, 137.

12 Richard Blome, *Britannia: Or a Geographical Description of the Kingdoms of England, Scotland and Ireland, with the Territories Thereunto Belonging* (London, 1673), 143; Donald Woodward (ed.), *The Farming and Memorandum Book of Henry Best of Elmswell, 1642* (London, 1984), 106.

13 *An Authentic Account Published by the King's Authority of all the Fairs in England and Wales* (London, 1756), 52-5; N.R. Wright, *Lincolnshire Towns and Industry,* 1700-1914 (HL 11, 1982), 25.

28. MARITIME TRADE AND FISHING IN THE MIDDLE AGES
Note

1 B.W. McLane (ed.), *The 1341 Royal Inquest in Lincolnshire* (LRS 78, 1987), nos. 16 and 177.

Bibliography

M.W. Barley, 'Lincolnshire rivers in the middle ages', *LAASRP* 1 (1936), 1-21.

E.M. Carus-Wilson, 'The medieval trade of the ports of the Wash', *Medieval Archaeology* 6-7 (1962-3), 182-201.

S. Pawley, 'Lincolnshire Coastal Villages and the Sea' (unpublished Leicester University Ph.D. thesis, 1984 copy at LAO L333.917).

G. Platts, *Land and People in Medieval Lincolnshire* (HL 4, 1985).

D.N. Robinson, *The Book of the Lincolnshire Seaside* (Buckingham, 1981).

29. MARITIME TRADE AND FISHING, 1500-1700
Notes

1 Boston was 'Head Port' for the southern part of the Lincolnshire coastline and Hull for the north. Grimsby was designated a 'Member' or sub-port of Hull. All other places were classified as 'Creeks', having so little trade that they did not require a resident customs officer. These arrangements reflect the extent to which Hull had displaced Boston as the major port in the area by the middle of the 16th century; although the control exercised by either place over the creeks attached to it is questionable.

2 Tobias Gentleman, *England's Way to Win Wealth* (London, 1614), reprinted in *Harleian Miscellany* 3 (1808).

Bibliography

R.W. Ambler and B.R. Watkinson (eds.), *Farmers and Fishermen: The Probate Inventories of the Ancient Parish of Clee 1536-1742* (Hull, 1987).

R.W.K. Hinton (ed.), *The Port Books of Boston 1601-1640* (LRS 50, 1956).

S. Pawley, 'Lincolnshire Coastal Villages and the Sea' (unpublished Leicester University Ph.D. thesis, 1984, copy at LAO L333.917).

D.N. Robinson, *The Book of the Lincolnshire Seaside* (Buckingham, 1981).

C.J. Sturman, 'Salt making in the Lindsey marshland in the 16th and early 17th centuries' in *A Prospect of Lincolnshire,* eds. N. Field and A. White (Lincoln, 1984), 50-56.

J. Thirsk, *English Peasant Farming: the Agrarian History of Lincolnshire from Tudor to Recent Times* (London, 1957).

30. THE LINCOLNSHIRE RISING
Notes

1 Anne Ward, *The Lincolnshire Rising 1536* (WEA East Midlands District, 1986) provides a lively and entertaining account, although it is perhaps over-reliant on evidence that was extracted under duress.

2 For a discussion of this, see Ward, *Lincolnshire Rising,* 7-9.

3 Louth, Caistor, Market Rasen, Kirton, Horncastle, Stainsby, Belchford, Apley, Nettleham, Goltho, Snelland, Wragby, Fulnetby, Saxby, Bolingbroke, Horkstow, Barton on Humber, Stainton, Alford, Bilsby, Spilsby, Donington, Maltby, Stewton,

Manby, Welton in the Marsh, Somercotes, Muckton, Linwood, Halton, Waddington, Immingham, Hackthorn, Sotby, Humberston, Thimbleby, Grimoldby, Croft, Braytoft, Partney, Willoughby, Lower Toynton, Hainton, Nun Ormsby, Hallington, Saleby, Biscathorpe, Mablethorpe, Markby, Brigg, Barnetby, Potterhanworth, Maindenwell, Farforth, Tetney, Croxton, Alvingham, Cockerington, Middle Rasen, Fulstow, Gayton, North Willingham, Butwell, North and South Covenham, Toynton St Peter, Fulletby, West Rasen, Legbourne, Binbrook, Stainton le Vale, Roxby cum Risby (71).

4 J. Thirsk, *English Peasant Farming: the Agrarian History of Lincolnshire from Tudor to Recent Times* (London, 1957), map II, 11.

5 In fact Lord Burgh ordered his town of Gainsborough not to join the Rising.

6 Thirsk, *English Peasant Farming,* Chapters 1, 2 and 3, *passim.*

7 Compare Julian Cornwall, 'The squire of Conisholme' in *Rural Change and Urban Growth 1500-1800: Essays in English Regional History in Honour of W.G. Hoskins,* eds. C.W. Chalklin and M.A. Havinden (London, 1974), especially pp.47-9.

8 Compare N.W. Davis, 'The rites of violence: religious riot in sixteenth century France', *Past and Present* 59 (1973), 51-91.

31. THE EARLS OF YARBOROUGH: INTERESTS AND INFLUENCES
Notes
1 LAO, Yarborough deposit.

2 N. Pevsner and J. Harris, *The Buildings of England: Lincolnshire* (2nd edition, revised by N. Antram, 1989).

3 LAO, Yarborough. 9/16. Letter written by Lord Yarborough to Lord Landsdowne, 1846.

4 C. Rawding, 'The iconography of churches: a case study of landownership and power in nineteenth-century Lincolnshire', *Journal of Historical Geography* 16 (1990), 157-76.

32. THE CIVIL WAR IN LINCOLNSHIRE
Bibliography
I.S. Beckwith, *The Book of Gainsborough* (Buckingham, 1988).

Sir Francis Hill, *Tudor and Stuart Lincoln* (Cambridge, 1956).

C. Holmes, *Seventeenth Century Lincolnshire* (HL 7, 1980).

34. LINCOLNSHIRE BUILDINGS: THE DISTRIBUTION OF DOMESTIC CROWN POST AND KING POST ROOFS
Notes
1 See E. Mercer, *English Vernacular Houses* (Royal Commission on Historical Monuments, London, 1979), pl. 17L, 53R.

2 D.W. Black [*et al.*] *Houses of the North York Moors* (Royal Commission on Historical Monuments, London, 1987).

3 These can also be compared with those of Framsden Hall (Suffolk), Selby's Farm, Hildenborough, and Headcorn Manor House (both Kent), all 15th century. See Mercer, *English Vernacular Houses,* pl. 56L, 57L, 66.

4 For instance at Hookstone Farm, Chobham (Surrey) and in a barn at Horsmonden (Kent) of

*c.*1500: Mercer, *English Vernacular Houses,* pl. 59.

5 D. Roberts, 'Kirkgate, Newark on Trent', *Transactions of the Thoroton Society 75* (1971), 79-80.

6 S.R. Jones, 'Ancient domestic buildings and their roofs', *Archaeological Journal* 131 (1974), 309-13; M.W. Barley *et al.,* 'The medieval parsonage house, Coningsby, Lincolnshire', *Antiquaries Journal* 49 (1969).

7 *The Building Accounts of Tattershall Castle, 1372-1434,* ed. W.D. Simpson (LRS 55, 1960); N. Pevsner and J. Harris, *The Buildings of England: Lincolnshire* (2nd edition, revised by N. Antram, 1989), 166-7.

8 See V. Parker, *The Making of King's Lynn* (London, 1971), 71.

9 To those examples already mentioned must be added the large and important group discovered by Vanessa Parker just outside King's Lynn in 1971.

10 Coningsby had, by tradition, a market in the medieval period.

35. THE POOR LAW, 1601-1834
Notes
1 43 Eliz I, c.2. This Act re-enacted in a revised form the earlier Act, 39 Eliz I, c.3 (1597).

2 Reports of the Commissioners appointed ... to inquire concerning charities and education of the poor (*House of Commons, 1815-1839*).

3 For example: LAO, LEVERTON PAR 13/1.

4 9 Geo I, c.7, 'The Workhouse Test Act'.

5 22 Geo 111 c.83, 'Gilbert's Act'.

6 For example at Alford and Spilsby. See F.M. Eden, *The State of the Poor* (ed. A.G.L. Rogers: London, 1928).

7 Abstract *of the returns made by the overseers of the poor* (Sessional Papers 1777, xxxi).

8 Report of the Poor Law Commissioners (*Parliamentary Papers* 1804 xiii).

9 Report of the Poor Law Commissioners (*Parliamentary Papers* 1818 xix).

10 *Report on the Administration of the Poor Laws and the Management of the Poor,* pt II (1834).

11 Major W. Wylde, the Poor Law Commissioner who surveyed Lincolnshire in 1834, commented that the 1831 Census showed that, except for Westmorland, Lincolnshire was the most sparsely populated county in England *(Report on the Administration of the Poor Laws and the Management of the Poor,* Pt 11 (1834)).

36. DRAINAGE AND RECLAMATION
Notes
1 In addition, the years 1570-1 were very wet with a disastrous tidal surge and widespread coastal damage and inland flooding.

2 The controversial feature of the East Fen was the 14-mile Hobhole Drain for the meres (former peat cuttings); other existing drains were extended, with the linking Cowbridge Drain to the Hobhole as a flood relief channel for Boston.

Bibliography
D.N. Robinson, *The Book of the Lincolnshire Seaside* (Buckingham, 1981).

W.H. Wheeler, *A History of the Fens of South Lincolnshire* (Boston, 1898 and Stamford, 1990).

V. Cory, *Hatfield and Axholme: an historical review* (Ely, 1985).

J. Dear and T. Taylor, A *History of the Fens North of Boston* (Spalding, 1988).

A. Straw, 'The Ancholme Levels North of Brigg', *East Midland Geographer*, 1955, 37-42.

37. PROTESTANT NONCONFORMITY, c.1700-1851
Notes

1 *Speculum Dioeceseos Lincolniensis ... 1705-1723,* ed. R.E.G. Cole (LRS 4, 1913), p.ix; *Minutes of the General Assembly of the General Baptist Church in England, with Kindred Records, Vol I, 1654-1728,* ed. W.T. Whitley (Baptist Historical Society, 1909), lxii.

2 Dr. Williams's Library, MS 38.4 (The John Evans List of Dissenting Congregations, 1715-1729).

3 Dr. Williams's Library, MS 38.5-6 (Josiah Thompson's List of Dissenting Congregations in England and Wales, 1715-1773).

4 LAO, Society of Friends (Calendar of Manuscripts, photocopy of David M. Butler, *Quaker Meeting Houses: a concise list of the meeting houses in each county, arranged in order of acquisition,* 1967).

5 Joan Varley, 'Dissenters' Certificates in the Lincoln Diocesan Records', *Lincolnshire Historian 4* (1949), 172-3, with amended numbers of certificates in Frank Baker, 'The Beginnings of Methodism in Lincolnshire', *Journal of the Lincolnshire Methodist History Society* (subsequently *JLMHS*) 4(1) (1988), 4.

6 For a survey of attendance in 1851, see Map 51.

7 Number of chapel buildings calculated from Baker, 'Beginnings of Methodism', 8, 10, 12-16; William Leary, 'Lincolnshire's First Chapel', 'A Survey of Lincolnshire Methodism in the Eighteenth Century' and 'Eighteenth Century Chapels', *The Epworth Witness and JLMHS* 15(6) (1966), 13; *ibid.,* 1(9) (1967), 11-12; *ibid.,* 1(12) 1969, 515; William Myles, A *Chronological History of the People called Methodists, of the Connexion of the late Rev. John Wesley; from their Rise in the year 1729, to their last Conference in 1802* (3rd edition, London, 1803), 329. The 1851 Census of Religious Worship identified 26 places of worship belonging to the Wesleyan Methodists which were said to have been built or used before 1802 (Parliamentary Papers, 1852-3 LXXXIX (1690) Population of Great Britain, 1851; Religious Worship (England and Wales) (subsequently 1851 Report), ccxliii.

8 J.T. Barker, *Congregationalism in Lincolnshire* (London, 1860), 19-20; G.F. Nuttall, 'The Rise of Independency in Lincolnshire: Thomas Wilson and the Students', *Journal of the United Reformed Church Historical Society* 4(1) (1987), 35-50.

9 *Lincolnshire Returns of the Census of Religious Worship, 1851,* ed. R.W. Ambler (LRS 72, 1979), lxiii.

10 *1851 Report,* ccxi.

38. ELEMENTARY EDUCATION TO 1830
Note

1 *Reports of the Charity Commissioners, xviii, County of Lincoln* (1815-1839).

39. TURNPIKES AND STAGE COACHES
Bibliography

A. Bates, *Directory of Stage Coach Services 1836* (Newton Abbot, 1969).

M.J.T. Lewis, *Dunham Bridge: A Memorial History* (Lincoln, 1978).

Ordnance Survey, One Inch Series (reprint, Newton Abbot, 1970-71).

Stamford Mercury.

P. White, *Guide Notes for a Tour of New Holland and Barton on Humber* (Grimsby, 1967).

N.R. Wright, *Sutton Bridge and Long Sutton, Lincolnshire: An Industrial History* (Lincoln, 1980).

N.R. Wright, *Lincolnshire Towns and Industry 1700-1914* (HL 11, 1982).

40. NAVIGABLE WATERWAYS AND CANALS
Bibliography

Lincoln's Waterways: Trail 1 (Lincoln, 1983).

Lincoln's Waterways: Trail 2 (Lincoln, 1984).

N.C. Birch, *Waterways and Railways of Lincoln and the Lower Witham* (Lincoln, 1968).

J. Boyes and R. Russell, *The Canals of Eastern England* (Newton Abbot, 1977).

J.N. Clarke, *The Horncastle and Tattershall Canal* (Oxford, 1990).

C. Hadfield, *The Canals of the East Midlands* (Newton Abbot, 1970).

S. Pawley, *Sleaford and the Slea* (Penkridge, 1990).

Joseph Priestley, *Navigable Rivers and Canals* (London, 1831).

A.W. Skempton, 'The engineering works of John Grundy (1719-1783)', *LHA* 19 (1984), 65-82.

W.H. Wheeler, *A History of the Fens of South Lincolnshire* (2nd edition, Boston, 1896).

N.R. Wright, *Lincolnshire Towns and Industry 1700-1914* (HL 11, 1982).

N.R. Wright, *John Grundy of Spalding, Engineer, 1719-1783: His Life and Times* (Lincoln, 1983).

41. PARLIAMENTARY AND OLDER ENCLOSURE IN LINCOLNSHIRE
Notes

1 In those few cases where the bulk of a parish had been enclosed privately but within which small acreages were later enclosed by act, those parishes also appear shaded. Examples of these are North Somercotes, where 397 acres were enclosed between 1837 and 1842, and Reepham, where 19 acres were enclosed in 1865.

2 See, for example, *The Barrow Town Book,* ed. Maurice Barley, reprinted in *Aspects of the History of Barrow on Humber, c.1713 to 1851* (1988).

3 See Eleanor and Rex C. Russell, *Parliamentary Enclosure and New Lincolnshire Landscapes* (Lincoln, 1987), Appendices A and B.

4 *Ibid.*

5 Rex C. Russell, *The Enclosures of Market Rasen 1779-1781 and of Wrawby cum Brigg 1800-1805* (Market Rasen WEA, 1969).

Bibliography

T.W. Beastall, *The Agricultural Revolution in Lincolnshire* (HL VIII, 1978).

C. Brears, *Lincolnshire in the Seventeenth and Eighteenth Centuries* (London, 1940).

D.B. Grigg, *The Agricultural Revolution in South Lincolnshire* (Cambridge, 1966).

S.A. Johnson, 'Some aspects of enclosure and changing agricultural landscapes in Lindsey from the sixteenth to the nineteenth century', *LAASRP* 9/2 (1962), 134-50.

J.A. Johnston, '17th-century agricultural practice in six Lincolnshire parishes', *LHA* 18 (1983), 5-14.

N. Lyons, *Enclosure in Context in North-West Lincolnshire* (Scunthorpe, 1988).

E. and R.C. Russell, *Landscape Changes in South Humberside* (Hull, 1982).

E. and R.C. Russell, *Making New Landscapes in Lincolnshire* (Lincoln, 1983).

E. and R.C. Russell, *Old and New Landscapes in the Horn-castle Area* (Lincoln, 1985).

E. and R.C. Russell, *Parliamentary Enclosure and New Lincolnshire Landscapes* (Lincoln, 1987)

R.C. Russell, *The Logic of Open Field Systems* (London, 1974).

R.C. Russell, *The Enclosures of Market Rasen 1779-1781 and of Wrawby cum Brigg 1800-1805* (Market Rasen WEA, 1969).

T.H. Swales, 'The parliamentary enclosures of Lindsey', *AASRP* 42 (1935), 233-274, and *LAASRP* 1 (1936), 85-120.

J. Thirsk, *English Peasant Farming: the agrarian history of Lincolnshire from Tudor to recent times* (London, 1957).

M. Turner, *English Parliamentary Enclosure* (Folkestone, 1980).

42. ENCLOSURE AT THE PARISH LEVEL
Note

1 Arthur Young, *A General View of the Agriculture of the County of Lincolnshire* [1813] (reprinted Newton Abbot, 1970), 488.

43. POPULATION TRENDS, 1801-1991
Notes

1 The actual population of the County of Lincolnshire was 58,453, based on the 1991 Census Returns. The population of those parishes of the historic county which now form South Humberside was estimated at 310,090, based on the Registrar-General's mid-1989 figures, published in *Humberside Facts and Figures* (Humberside County Council, 1991).

2 The parish totals for the period 1801-1901 are tabulated in *VCH Lincs.*, 356-79.

44. FRIENDLY SOCIETIES IN LINCOLNSHIRE
Notes

1 Many different kinds of organisation were included in friendly society legislation, including trade unions, savings banks, building societies, medical societies, cattle clubs, loan clubs, coal clubs, shop clubs, working men's clubs, literary institutions.

2 *Report of the Chief Registrar of Friendly Societies 1905.* These clubs were still in existence at the beginning of the 20th century.

3 *Abstract of the answers and returns made pursuant to ... 'An Act for procuring returns relative to the expenses and maintenance of the poor in England'* (London, 1803).

4 *Report of the Chief Registrar of Friendly Societies 1905.* In Lincolnshire in 1905 there were over 21,000 members of ordinary societies, and over 48,000 members of affiliated orders. It is not possible to establish how many Lincolnshire residents belonged to the collecting societies which were not based in the county. Hence the numbers quoted here are likely to underestimate the total of friendly society members.

5 *Report of the Chief Registrar of Friendly Societies 1905.* The total number of friendly society members was probably considerably higher as these figures include evidence from registered societies only. Registration of friendly societies has never been compulsory and even by the 20th century there were still many unregistered societies whose membership would not be reflected in these figures.

6 The percentage grew from 3.6 per cent in 1803 to 13.1 per cent in 1905: *Abstract of answers and returns* (1803); *Report of Chief Registrar* (1905); *Census Abstracts*, 1801 and 1901.

7 It is not known how many female societies existed in Lincolnshire; none appears in the 1803 list, three were included in a list of registered friendly societies dated 1855 and four in the 1905 list.

Bibliography

P. Gosden, *Friendly Societies in England 1815-75* (Manchester, 1961).

D. Neave, *Mutual Aid in the Victorian Countryside: Friendly Societies in the Rural East Riding 1836-1914* (Hull University Press, 1991).

J. O'Neill, *On The Club: A History of Friendly Societies in Nottinghamshire*.

R.C. Russell, *Friendly Societies in the Caistor, Binbrook and Brigg Area in the Nineteenth Century* (Nettleton W.E.A., 1975).

45. AGRICULTURAL LAND USE IN 1801
Notes

1 PRO, HO 67; *Home Office Acreage Returns (HO 67), List and Analysis, ii, Jersey-Somerset, 1801,* List and Index Society 190 (1982).

2 PRO, MAF 68 Agricultural Statistics: parish summaries. See PRO Leaflet 14.

3 The map was drawn by combining parishes into units of 28-42,000 acres (with the exception of the Isle of Axholme (54,933 acres)). Varying parish size and size of physical regions prevented stricter controls on unit area. Where parishes straddled physical regions, they were included entirely in the region which comprised the larger portion of the parish. Physical regions have been simplified to maintain clarity on the map. All these limiting factors need to be taken into account when interpreting the map. For a discussion of mapping the 1801 Returns, see D. Thomas, 'The statistical and cartographic treatment of the Acreage Returns of 1802', *Geographical Studies* 5 (2) (1959).

4 Arthur Young, *A General View of the Agriculture of the County of Lincoln* (1813), 116-17.

5 Young, *General View,* 201.

6 The figures for Deeping Fen have not been included in the table, although they are shown on the map, since they comprise an estimate given in the correspondence, not in the returns.

7 T.W. Beastall, *Agricultural Revolution in Lincolnshire* (HL 8, 1978), 66-7.

46. LANDOWNERSHIP AND PARISH TYPE
*c.*1830
Notes

1 LAO, KQS Land Tax Duplicates 1831; LAO, LQS Land Tax Duplicates 1830 and 1831; LAO, HQS Land Tax Duplicates 1831 (North Holland), 1826 (South Holland).

2 See D.R. Mills, *Lord and Peasant in Nineteenth Century Britain* (London, 1980), 116-18.

3 A. Young, *General View of Agriculture in Lincolnshire* [*1813*], (reprinted Newton Abbot, 1970), 464.
4 *Ibid.*, p.468.
5 'Let the Magistrates be ever so active, let the resident clergy be ever so attentive, while the property of this large parish continues divided and in so many hands, each individual proprietor will consider himself at liberty to act independently. His example is insensibly imitated by his inferiors who, gradually, growing up in ... lawless habits, have no notion of that deportment and necessary subordination visible in the market towns and villages belonging solely to either some virtuous nobleman, or to a resident gentleman.' LAO, Misc Don 1/10 (Notebook of Samuel Hopkinson, Vicar of Hacconby with Morton 1795-1841).
6 Report from the Committee of Settlement and Removal (*Parliamentary Papers* 1847 xi), 71.

47. SWING RIOTS IN LINCOLNSHIRE, 1830

Notes

1 E.J. Hobsbawm and G. Rudé, *Captain Swing* (London, 1969), 199-202.
2 *Stamford Mercury,* 12 December 1830.
3 LAO, 4BNL Box 2 (Correspondence).
4 LAO, KSB Epiphany 1831.
5 LAO, 4BNL Box 2 (Commissioner of the Peace).
6 LAO, KQS 1830/7/2/3 (Clerk's Papers).

Bibliography

John E. Archer, *'By a Flash and a Scare': Arson, Animal Maiming and Poaching in East Anglia, 1815-1870* (Oxford, 1990).
Class, Conflict and Protest in the English Countryside, 1700-1880, eds. M. Reed and R. Wells (London, 1990).
Barry Reay, *The Last Rising of the Agricultural Labourer* (Oxford, 1990).

48. ELEMENTARY EDUCATION, 1833-70

Note

1 Under the Child Labour Employment Act 1867, no-one under the age of eight was to be employed. By 1873 it was laid down that no child under ten was to be in an agricultural gang; 250 attendances at school were required per year.

Bibliography

Further information can be obtained from the Return *Non-provided Schools, Lincolnshire* (23 February 1906).

49. THE INTRODUCTION OF THE NEW POOR LAW, 1834-46

Bibliography

LAO, Poor Law Union records.
A. Digby, *The Poor Law in 18th Century England and Wales* Historical Association, General Series, 104, 1982).
J.A.H. Brocklebank, 'The New Poor Law in Lincolnshire', *Lincolnshire Historian* 2(8) (1962), 21-33.
A. Brundage, *The Making of the New Poor Law 1832-9* (London, 1978).
M.E. Rose, *The Relief of Poverty 1834-1914* (Basingstoke, 1972).

50. THE COUNTY ELECTION, 1841

Notes

TABLE 1

Northern Division		Southern Division	
Worsley	5401	Turnor	4581
Christopher	4522	Trollope	4563
Cust	3819	Handley	2948

2 The franchise in boroughs was also based on a property qualification of being an owner or tenant of a building valued at £10 per annum.
3 *The Poll Book for the Election of Two Members to Represent in Parliament the Southern Division of the County of Lincoln* (Sleaford, 1841); *The Poll Book for the Parts of Lindsey in the County of Lincoln* (Lincoln, 1841).

Bibliography

R.J. Olney, *Lincolnshire Politics* (Oxford, 1972).
R.J. Olney, *Rural Society and County Government in Nineteenth Century Lincolnshire* (HL 10, 1979).
J. Varley, *The Parts of Kesteven: Studies in Law and Local Government* (Sleaford, 1974).

51. ATTENDANCE AT RELIGIOUS WORSHIP, 1851

Notes

1 R.W. Ambler (ed.), *Lincolnshire Returns of the Census of Religious Worship 1851* (LRS 72, 1979), vii-viii. This volume also contains a transcription of the detailed returns for Lincolnshire.
2 Where the districts overlap the county boundary, the figures have been recalculated to include places in the county only, except for the single parishes of Crowland and Luddington which were in the Peterborough and Goole districts. The national report on the religious census was published as Parliamentary Papers 1852-3, lxxxix (1690) Population of Great Britain, 1851, Religious Worship (England and Wales). For the analysis of the returns for Lincolnshire, see pp.ccxi, ccxxxvii, ccxliii, cclxxxix, ccxcvii, 81-5.
3 For a discussion of these measures of attendance, see B.I. Coleman, *The Church of England in the Mid-Nineteenth Century: A Social Geography* (London, 1980), 6.

52. COUNTRY SEATS OF THE GENTRY

Notes

1 LAO, WILLSON/1/542-5.
2 Only 17 of the 157 south Lindsey parishes identified as close parishes by Obelkevitch had resident squires in 1851 (J. Obelkevitch, *Religion and Rural Society: South Lindsey 1825-75* (Oxford, 1976), 12, 30). This proportion can be compared with figures for Leicestershire, where 39 out of 134 close parishes contained a resident squire (D.R. Mills, *Lord and Peasant in Nineteenth-Century Britain* (London, 1980), 77.
3 Figures calculated from F.M.L. Thompson, *English Landed Society in the Nineteenth Century* (London, 1963), 32, 113, 117.

53. PARLIAMENTARY BOUNDARIES
I: BEFORE 1885

Note

1 The only change to the borough boundaries in 1867 was a further small extension to Stamford in St Martin's parish (not shown on the map).

Bibliography

Reform Act 1832 (2 and 3 William IV, cap. 45).

Reform Act 1867 (30 and 31 Victoria, cap. 102).

Reports of Boundary Commissioners *(Parliamentary Papers* 1831-2 xxxix, 1867-8 xx).

R.J. Olney, *Lincolnshire Politics 1832-1885* (Oxford, 1973): see especially pp.72-3, 80-3, 162-3, 204-5.

R.J. Olney, *Rural Society and County Government in Nineteenth-Century Lincolnshire 10, 1979*: for wapentake boundaries, see pp.7 (map) and 130-1.

54. PARLIAMENTARY BOUNDARIES, II: 1885-1948

Bibliography

Redistribution of Seats Act 1885 (48 and 49 Victoria, cap. 23).

Representation of the People Act 1918 (7 and 8 George V, cap. 64).

Representation of the People Act 1948 (11, 12 and 13 George VI, cap. 65).

Reports of Boundary Commissioners *(Parliamentary Papers* 1884-5 xix, 1917-18 xiii, 1947-8 xv).

55. RAILWAYS AND DOCKS

Bibliography

British Railways Pre-Grouping Atlas and Gazetteer (5th edition, London, 1980).

G. Dow, *Great Central* (London, 1959-65).

R.E. Pearson and J.G. Ruddock, *Lord Willoughby's Railway—The Edenham Branch* (Grimsthorpe, 1986).

J.G. Ruddock and R.E. Pearson, *The Railway History of Lincoln* (Lincoln, 1974).

S.E. Squires, *The Lincolnshire Potato Railways* (Oxford, 1987).

S.E. Squires, *The Lost Railways of Lincolnshire* (Ware, 1988).

N.R. Wright, *The Railways of Boston* (Boston, 1971).

N.R. Wright, *Lincolnshire Towns and Industry 1700-1914* (HL 11, 1982).

J. Wrottesley, *The Great Northern Railway* (London, 1979-81).

56. IRONSTONE MINING

Bibliography

R.W. Ambler (ed.), *Workers and Community: The People of Scunthorpe in the 1870s* (Scunthorpe, 1980).

M.E. Armstrong (ed.), *An Industrial Island: A History of Scunthorpe* (Scunthorpe, 1981).

I.J. Brown, 'Gazetteer of ironstone mines in the East Midlands: Lincolnshire section', *Lincolnshire Industrial Archaeology* 6 (2/3) (1971).

F. Henthorn (ed.), *Letters and Papers concerning the Establishment of the Trent, Ancholme and Grimsby Railway 1860-62* (LRS 70, 1975).

H.B. Hewlett, *The Quarries—Ironstone, Limestone and Sand* (Stanton, 1935).

D.R. Mills (ed.), *Twentieth Century Lincolnshire* (HL 12, 1989).

S.E. Squires, *The Lost Railways of Lincolnshire* (Ware, 1988).

G.R. Walshaw and C.A.R. Behrendt, *The History of Appleby-Frodingham* (Scunthorpe, 1950).

N.R. Wright, *Lincolnshire Towns and Industry 1700-1914* (HL 11, 1982).

57. BRICK AND TILE MAKING

Notes

1 At South Ormsby, two men could make 48,000 bricks in one firing at 6s. per thousand which was one-third of the cost of buying.

2 For the construction of the Royal Dock at Grimsby, opened 1852, silt was dug from the bed of the Humber and burnt in close clamps being fired with layers of small coal. When first dug the silt was dark blue, changing to brown on exposure, and the bricks varied from dark purple to dirty white. A million bricks were used in building the Dock Tower.

3 The Frank brothers, who had extensive brickworks alongside the Ancholme from Horkstow to South Ferriby, also had a F-shaped dowel to pierce the brick, and the company produced special shaped bricks for churches, trimming with a wire to the required design after moulding.

Bibliography

A. White, *Guide to Early Brick Buildings in Lincolnshire* (Lincoln, 1982).

S.A. Holm, *Brick and Tile Making in South Humberside* (Scunthorpe, 1976).

A.E. Truman, 'The Lias Brickyards of South-West Kesteven', *Transactions Lincolnshire Naturalists' Union* (1916) 48-53.

White's and Kelly's *County Directories*.

58. MALTING AND BREWING

Bibliography

T. Barlow, 'Maltings, Brayford Wharf North', *LHA* 19 (1984), 114-17.

N.C. Birch, *Stamford: An Industrial History* (Lincoln, 1972).

Kelly's Directory of Lincolnshire (8th edition, London, 1913).

W. White, *History, Gazetteer and Directory of Lincolnshire* (2nd edition, Sheffield, 1856).

N.R. Wright, *Lincolnshire Towns and Industry 1700-1914* (HL 11, 1982).

59. BANKING

Bibliography

W.F. Crick and J.E. Wadsworth, *A Hundred Years of Joint Stock Banking* (London, 1936).

S.N. Davis, *Banking in Boston* (Boston, 1976).

Kelly's Directory of Lincolnshire.

P.W. Matthews and A.W. Tuke, *History of Barclays Bank Ltd.* (London, 1926).

H. Porter, 'Old private bankers of south Lincolnshire', *Lincolnshire Magazine 2* (1935), 77-82.

H. Porter, 'Old private bankers of north Lincolnshire', *Lincolnshire Magazine 2* (1936), 289-96.

White's Directory of Lincolnshire.

N.R. Wright, *Lincolnshire Towns and Industry 1700-1914* (HL 11, 1982).

60. SEASIDE RESORTS AND SPAS

Notes

1 Similarly, sea bathing ceased at Saltfleet when the marsh frontage was enclosed in 1854.

2 In 1791, John Byng called the Dolphin 'the best of the Lincolnshire bathing shops'.

3 This hotel was taken down after flood damage in the early 1920s.

4 The layout included pleasure grounds (Tower Gardens) and Sea Water Baths.

5 Cleethorpes pier was breached as an anti-invasion

precaution in 1940 and the seaward portion taken down after the war. Skegness pier was largely destroyed in the storm of 12 January 1978. Its other symbol, the Clock Tower, erected 1898-9, still stands at the head of the Tower Esplanade.

6 The worst of these settlements were removed under the Lindsey Sandhills Act 1932 and others failed. Humberston Fitties, however, grew from a handful of huts in 1925 to around 300 now.

7 The third hotel was the *Eagle House*, refurbished as such in the 1880s. *Petwood House*, built in 1905 for Grace Maple, was turned into a hotel in 1933. Visitors to Woodhall Spa came from all parts of the British Isles as well as Europe, India, Australia, South Africa and North and South America.

8 The water was described as having 'remarkable purity and abundance of gaseous constituents, rendering it eminently suitable for drinking dietetic purposes'.

9 These attempts included bottling the waters for sale.

Bibliography
D.N. Robinson, *The Book of the Lincolnshire Seaside* (Buckingham, 1981).

D.N. Robinson, *Beside the Seaside: Lincolnshire In Camera* (Buckingham, 1991).

D.N. Robinson, *The Book of Horncastle and Woodhall Spa* (Buckingham, 1983).

C. Ekberg, *The Book of Cleethorpes* (Buckingham, 1986).

W. Kime, *The Book of Skegness* (Buckingham, 1986).

61. THEATRES AND CINEMAS
Bibliography
D.W. Clementson, 'The Theatre Royal, Lincoln' (unpublished B.Ed. thesis, Lincoln, 1961).

T. Gilliland, *The Dramatic Mirror: containing the history of the stage* (London, 1808).

F. Hance, *Stamford Theatre and Stamford Racecourse* (Stamford, n.d.).

Kelly's Directory of Lincolnshire (8th edition, 1913).

Kelly's Directory of Lincolnshire (14th edition, 1937).

B.J. Parker, 'The theatre of Gainsborough: from 1772 until 1850' (unpublished thesis).

Stamford Mercury.

L. Warwick, *Drama That Smelled* (Northampton, 1975).

N.R. Wright, *Lincolnshire Towns and Industry 1700-1914* (HL 11, 1982).

62. THE DECLINE OF THE LIBERALS, 1918-31
Notes

1 For a very readable account of the Liberal decline nationally see Roy Douglas: *History of the Liberal Party 1895-1970* (1971).

2 See Keith Laybourn, *The Rise of Labour* (1988), especially chapters 4-6.

3 The *Grantham Journal* covers this election campaign, week by week, in great detail.

4 See, for instance, the Lincoln Liberal Association minute book and subscription book in Lincolnshire Archives.

5 In 1886 the Liberals split over Irish Home Rule. Approximately 1/3 of Liberal MPs formed the Liberal Unionists who by 1911 had joined the Conservatives. In 1918 about half the Liberal MPs supported Lloyd George's coalition while the other half supported Asquith, in opposition. In 1931 the Liberals split three ways–the General Election returned 33 genuine Liberals, 35 Liberal Nationalists or National Liberals who eventually became Conservatives, and 4 independent Liberals.

6 Explanation may lie in the occupational structure, or perhaps the religious affiliation, or perhaps the influence of the local press, the politics of local landowners or employers, or perhaps some as yet unidentified factor.

63. DISPENSARIES AND HOSPITALS TO 1937
Notes

	Establishment of		
	Hospitals	Dispensaries	Population
Lincoln	1769	1828	7,205 (1801)
Stamford	1828		5,797 (1831)
Grimsby	1866		11,067 (1861)
Market Rasen	1869	1856	2,815 (1871)
Boston	1871	1852	15,156 (1871)
Louth	1873	1803	10,500 (1871)
Grantham	1874	1837	13,225 (1871)
Willingham by Stow	1880		460 (1881)
Spalding	1881		9,260 (1881)
Frodingham (Scunthorpe)	1886		4,296 (1881)
Woodhall Spa	1890		671 (1891: with Woodhall)
Bourne	1900		4,191 (1901)
Spilsby	1902		2,060 (1901: with Hundleby)
Gainsborough	1913	1828	20,587 (1911)
Skegness	1913		3,775 (1911)
Alford	1921		2,194 (1921)
Horncastle	1924	1789	3,461 (1921)

Notes

1 N. R. Wright, *Lincolnshire Towns and Industry 1700-1914* (HL 11, 1982), 234.

2 Grimsby Hospital Management Committee, *Hospital and Health Services Handbook* (London, c.1956), 40.

64. THE RAF IN LINCOLNSHIRE
Bibliography
R. Blake, M. Hodgson and W.J. Taylor, *The Airfields of Lincolnshire Since 1912* (Leicester, 1984).

B.B. Halpenny, *Action Stations 2: Military Airfields of Lincolnshire and the East Midlands* (Cambridge, 1981).

T.N. Hancock, *Bomber County* (Lincoln, 1978).

T.N. Hancock, *Bomber County 2* (Lincoln, 1985).

M. Ingham, *The Polish Air Force in Lincolnshire* (Nettleham, 1988).

M. Ingham, *The Air Force Memorials of Lincolnshire* (Nettleham, 1990).

D. Willis and B. Hollis, *Military Airfields in the British Isles 1939-1945* (Newport Pagnell, 1987).

65. EVOLVING LINCOLN
Bibliography
Sir Francis Hill, *A Short History of Lincoln* (Lincoln Civic Trust, 1979).

Lincoln: 21 Centuries of Living History (Lincoln Archaeological Trust, 1984).

Planning our Future (Lincoln City Council, 1991).

INDEX

Parts of Lindsey

#	Name	#	Name	#	Name	#	Name
1	Aby with Greenfield	117	Dalby	233	Kirkstead	349	Snitterby
2	Addlethorpe	118	Dalderby	234	Kirmington	350	Somerby
3	Aisthorpe	119	Donington upon Bain	235	Kirmond le Mire	351	Somercotes North
4	Alford	120	Driby	236	Kirton in Lindsey	352	Somercotes South
5	Alkborough	121	Dunholme	237	Knaith	353	Somersby
6	Althorpe	122	Eastoft	238	Laceby	354	Sotby
7	Alvingham	123	Eastville	239	Langriville	355	Southorpe
8	Amcotts	124	Edlington	240	Langton nr Horncastle	356	Spilsby
9	Anderby	125	Elkington North	241	Langton by Spilsby	357	Spridlington
10	Apley	126	Elkington South	242	Langton by Wragby	358	Springthorpe
11	Appleby	127	Elsham	243	Laughton	359	Stainfield
12	Asgarby	128	Epworth	244	Lea	360	Stainton by Langworth
13	Ashby	129	Faldingworth	245	Legbourne	361	Stainton le Vale
14	Ashby by Partney	130	Farforth cum Maidenwell	246	Legsby	362	Stallingborough
15	Ashby-with-Fenby	131	Farlesthorpe	247	Limber Great	363	Steeping Great
16	Ashby Puerorum	132	Fenton	248	Linwood	364	Steeping Little
17	Ashby West	133	Ferriby South	249	Lissington	365	Stenigot
18	Asterby	134	Ferry East	250	Louth	366	Stewton
19	Aswardby	135	Fillingham	251	Louth Park	367	Stickford
20	Atterby	136	Firsby East	252	Ludborough	368	Stickney
21	Authorpe	137	Firsby West	253	Luddington	369	Stixwould
22	Aylesby	138	Firsby	254	Ludford Magna	370	Stockwith East
23	Bag-Enderby	139	Fiskerton	255	Ludford Parva	371	Stow
24	Bardney	140	Flixborough	256	Lusby	372	Strubby with Woodthorpe
25	Barkwith East	141	Fotherby	257	Mablethorpe	373	Sturton
26	Barkwith West	142	Friesthorpe	258	Maltby le Marsh	374	Sturton Great
27	Barlings	143	Friskney	259	Manby	375	Sudbrooke
28	Barnetby le Wold	144	Frith Villa	260	Manton	376	Sutterby
29	Barnoldby le Beck	145	Frodingham	261	Mareham le Fen	377	Sutton in the Marsh
30	Barrow upon Humber	146	Fulletby	262	Mareham on the Hill	378	Swaby
31	Barton upon Humber	147	Fulnetby	263	Markby	379	Swallow
32	Baumber	148	Fulstow	264	Market Rasen	380	Swinhope
33	Beelsby	149	Gainsborough	265	Market Stainton	381	Tathwell
34	Beesby in the Marsh	150	Garthorpe	266	Marsh Chapel	382	Tattershall
35	Belchford	151	Gate Burton	267	Martin	383	Tattershall Thorpe
36	Belleau	152	Gautby	268	Marton	384	Tealby
37	Belton	153	Gayton le Marsh	269	Mavis Enderby	385	Tetford
38	Benniworth	154	Gayton le Wold	270	Melton Ross	386	Tetney
39	Bigby	155	Glentham	271	Messingham	387	Theddlethorpe all Saint
40	Bilsby	156	Glentworth	272	Midville	388	Theddlethorpe St Helen
41	Binbrook	157	Goltho	273	Miningsby	389	Thimbleby
42	Biscathorpe	158	Goulceby	274	Minting	390	Thonock
43	Bishop Norton	159	Goxhill	275	Moorby	391	Thoresby North
44	Blyborough	160	Grainsby	276	Morton	392	Thoresby South
45	Blyton	161	Grainthorpe	277	Muckton	393	Thoresway
46	Bolingbroke	162	Grange de Ligne	278	Mumby	394	Thorganby
47	Bonby	163	Grasby	279	Nettleham	395	Thornton
48	Bottesford	164	Grayingham	280	Nettleton	396	Thornton Curtis
49	Brackenborough	165	Greenhill and Redhill	281	Newball	397	Thornton le Fen
50	Bradley	166	Greetham	282	New Leake	398	Thornton le Moor
51	Brampton	167	Greetwell	283	Newstead	399	Thorpe in the Fallows
52	Bratoft	168	Grimblethorpe	284	Newton by Toft	400	Thorpe St Peter
53	Brattleby	169	Grimoldby	285	Newton on Trent	401	Toft next Newton
54	Brigg	170	Grimsby Great	286	Normanby by Spital	402	Torksey
55	Brigsley	171	Grimsby Little	287	Normanby on the Wolds	403	Torrington East
56	Brinkhill	172	Gunby	288	Northorpe	404	Torrington West
57	Brocklesby	173	Gunhouse	289	Orby	405	Tothill
58	Broughton	174	Habrough	290	Ormsby North	406	Toynton All Saints
59	Broxholme	175	Hackthorne	291	Ormsby South	407	Toynton St Peter
60	Brumby	176	Hagnaby	292	Owersby North	408	Toynton High
61	Bucknall	177	Hagworthingham	293	Owersby South	409	Toynton Low
62	Bullington	178	Hainton	294	Owmby	410	Trusthope
63	Burgh on Bain	179	Hallington	295	Owston	411	Tumby
64	Burgh in the Marsh	180	Haltham	296	Oxcombe	412	Tupholme
65	Burringham	181	Halton East	297	Panton	413	Twigmore
66	Burton by Lincoln	182	Halton Holegate	298	Partney	414	Ulceby with Fordington
67	Burton Stather	183	Halton West	299	Pilham	415	Ulceby
68	Burwell	184	Hemeringham	300	Raithby	416	Upton
69	Buslingthorpe	185	Hannah cum Hagnaby	301	Raithby cum Maltby	417	Usselby
70	Butterwick East	186	Hardwick	302	Ranby	418	Utterby
71	Butterwick West	187	Hareby	303	Rand	419	Waddingham
72	Cabourne	188	Harpswell	304	Rasen Middle	420	Waddingworth
73	Cadney cum Howsham	189	Harrington	305	Rasen West	421	Wainfleet all Saints
74	Caenby	190	Hatcliffe	306	Ravendale East	422	Wainfleet St Mary
75	Caistor	191	Hatton	307	Ravendale West	423	Waithe
76	Calceby	192	Haugh	308	Raventhorpe	424	Walesby
77	Calcethorpe	193	Haugham	309	Redbourne	425	Walkerith
78	Cammeringham	194	Hawerby cum Beesby	310	Reepham	426	Walmsgate
79	Candlesby	195	Haxey	311	Reston North	427	Waltham
80	Carlton Great	196	Healing	312	Reston South	428	Weelsby
81	Carlton Little	197	Heapham	313	Revesby	429	Well
82	Carlton North	198	Hemingby	314	Riby	430	Welton
83	Carlton South	199	Hemswell	315	Rigsby with Ailby	431	Welton le Wold
84	Carrington	200	Hibaldstow	316	Riseholme	432	Welton in the Marsh
85	Castle Carlton	201	Hogsthorpe	317	Rothwell	433	West Fen
86	Cawkwell	202	Holme	318	Roughton	434	West Ville
87	Cawthorpe Little	203	Holton cum Beckering	319	Roxby cum Risby	435	Whitton
88	Chapel St Leonard	204	Holton le Clay	320	Ruckland	436	Wickenby
89	Cherry Willingham	205	Holton le Moor	321	Saleby with Thoresthorpe	437	Wildmore Fen
90	Claxby	206	Horkstow	322	Salmonby	438	Wildsworth
91	Claxby by Normanby	207	Horncastle	323	Saltfleetby All Saints	439	Wilksby
92	Claxby Pluckacre	208	Horsington	324	Saltfleetby St Clement	440	Willingham
93	Claythorpe	209	Humberston	325	Saltfleetby St Peter	441	Willingham North
94	Cleatham	210	Hundleby	326	Sausthorpe	442	Willingham South
95	Clee	211	Huttoft	327	Saxby	443	Willoughby with Sloothby
96	Cleethorpes	212	Immingham	328	Saxby All Saints	444	Willoughton
97	Clixby	213	Ingham	329	Scamblesby	445	Winceby
98	Coates	214	Ingoldmells	330	Scampton	446	Winteringham
99	Coates Great	215	Irby on Humber	331	Scartho	447	Winterton
100	Coates Little	216	Irby in Marsh	332	Scawby	448	Winthorpe
101	Coates North	217	Keadby	333	Scothern	449	Wispington
102	Cockerington North	218	Keal East	334	Scotter	450	Withcall
103	Cockerington South	219	Keal West	335	Scotton	451	Withern with Stain
104	Cold Hanworth	220	Keddington	336	Scrafield	452	Wold Newton
105	Coningsby	221	Keelby	337	Scremby	453	Wood Enderby
106	Conisholme	222	Kelsey North	338	Scrivelsby	454	Woodhall
107	Corringham	223	Kelsey South	339	Scunthorpe	455	Woodhall Spa
108	Covenham St Bartholomew	224	Kelstern	340	Searby cum Owmby	456	Wootton
109	Covenham St Mary	225	Kettlethorpe	341	Sibsey	457	Worlaby
110	Croft	226	Kexby	342	Six Hills	458	Wragby
111	Crosby	227	Killingholme North	343	Sixilby with Ingleby	459	Wrawby
112	Crowle	228	Killingholme South	344	Skegness	460	Wroot
113	Croxby	229	Kingerby	345	Skendleby	461	Wyham cum Cadeby
114	Croxton	230	Kirkby cum Osgodby	346	Skidbrook with Saltfleet Haven	462	Wykeham East
115	Cumberworth	231	Kirkby on Bain	347	Snarford	463	Yarburgh
116	Cuxwold	232	Kirkby East	348	Snelland		

Parts of K

1	Allington
2	Ancaster
3	Anwick
4	Asgarby
5	Ashby de la Lau...
6	Aslackby
7	Aswarby
8	Aubourne
9	Aunby
10	Aunsby
11	Barholm
12	Barkston
13	Barrowby
14	Bassingham
15	Bassingthorpe
16	Baston
17	Beckingham
18	Belton
19	Bennington Gran...
20	Bennington Long...
21	Billingborough
22	Billinghay
23	Birthorpe
24	Bitchfield
25	Blankney
26	Bloxholm
27	Boothby Graffoe
28	Boothby Pagnell
29	Boultham
30	Bourne
31	Braceborough
32	Bracebridge
33	Bracebridge Heat...
34	Braceby
35	Branston
36	Brant Broughton
37	Brauncewell
38	Burton Coggles
39	Burton Pedwardin...
40	Byard's Leap
41	Canwick
42	Careby
43	Carlby
44	Carlton le Moorl...
45	Carlton Scroop
46	Castle Bytham
47	Caythorpe
48	Claypole
49	Coleby
50	Colsterworth
51	Corby
52	Counthorpe
53	Cranwell
54	Creeton
55	Culverthorpe
56	Deeping St James
57	Deeping West
58	Dembleby
59	Denton
60	Digby
61	Doddington
62	Dogdyke
63	Dorrington
64	Dowsby
65	Dry Doddington
66	Dunsby
67	Dunston
68	Eagle
69	Eagle Hall
70	Easton
71	Edenham
72	Evedon
73	Ewerby
74	Fenton
75	Folkingham
76	Foston
77	Fulbeck
78	Gonerby Little
79	Gonerby Great
80	Grantham
81	Greatford
82	Gunby
83	Hacconby
84	Haceby
85	Haddington
86	Hale Great
87	Hale Little
88	Harlaxton
89	Harmston
90	Harrowby
91	Haverholme Prior...
92	Haydor
93	Heckington
94	Heighington
95	Helpringham
96	Holdingham
97	Holywell
98	Honington
99	Horbling
100	Hougham
101	Hough on the H...
102	Howell
103	Humby
104	Hykeham North
105	Hykeham South